ATTACHMENT THEORY

ATTACHMENT THEORY

Working Towards Learned Security

Rhona M. Fear

Routledge
Taylor & Francis Group
LONDON AND NEW YORK

First published 2017 by
Karnac Books Ltd.

2 Park Square, Milton Park, Abingdon, Oxfordshire OX14 4RN
52 Vanderbilt Avenue, New York, NY 10017

Routledge is an imprint of the Taylor & Francis Group, an informa business

First issued in hardback 2019

British Library Cataloguing in Publication Data

A C.I.P. for this book is available from the British Library

ISBN 978-1-78220-429-9 (pbk)
ISBN 978-0-367-32337-0 (hbk)

Edited, designed and produced by The Studio Publishing Services Ltd

www.publishingservicesuk.co.uk

e-mail: studio@publishingservicesuk.co.uk

CONTENTS

It gives me great pleasure in dedicating this book to my two beloved daughters. Louise Beattie, my elder daughter, has faithfully helped to edit both this book and my previous book, published by Karnac in 2015, on the subject of the Oedipus complex.

My younger daughter, Catherine Fear, has supported me emotionally through the year in which this book has come to fruition. More technically minded than me, she has helped me enormously with the frustrations of using the PC, as sometimes it is alien to me!

ACKNOWLEDGEMENTS

I would like to extend my thanks to all of the clients with whom I have worked during my years as a therapist. I have learned enormously from every one of them; I hope the satisfaction has been reciprocal. I am especially grateful to those clients who have given their permission to use the dynamics of their therapy in the case studies in this book.

I am deeply grateful to Robin Harriott, of Dilwyn, Herefordshire, for once again showing his assiduous care in editing this manuscript. He has given many hours of his time to the process he describes as "acting as midwife to the birth of this particular baby".

ABOUT THE AUTHOR

Rhona Fear, BA (Hons), MA, is a UKCP registered psychoanalytic psychotherapist and an accredited member of BACP. She has been in private practice in Worcestershire since 1994, where she specialises in working with clients in long term therapy. She first qualified as a counsellor with Relate in 1990. In order to broaden her horizons, she then undertook a Master's Degree in Counselling Studies at the University of Keele from 1994 to 1996. Shortly after this, she began training as a psychoanalytic psychotherapist in 1998 and qualified in 2004. This involved a number of years in five-times weekly therapy and considerable years of intensive supervision of her clinical work, as well as academic seminars and work with a number of twice-weekly training cases, prior to the presentation of a Final Qualifying Paper.

She has always maintained a keen interest in writing and in academia, especially since spending some years lecturing in Political Science and Sociology earlier in her career, following the attainment of her first degree. She has also taken an active political role in democratic government and in pressure-group politics. Previously, she contributed to the literature on the Integration debate within the field of counselling and psychotherapy, by publishing a number of refereed papers on the relationship between the counsellors' choice of theoretical orientation and the meta-theoretical assumptions of their underlying personal philosophies. She has also published a number of chapters in edited textbooks.

In 2015, Karnac published her first book, *The Oedipus Complex: Solutions or Resolutions?*

PREFACE

I decided to write this book because I have become certain, particularly over recent years, that the most important shifts in the client's psychic organisation are a result of the healing power of the therapeutic relationship. In an earlier book (Fear, 2015), where I detailed strategies employed in the resolution of the Oedipus complex, I grew to think that it is through the transference that mutative change can occur. I believe this still holds true. However, I remain convinced that the processes involved in the development and maturation of the real relationship are *also* of paramount importance. Here, I want to put forward the notion that the most significant change of all involves the client's experience of learning how it feels to enjoy, for an extended period of time, the dependability of recourse to a "secure base" (Bowlby, 1988) when anxiety is aroused. It is during this experience in therapy that the client's psychic organisation changes, and he can then transfer this learning to his relationships with significant others in the external world. The majority of the clients who present to me in long-term therapy suffer from either an insecure ambivalent or insecure avoidant attachment schema. This is as the result of developmental deficit during the individual's childhood, either in the form of a traumatological episode, or sustained lack of consistent, loving attention from their primary carer. The psychotherapy I offer aims to heal the effects of these developmental deficits and helps the client to change dysfunctional ways of relating.

Since I began to work as a noviate psychoanalytic psychotherapist two decades ago, during which time it has been my privilege to work with many clients in long-term therapy, I have gradually developed a way of working that I believe most effectively enables the clients to change their attachment schema so that they can begin to relate in a secure way. This occurs first in the consulting room with me, and then the client can reflect this learning experience in practical ways through his relationships in the external world.

I have always been deeply influenced by John Bowlby's concept of attachment theory, and have followed the development of his ideas by others since his death in 1990. Through extensive reading and research, I have also found that I am drawn to consider the underlying meta-theoretical assumptions of both Kohut's psychology of the self, and Stolorow, Brandchaft, and Atwood's intersubjective perspective. I have gradually sought to achieve an integration of these two theories together with attachment theory, and have developed the theory of learned security.

It has been my enormous privilege to work with hundreds of individuals during my twenty-seven years as a therapist. In a relationship built on trust and dependability, I hope that my clients have appreciated that I endeavour to hold them in mind throughout our work together. Years of clinical experience have enabled me to devise a method that I believe best enables the client to attain a sense of a secure base—something he has never before been fortunate enough to experience.

This book is divided into five sections. In Part I, I examine attachment theory, both as it was devised by John Bowlby and as developed by others in more recent years. We are fortunate that attachment theory has been extended through the work of a group of highly talented practitioners and theorists since Bowlby's time. In Chapter Four of this part of the book, I introduce the concepts of "earned security" and "learned security" which are, in fact, central to this book. Part II goes on to describe some of the ways in which, through traumatological life experiences, individuals develop insecure attachment schemas. Part III focuses upon the central purpose of the book: to explain the theory of learned security. Chapter Eleven seeks to explain how this integrative theory has been reached, while Chapter Twelve aims to put forward how practitioners may best put the theory into practice in the clinical setting of the consulting room. Chapters Nine and Ten present the central concepts of the two theories other than attachment theory that have been utilised in the integration. Part IV of the book presents four case studies: the aim of these is to evidence how the theory can be applied in the consulting room. Part V concludes the book, and offers a brief discussion of the ideas presented.

I am deeply indebted to the individual clients who have given their permission for the dynamics of their therapy to be used in the case studies. I would also like to thank the many other clients with whom it has been my privilege to work. I never cease to be astounded at the level of courage it takes for one to engage in long-term therapy at what usually is a very difficult point in life.

I am thrilled with the way that relational psychoanalysis has developed in the past two decades. There has been a paradigmatic shift away from the determinist and reductionist approaches in Freudian theory to an appreciation of the complexities of life and of environmental influence, and a growing understanding that attachment relationships have a biological significance. I have found it particularly efficacious to combine the central tenets of attachment theory with the approaches of Kohut and those of Stolorow, Brandchaft, and Atwood. A state of learned security occurs when the client gains a sense of having a secure base to which to return and refuel in times of emotional doubt or trauma, and through which he learns to self-regulate his emotions.

I am aware that the ideas presented in this book might encounter some resistance, especially from those of you who believe that intrapsychic conflict is the cause of neurosis, rather than inopportune environmental factors. However, as testified in a previous book, I am not proposing that intrapsychic conflict is not a causative factor in dis-*ease*; I believe that the answer lies somewhere along a continuum between the two poles. Even within the attachment fraternity, I think that the book might arouse some debate. I hope, above all, that the ideas in this book will lead to further debate and discussion about the valuable concepts of attachment theory that John Bowlby bequeathed us in his legacy.

I conclude this Preface with a few words about the terminology that I have used in writing this book. I have long pondered on the appropriate term of reference for those courageous individuals who arrive in our consulting rooms and devote their attentions, energies, and finance to long-term therapy. Consequently, I have decided to refer to those individuals as my clients rather than my patients. I have always been uneasy about the use of the term "patient". My associations to the word are bound up with the medical model, and I am firmly of the belief that the use of this terminology suggests a particular power discourse between practitioner and patient. On the other hand, I truly believe that the word "client" makes an attempt to give the analysand the possibility of controlling his own destiny and his own therapy.

I have used the masculine pronoun to refer to the clients (except when I am writing about specific individuals), and the female pronoun to refer to the therapist. This is just a mechanism that I have employed for the purpose of clarity; in reality, it could just as well be either sex in either of the roles.

Similarly, I have generally used the word "therapy" instead of psychoanalysis or psychotherapy in the narrative of the book, although I think the three words, dependent upon context, are used in the text at different points interchangeably. This book is aimed to appeal to all counsellors, psychotherapists, and psychoanalysts, and purposely attempts to be inclusive. However, as I state clearly in Chapters Four and Twelve, my discussion of the best way to act as a therapist will not appeal to everyone. Clients in long-term learned security therapy will, by its very nature, become very dependent at times, and so this type of therapeutic process might not suit everyone.

Introduction

In this book, I focus on a new model of therapy that is largely a result of the development of concepts promulgated originally by John Bowlby and Mary Ainsworth from the 1940s until Bowlby died in 1990. Bowlby's research supported his notion that it is crucial for the child to receive the consistent loving care of a physically and emotionally available parental figure throughout childhood and adolescence. Bowlby's seminal concepts in developing attachment theory, including the prescient belief that we should all have a "secure base", have had far-reaching ramifications upon some sectors of the therapy world.

There have been many developments in attachment theory, both during Bowlby's lifetime and since his death. Mary Ainsworth's "strange situation" test is world-renowned in the field of psychotherapy, as is the adult attachment interview (AAI). There have been other developments emanating from attachment theory by individuals such as Peter Fonagy, Howard and Miriam Steele, Bateman, Target, Gergely, and Allen. Fonagy and colleagues' (Bateman & Fonagy, 2004; Fonagy et al., 2002) recognition of the concept of mentalization, and then the development of it as a body of thought, is just one example of individuals determined to develop psychoanalytic concepts in the footsteps of Bowlby.

More recent developments and debate about psychotherapy based on the ideas of attachment theory have begun to claim the interest of many in the attachment fraternity, as relational models of psychotherapy have gained ascendency in the psychoanalytic world. I have been persuaded by the underlying meta-theoretical assumptions of attachment theory ever since I first entered the therapy world in 1989. My initial training in counselling was with Relate, and, in those days, the theoretical approach taught was essentially eclectic. We were trained as counsellors to recognise a range of different theoretical modalities, and learnt to apply different theories according to their suitability. It was as if we had a metaphorical toolbox from which we pulled, in each counselling session, the most appropriate instrument to help the relationship to recover, or, alternatively, to enable the couple to separate without undue animosity. However, even in these early years of eclectic practice, I was drawn towards John Bowlby's theory of attachment. It resonated with me, undoubtedly because of my own personal history, although I had no conscious awareness of this at the time.

Perhaps as a consequence of a combination of this early training and my own personal history, some years later, in 1997, I decided to train as a psychoanalytic psychotherapist in order to specialise in the theoretical orientation that I found most appealing and efficacious in the consulting room. Since qualifying in 2004, I have specialised in working long term with the majority of my clients. I have gradually devised a way of working that aims to repair the developmental deficits that clients have encountered because of traumatological experiences in their earlier years, and this method of working has so inspired me that it has provided the motivation to write this book. I hope that the reader will be as enthusiastic about the ideas in the book as I am, and that it might modify your way of working with your clients. For others, it might not motivate you to change your entire way of working, but I do hope, nevertheless, that it might stimulate your thought processes. Others of you, who do not believe in the radical effects of environmental trauma, might find yourselves reacting negatively to the ideas in this book. It is not that I think that intrapsychic conflict does not cause neurosis; I think, instead, that the answer to the conundrum of what causes neuroses lies in the rationale that we need to take into account both environmental effect and intrapsychic conflict.

Since my qualification as an analytic therapist, I have worked with many clients suffering from neurotic symptoms and I have grown to appreciate that I do not believe that rigorous interpretation of the transference and countertransference and use of psychoanalytic interpretations are sufficient methods to employ alone in psychotherapy where one is trying to help clients to achieve psychic change. As a mature therapist, I am now no longer idealistic enough to believe and hope for a complete "cure". One can, at best, hope that the client may learn through therapy to avoid repeating dysfunctional patterns of behaviour that are linked historically to his experience in the past, and that he will come to feel more at peace with life. One comes to recognise, as a therapist, that there remains an inevitable tendency within an individual's psyche to revert to old habits and pre-existing patterns of thought and behaviour in times of stress or under circumstances that replicate old memories. In summation, it seems to me that individuals rarely manage, with the help of their therapist, to eradicate their pathologies entirely.

Given the caveat that one might be unable to achieve a complete cure for the client, what, then, is the theoretical approach that is best suited to help the client's recovery? After a lot of soul-searching, I have come to believe that the application of the core conditions of empathy, acceptance, and congruence (which form the basis of person-centred counselling, as popularised by Carl Rogers (1961, 1980)) are of inestimable value in the consulting room if we are to help clients to regain a pathway to ordinary, everyday living. This might seem like heresy to those of you of a strict psychoanalytic persuasion, but I do believe that the use of the core conditions is vital in order to help to establish and maintain a relationship where the therapist can be seen as a secure base.

It is common for clients to present with issues concerning their relationships: these may be their core romantic relationships, or relationships with parents or other relatives, or sometimes with friends or work colleagues. Attachment theory provides us with the meta-theoretical, underlying beliefs that underpin how best to work with these individuals. However, while John Bowlby was a giant among individuals as a theoretician, he was not a well-practised clinician. He maintained a small clinical practice, working mostly at the Tavistock Centre, while his primary interest lay in research and academia rather than in the practical application of his theory. A similar point may be made regarding Ainsworth and colleagues (strange situation test, 1978) and George and colleagues (who developed the adult attachment interview, 1985).

I have always been interested in academia and in the meta-theoretical underpinnings of belief systems. To my mind, it is better to underpin one's work with a theoretical rationale than to rely purely upon an eclectic toolbox of skills, for the latter might be underlain with unexamined prejudice. My dissertation for my MA focused on the meta-theoretical assumptions and *weltanschauung* underlying each of the principal categories of different theoretical orientations. Subsequently, I co-wrote and published a number of academic papers and chapters in books during the 1990s and the millennium on the subject of integration of theories in counselling and psychotherapy (Fear & Woolfe, 1996, 1999, 2000). I have followed the integration debate for over twenty years. In 1996, a colleague and I published (Fear & Woolfe, 1996) an attempted integration of Wachtel's cyclical psychodynamics (Wachtel & McKinney, 1992) and attachment theory. Even twenty years ago, I was not convinced that attachment theory alone provided the optimum solution for many individuals in therapy.

I would now like to consider the possibility of how we might employ the concepts of empathy, acceptance, and congruence as valuable adjuncts to the underlying core modality of psychoanalysis. Unlike Carl Rogers, however, I do not believe that they are "the necessary and sufficient requirements for change" (Rogers, 1957) to be engendered. Anyone who is familiar with the session of Carl Rogers and his client Gloria in that delightful and fascinating work (*Three Approaches to Psychotherapy*, filmed by Dr Everett Shostrom, 1964) detailing her sessions with therapists of differing theoretical persuasions (Albert Ellis, Carl Rogers, and Fritz Perls, respectively) might also remember that while she found Carl Rogers' session the most comforting and empathic, she did not see it as enabling the most progress to be made.

Consequently, it appears to me that although these core conditions are useful, they are insufficient in themselves. Thus, I am aware that we need the skills of timely interpretations, of proactive use and interpretation of the transference and countertransference, and the linking of past and present, if one is to achieve insight and psychic change for the client. Alongside these skills, I believe that we need a working knowledge of the psychoanalytic theories we can apply in analytic practice (as can be seen in my previous book concentrating on the use of the theories of the Oedipus complex (Fear, 2015)). However, extending the concepts of Bowlby's attachment theory, I have come to believe that the therapist needs (in long-term therapy) to create and foster a relationship that enables the client to enjoy the healing experience of "knowing" what it is to have a "secure base". Through the practical application of my theory, which I have named the theory of learned security, I believe that the therapist can help her client to recover from the developmental deficit(s) suffered in earlier years. It is often precisely as a result of the lack of a secure base that a client will present in therapy, although clients do not tend to attend early sessions with a formulated notion of this. Few clients ever present in our consulting rooms with a secure attachment schema. This is due to the simple fact that individuals who have experienced a secure base, while suffering the same vicissitudes in life as those who tread a path to our doorways, are able to withstand and deal with the crises and life difficulties that befall them, without the need for recourse to professional help.

It seems to me that the individuals who *do* require our help are most often in need of a secure base experience, in order to enable them to gain the fortitude and resilience to face life's difficulties robustly and to comprehend their meaning. By the therapist's provision of a secure base on which to lean in times of difficulty, they not only overcome the presenting problem, but also are given the tools with which to manage whatever else life may throw at them in the future.

As has been intimated before, I do believe that psychoanalytic and psychodynamic interpretations are not sufficient in themselves to provide the experience of learned security. I think similarly of the Rogerian core conditions. The deficit here necessitates that we employ and integrate some person-centred techniques with those of psychoanalysis. To this end, I have drawn upon a number of theories: the intersubjective perspective of Stolorow and colleagues (1983, 1995), and Kohut's ideas in self psychology as well as Bowlby's attachment theory. In Chapter Eleven, I put forward an integration of these three theories; additionally, I have employed the use of the core conditions in describing how to use this integrative theory in a therapeutic setting (Chapter Twelve).

In order to achieve theoretical integration, one must seek recourse to a higher level of abstraction. It is a matter of finding common underlying meta-theoretical assumptions and concepts within the theories. It is helpful if there is a common *weltanschauung* (or world view) underlying the theories one has chosen to integrate. One of the taxonomies of world view was inaugurated by Northrop Frye (1957, 1964) in his analysis of Shakespearean literature. It was then taken up by Messer and Winokur (1984), and Shafer (1976), who applied Frye's taxonomy to psychoanalytic theory. Frye identified four major visions of reality: tragic, comic, romantic, and ironic (See Fear & Woolfe, 1999, 2000 for a detailed exposition of these visions). Each of these visions, while essentially different in their approach to life, have at their core some overlapping meta-theoretical concepts such as optimism/pessimism; the degree to which self-actualisation is possible; positive/negative stance on life; internal/external locus of control.

I discovered, by analysing the theories of Stolorow and colleagues, Bowlby, and Kohut, that all three theories are, in essence, relational models (rather than being drive models, as in Freudian theory). All three theories share the meta-theoretical assumption that relationships in life are of pre-eminent importance. In terms of integration, they are all underpinned by a tragic view of reality. In short, this encompasses the beliefs that not all is redeemable; neither can everything be remedied in life. As Shafer (1976) puts it:

> it requires one to recognise the elements of defeat in victory and victory in defeat; the pain in pleasure and the pleasure in pain; the guilt in apparent justified action; the loss of opportunities in every choice and by growth in every direction. (Shafer, 1976, p. 35)

All three theories stress highly the provision of empathic attunement; they also give due regard to the healing power of the transference between therapist and client. In the theory of learned security, I have developed the concept of empathy to have a specific meaning. I am putting forward the notion that intersubjective empathy involves a collaborative experience: it refers to the need for the therapist to consistently engage with the client by actively checking out with him if she is "alongside him". I am talking about a co-constructive process where the therapist actively seeks the feedback of the client. Similarly, I believe that we need to employ a co-constructive process when helping the client to create a sense of autobiographical competence (Holmes, 1993). In the theory of learned security, this is also one of the important underlying purposes of long-term therapy. All three theories focus on the interpersonal, on both the "real" and transference relationships between the therapist and client, and also give priority to the client's relationships in his external world.

I am indebted to Jeremy Holmes (2010) and several others for the initial concept of earned security. This concept has begun to take root within the attachment fraternity. However, I have been frustrated by the fact that I have not been able to trace very many books, apart from Holmes (2010) and Odgers (2014), that focus on precisely how this sense of earned security is to be achieved by the therapy dyad. In Odgers' book (2014), there are three chapters describing case studies (Haynes & Whitehead; Patrikiou; Richards) that give examples of how earned security might manifest itself in the clinical setting of the consulting room. These two books have served to increase my dedication to the integration put forward in this book. However, I am not aware of any treatise on the underlying theory that incorporates concepts from Kohut and from Stolorow, Brandchaft, and Atwood. I believe that concepts from these theories are needed to achieve the endpoint of learned security. I hope that this book may help other therapists to develop such a way of working. I have named this theory the theory of learned security (*learned* rather than *earned*) for two reasons: first, it has a number of essential differences from earned security and, thus, requires a separate delineation. Second, I believe this title signifies more directly the informal learning process that is involved in helping individuals to intuitively learn experientially what it means to have a secure base.

The book is divided into four sections. In Part I, I provide an exposition of attachment theory; developments in theory post-Bowlby and a description of the concept of mentalization, which has been developed in this century. I believe Bowlby's theory clearly states that emotional security depends indubitably on whether there is a deficit in childhood, and whether a satisfactory close emotional attachment is made to a reliable, responsible, and attuned parental figure. However, I am convinced that "loss" does not only encompass physical loss, but also the intrinsic loss of emotional connectedness that constitutes a major reason for individuals unable to grow up with a secure base.

In the four chapters of Part II, I focus upon differing ways in which one's experience of childhood might lead to a loss of emotional connectedness, and how this, in turn, prevents an experience of "containment" (Bion, 1984). In Chapters Four to Six, I provide an exposition of the effects of toxic nourishment, maternal deprivation, and the results of an attachment figure being emotionally unavailable. I look, in Chapter Seven, at the biological effects on an infant's brain of emotional unavailability by a parental figure who is not emotionally attuned to the child. I am indebted to Sue Gerhardt for her seminal book, *Why Love Matters: How Affection Shapes a Baby's Brain* (Gerhardt, 2015) for the facts that she has collected there. Here, at last, there is physiological evidence for John Bowlby's beliefs that such emotional attunement and "companionable interaction" (Heard & Lake, 1997) between parent and infant are so life changing. This research unquestionably shows us now that there are biological ramifications if the child is not in receipt of emotional connectedness. The fact that Romanian orphans, whose early childhood consisted of lying in a cot without the emotional stimulation of adult figures, effectively have a "black hole" in their brains due to the failure of the orbitofrontal cortex to develop is quite shocking. It is also worth noting that negative emotions can actually prevent the baby's brain from developing because they lead to the production of cortisol, and this, in turn, stops the development of endorphins and dopamine, creating a circularity whereby glucose is not manufactured. The brain requires glucose to develop.

Part III of the text concentrates upon the theoretical underpinnings of the theory of learned security. In Chapters Nine and Ten, I put forward a summation of the other two theories (the psychology of the self and the intersubjective perspective) that have been utilised to reach this integration. In Chapter Eleven, I present the integration of these three theories, which underlies the practical application of the concepts used in the theory of learned security. Chapter Twelve concludes this section by focusing upon the way in which I think that one needs to engage in the therapeutic process if one is convinced that there is a need for the client to gain a sense of earned security or learned security.

Part IV consists of case studies of four individuals with whom I have worked for some considerable time. Here, I attempt to show the reader how the therapist plays an essential role in enabling the client to "know" what it means to truly experience a secure base on whom he can rely. I also examine the effect of this upon the client's emotional and psychological self. I am particularly indebted to one client, Nick, who has written a narrative of what therapy has meant to him. The reader is given the opportunity to appreciate how the client may assimilate and view his therapy from a subjective perspective.

I hope that the book will serve to make you think about the purpose of psychotherapy. I have been passionate in my motivation to write this book, just as my years in clinical practice, honing the therapy that I describe, have been challenging, stimulating, and hugely rewarding. I hope that other therapists among you may learn from this book, and that it fosters debate in order to enable individuals to continue along the path that I have outlined. Some theoreticians and clinicians might take the ideas in other directions that they deem worthwhile and exciting. I trust that others of you may find the energy and motivation to develop the ideas that I have suggested here, in order that we as an analytic community continue to employ the initial concepts developed and promulgated by John Bowlby.

My thanks go to all of the clients with whom I have worked over the past twenty-seven years. Had it not been for you, the writing of this book would never have been possible. It takes a lot of courage to present oneself in psychotherapy, and a dedication to the process if one is to achieve significant change together with the help of the therapist. I am particularly indebted to the four clients who have allowed me to use the dynamics of their time in therapy with me, so that I can share with you the way that the theory of learned security works in practice.

PART I

ATTACHMENT THEORY AS THE UNDERLYING BASIS OF THE THEORY OF LEARNED SECURITY

CHAPTER ONE

Origins of attachment theory

Introduction

Attachment theory, as first developed by John Bowlby, is at the very heart of this book. It is to John Bowlby that I owe the nascent ideas that led me to develop an integration of three psychoanalytic theories (described in Chapter Eleven) which, when employed in concert, I believe to be more effective in enabling the healing process of my clients to take place than if one employs a single theoretical model. I undertook to write this book in order to share with a wider audience of practising psychotherapists and counsellors this integrative approach to psychotherapy. I hope that it may encourage further debate that will lead to further development.

This book is an attempt to present the underlying ideology that has been born over many years as a practising psychoanalytic psychotherapist. Above all, the theory of learned security represents a summation of the way in which I think psychotherapy can best function as an effective instrument, carefully crafted by the therapist and used with skill to assist her client to develop a clearer sense of "autobiographical competence" (Holmes, 2010, p. 49) and a stronger and more sustainable sense of self by the time he ends long-term therapy.

These two aims—autobiographical competence and the ability to feel secure within oneself—are, to my mind, the most important gains of long-term therapy. They are frequently not the stated, conscious aims of the client, who might often actually present with more pressing concerns about external environmental factors which are troubling him.

It is my contention that it is one of the foremost aims of many therapists, though perhaps not always consciously recognised, to help the client move from a fractured, conflictual approach to relationships to a more satisfying way of relating. The conflictual mode of relating is almost always evidenced in the very first few sessions of therapy, embroiled in the issues with which the client presents. In my experience of over twenty-seven years in practice, the presenting problem is nearly always due to difficulties in relationships, whether these relationships concern a core partnership, interactions with a child or another family member, or, alternatively, with individuals at work or within the social milieu. Thus, I believe that one needs to tackle the way in which the client relates to others, and, of course, this will be revealed in the "here and now" of the transference and countertransference, and by the growth of the real relationship which underpins the working alliance.

Attachment theory: the precedence of external traumata

I am concentrating here upon attachment theory, so it seems expedient to talk about John Bowlby's life from a psychodynamic perspective, in order to provide some insight into the reasons that Bowlby perhaps devoted his time to the invention and development of attachment theory and its clinical applications. In so doing, Bowlby's career involved him in a grand schism with the majority of the psychoanalytic world, including The Psychoanalytical Society and its main proponents. The inevitability of the schism essentially lay in the fact that Bowlby believed that environmental failures were pre-eminent in adversely influencing the mental health of individuals, rather than a person's intrapsychic phantasies and motivations being at odds with his expressed conscious intentions and stated aims. In short, the client is understood by traditional psychoanalysts to be suffering from intrapsychic conflict rather than the result of environmental failure. In addition, Bowlby also believed that psychoanalysis, by the mid twentieth century, had lost its scientific basis, as put forward by Freud, and had been replaced by the intuitive and hermeneutic approach of Melanie Klein and Anna Freud.

In contradicting the underlying philosophical assumptions of traditional psychoanalysis, Bowlby attacked the basic tenet of psychoanalysis, and has never been forgiven. Some rapprochement has been seen over the past sixty years, but it is my guess that even this book, which adheres to the Bowlbian principle that environmental failure is more important than, or at least as important as, intrapsychic conflict will be poorly received in some circles. It has been my own experience, during my training as a psychoanalytic psychotherapist in the 1990s, to find the theoretical ideas of Bowlby dismissed as banal and bland. I had intended to write my second year extended theory essay on attachment theory, and was told in no uncertain terms that this would not be well received and I should consider another subject.

Furthermore, when I was undertaking an assessment during my training, I presented a patient who had suffered from extreme environmental traumata, through the horrific death of both of his parents when he was a teenager. Following this trauma, my patient was later affected directly by two close friends' attempted suicides. During the presentation of the case at my interview, I recalled that he cried for the first time ever during this session with me, believing it to be an important moment of emotional cathexis. I believe that when a client starts to feel safe and securely held in therapy, then he starts to be able to voice his deepest anxieties and hurts. For this reason, I believed that my client being able to cry, for the first time ever, represented a defining moment in his therapy. However, the assessor did not agree with me, probably because she gave no credence to attachment theory or the growth of an affective relationship between client and therapist. She focused entirely upon the negative transference, saying that my client was simply seeking to satisfy me by acting out a show of being upset. I was told that I should have tackled the negative transference and not have been taken in by my client's distress. I am speaking about the reality, prevalent in the 1980s and 1990s when I trained, when clients were referred to with a very superior and arrogant tone of voice; clients seen as being intrinsically less "knowing" than ourselves as psychoanalytic psychotherapists. I am not alone in this view; Gerhardt (who also trained in the 1990s) speaks similarly in her chapter in Odgers' (2014) book, where she describes a supervisor instructing her very clearly "to *destroy* her client's masochism" (my emphasis).

In fact, research shows that there is an inverse correlation between repeated insistence on interpreting the negative transference and drop out in therapy because the client experiences therapy as punitive. Personally, I am not surprised by this summation. The use of unkind language, which has been used on some courses (which also tend to give apostolic power to senior analysts) by the reference to their clients as "babies" and "victims" has a knock-on punitive effect upon the actual therapy relationship in the consulting room. If we refer to our clients privately in such negative terms, and with a superior demeanour, we cannot hope to enable the client to gain a sense of "learned security". The real power of the therapist lies not in being the only one who "knows" the "unthought known" (Bollas, 1987), but in the fact that she is the supplier of the "secure base" (Holmes, 2010, p. 6). Unless the client can gain a sense of security, their accompanying anxiety will be such that they are unable to voice the true feelings and beliefs that will enable them to work through their neurosis, assisted by the making of the unconscious conscious.

It was my contention, at that assessment, that my client had formed an internal working model of relationships in that he believed there was intrinsically something so abhorrent about him that each individual with whom he became involved took it upon themselves to leave him. It was this interpretation, rather than some deep Kleinian transference interpretation, that I thought more applicable at that point in the therapy. I believed that by this interpretation, I gave to my client the power that comes with knowledge: having started to make the unconscious conscious, he would then have the choice to continue to think that way about his life, or the choice to reassess and continue from thenceforward differently.

In *The Oedipus Complex: Solutions or Resolutions?* (Fear, 2015), it will be seen that I give due credence to intrapsychic conflict. An Oedipus complex manifests itself in the transference as well as in the client's everyday life, and is the result of intrapsychic conflict. Six case studies therein provide detailed analysis of how the work in the transference led to a more permanent resolution of oedipal conflict for each of these clients with whom I worked.

However, it is my contention that we must work towards an integration of theories, where we accept that the anguish that individuals suffer is a mix of both intrapsychic and interpersonal conflict. I have written previously (Fear & Woolfe, 1996, 1999, 2000) of my determination and my wishes to pursue a philosophical path via a process of dialectical thinking. It is through thinking dialectically that one can look for a common range of concepts that, employed together, marry up seemingly irreconcilable differences. I voyaged some way down the path of dialectical thinking in an earlier paper (Fear & Woolfe, 1996), as I mentioned in the Introduction.

I have remained, throughout the intervening twenty years, a staunch believer in the centrality of attachment theory, and in John Bowlby's ideas. But, first of all, it is to John Bowlby's life story that I turn, in order to explore his own psychodynamic history. I hope that, in so doing, we will be better able to appreciate why this enigmatic man, so sensitive to the emotional needs of others and yet so unable to share his own feelings with his contemporaries, devoted his life to the pursuit of a world in which privation of emotional nurturance from one's mother would become a thing of the past.

A psychodynamic approach to John Bowlby's history

John Mostyn Bowlby was born on 26 February 1907 to May Mostyn and Major-General Sir Anthony Bowlby (1855–1929), who had been rewarded with a knighthood for his appointments as Royal Surgeon to King Edward VII and King George V. Sir Anthony had only felt himself free to look for a wife following the death of his widowed mother. He had appointed himself as the latter's carer, after the murder of his father in Peking in 1861 when he was a small boy.

John was one of six children, his parents being middle-aged when he was born: his mother being forty when she gave birth to him, his father fifty-two. As so many parents of their class and generation, they left the care and upbringing of their children mainly to a succession of trusted nannies, servants, and the rigid discipline of boarding schools. As a consequence, it might well be appropriate to surmise that John Bowlby suffered the maternal deprivation that he found so abhorrent and which motivated him to campaign for radical change to the circumstances in which children were brought up. In 1944, he wrote "Forty-four juvenile thieves: their characters and home life", a paper about the way in which ten of the twelve of those whom he termed "affectionless psychopaths" had been subjected to the protracted loss of maternal care during their childhoods. Admittedly, in contrast, John had a physically available mother. (His mother was available for an hour from 5.00 p.m. to 6.00 p.m. each evening after nursery tea, so, at times, she was physically available!) It is questionable, however, whether she was really emotionally available to him. Father, too, was an unavailable, distant object, having given most of his time to his vocation. John's upbringing meant, in reality, that while he remained a devoted campaigner for the rights of the child, sensitive and with "an inner calm" (Phelps Brown, 1992), he would allow few people to get close to him. It is possible that if he had undertaken Mary Ainsworth's strange situation test, he would have been categorised as insecure–avoidant (I define this typology later in this chapter). This is as a result of having a carer who was only available on her terms. He was, thus, unsure, I surmise, whether he was ever going to get the attention he desired. Again, had he submitted to Main's adult attachment interview (AAI), he might well have been analysed as distant and unemotional, and not very responsive or attuned as a parent himself. This could well be because it would have been too embarrassing to admit to any level of vulnerability. One can also surmise that he felt very severely the lack of a close emotional bond with either his mother or father, and, undoubtedly, it was this that partially motivated him to pursue the innovative and unique path that he trod, resulting in a silver lining to the cloud for all of us in the psychoanalytic world.

John grew up alongside one particular brother, Tony, and a very competitive relationship developed. This affected him significantly. Tony was thirteen months older than he, but the two were often treated as twins. In consequence, John was forever caught up in a struggle to be "equal" or "better than". Tony was destined to follow his father into medicine, but chose not to, in order to perhaps avoid feelings of failure in comparison to his father's prowess. This left the path to a career in medicine open to John, and, following a false start in a naval career at Dartmouth, he went up to Trinity College, Cambridge. There, he read for a first class honours degree in pre-clinical sciences and psychology.

It was expected that he would then go to London and study clinical medicine, but, ever the renegade (if quietly so), he sought a position in a progressive school for maladjusted children. While there, two experiences radically affected his entire professional career thereafter. First, he found that he could communicate with the disturbed children at the school, and found, moreover, that their psychological problems seemed to be linked to their unhappy and disrupted childhoods. This factor was to direct his course, like a compass, for the remainder of his professional days. Second, he met and became friends with John Alford, who himself had enjoyed some personal therapy, and who advised John to undertake training as a psychoanalyst. Again, perhaps because of both his level of interpersonal and intrapsychic conflict, John found the path to analysis inviting at a personal level.

While at University College London (1929) during his clinical medical training, he entered the Psychoanalytic Society and undertook analysis with Joan Riviere, a friend and follower of Melanie Klein. After medical qualification in 1933, he went to the Maudsley, where he started training as an adult psychiatrist. He qualified as an analyst in 1937, and immediately commenced training in child analysis with Melanie Klein. While he believed in the practical efficacy of analysis, he questioned its theoretical underpinnings for two reasons. First, he felt that, under the directions of Anna Freud and Melanie Klein, analysis had become a discipline removed from the rigours of science, relying far more on intuition and intellectual premise. Second, he disagreed (as I have stated before) with the primacy given to intrapsychic conflict and phantasy, and to Freud's "homuncular" model (that is, that each developmental stage is predetermined and succeeds the previous one in a pre-existing planned order). Instead, he felt that each individual develops in his or her own particular way, at a varying rate (an epigenetic model), and that environment rather than the internal world of phantasy is of paramount importance to the development of the human being.

Despite his misgivings concerning the Psychoanalytic Society, and his continuous disquietude with the prevailing attitudes, Bowlby was elected as Training Secretary in 1944, although he was not an appointed training analyst. He disliked the fact that the Society dissociated itself from the beginnings of the National Health Service (NHS, which was clearly going to come into being (as it did in 1948) following the Second World War, and it seems to me that, in consequence of this, psychoanalysis did itself a grave disservice.

We have all suffered the legacy of the arrogance of this attitude, for, as a result, psychoanalysis and psychoanalytic psychotherapy (by association) have never been politically accepted by government, whatever party may be in power. Contrast this with the profession of psychology, which aligned itself to the NHS, in consequence of which it is an accepted part now of NHS provision in the field of mental health, especially since the implementation of the Improving Access to Psychological Therapies (IAPT) programme. Concomitantly, psychologists in NHS practice or private practice can charge far higher fees than qualified analysts or psychoanalytic psychotherapists, despite the latter groups' difficult, equally arduous and expensive training. This, it seems to me, is the political rationale for this discrepancy, which clearly exists, despite the evidential fact that neither psychologists nor psychoanalysts are qualified to prescribe medicine, or, *de rigueur*, receive a medical training.

In 1944, Bowlby had to read a paper to the Psychoanalytic Society in order to achieve full voting rights. He prepared and then read his seminal paper, "Forty-four juvenile thieves: their characters and home life" (Bowlby, 1944). In this paper, he made the point that of twelve "affectionless psychopaths", ten had suffered maternal loss under the age of ten. In similar vein, forty per cent of them had suffered severe maternal deprivation and, as a result of this (he believed), there was a correlation between deprivation and alienation and anomie regarding societal norms. While such small sample numbers, without any control groups, would not be accepted as statistically significant nowadays, the evidence was convincing enough to have an impact in the 1940s. However, the Society disliked Bowlby's emphasis on the effect of environment rather than intrapsychic conflict as the cause of neurosis, and he was noticeably shunned and marginalised.

Further papers, presented between 1957 and 1959, led to debate but little enthusiasm, and downright hostility from the Kleinian contingent. Note that I was in receipt of the same hostility in the 1990s during my training. It makes me wonder whether the prevailing ideology in psychoanalysis has really changed. Jeremy Holmes is a little more optimistic than me. He writes, in *John Bowlby and Attachment Theory*,

> But times have changed. The old certainties no longer hold. Psychoanalysis has lost its dogmatism and is much more open to empirical evidence and to cross-disciplinary influence. The Berlin wall which separated psychoanalysis from the superficiality but also the stimulus of other disciplines has come down. (Holmes, 1993, p. 7)

It is true that attachment theory can seem banal, even bland at times. It has a quality of "obviousness", of which, once the concepts are pointed out, one tends to say, "Why did I not think to say that? I sort of knew it all along!" Perhaps this is as a result of it resonating with our own life experience. However, the truth is that *no one did say it* until Bowlby stuck his head above the parapet, and was promptly decapitated! Indeed, attachment theory lacks the intellectual sophistication and abstract nature of the concept of intrapsychic conflict, of defence mechanisms such as projective identification, of the Freudian concepts of ego and id. However, it does win hands down in the stakes of being easily understood, and of being readily applicable to the life situations of many clients who present in our consulting rooms. Furthermore, when I move on, in later chapters, to post-Bowlbian ideas of earned security and learned security, and its links with Stolorow, Brandchaft, and Atwood's (1995) intersubjective approach, I think its possibility as a sophisticated theory becomes apparent.

In 1952, Bowlby and James Robertson co-operated in the study of the effect on young children (aged 1–5) of separation from their parents during residential stays in hospital. This resulted in James Robertson's classic film, *A Two-Year-Old Goes to Hospital* (Bowlby & Robertson, 1952a). This film, hard to watch without tears in one's eyes, and the accompanying evidence (Bowlby & Robertson, 1952a), was to rock the foundations of the NHS and led to wide-ranging changes in the attitude to parental visiting and access to children while in hospital.

It was with James Robertson that Bowlby developed the theory that the separation of infant from carer gives rise to three stages: protest, despair, and then detachment. Protest involves the child crying, shouting, calling out in order to attempt to make mother return to him. All of these behaviours are motivated by this same factor: the wish to make it clear that he wants mother to return. I would add that I think this stage also involves some cathartic (emotional) release. This stage may go on for up to a week. As an example of this, my little puppy cries forlornly when his main attachment figures leave him. He is trying his best to protest, and make us return to him.

The second stage involves despair. The child might alternate between being withdrawn and being sad. Tears are in evidence during this period. He might not actually cry tears that are visible to the onlooker, but internally he is in a state of mourning and cannot think of anything else beyond his loss. The child is listless, tends not to be interested in anything much, even favourite toys. I can remember myself feeling like this while in hospital at age three, where I was an in-patient for four weeks and was only allowed parental visiting on three occasions. The little one is adjusting psychologically to a new reality. He is in grief and this evidences itself in a mood of despair.

Detachment is the third stage and involves a point being reached when the child *appears* to have accommodated the loss and *appears* to have returned to normal. There is a resumption of play and interest in life, and he smiles again. This is, in fact, deceptive: in reality, the child has withdrawn into an "alone world" where, as Bowlby put it, he has decided unconsciously not to risk again getting close to anyone, in case it should result in a repetition of the crushing, unbearable pain he has suffered in the first stage of abandonment. Sometimes, this stage cannot be mended in psychotherapy, but often therapy is successful in relation to this and the client dares to become intimate again, although he might act cautiously at first. Personally, I believe that children who have reached this stage have a psychological frailty that is unlikely to be repaired without long-term psychotherapy.

During the same post-war period that James Robertson and John Bowlby were collaborating, Mary Ainsworth (co-founder of attachment theory) joined Bowlby's team. She is said to have remembered that the idea of attachment theory came to Bowlby "in a flash" when, in 1952, he heard about, and then read of, Lorenz's work with greylag geese in "King Soloman's ring" (Lorenz, 1959). Lorenz discovered that goslings pass through a stage for a discrete, short period of time where they will be become attached to any moving object that is set before them. This is called "imprinting". His research proved that a gosling might even become attached to a moving cardboard box, or himself, if placed before it at the correct time. By recourse to the scientific discipline of ethology (the scientific and objective study of animal behaviour), Bowlby began to find that he could marry together hermeneutics (the theory and methodology of interpretation) in psychoanalysis with that of the biological scientific approach. Ainsworth, meanwhile, moved on to live in Uganda, and eventually settled in Baltimore, Maryland, where she devoted her time to developing a way of measuring the attachment schema of young children. She developed the strange situation test, from which emanates the four-part typology of attachment schema, or "internal working models", as John Bowlby liked to call them. Later in this chapter, the typology will be discussed and described.

During the post-war era, Bowlby was chosen by the World Health Organization (WHO) as the obvious person to prepare a report on the mental health of homeless children. It is worth mentioning that the political and sociological awareness of the issues of loss and trauma following the Second World War (1939–1945) worked in Bowlby's favour. These issues, so much the common currency of the governments of the day, and of the academic sociologists, political scientists and psychologists, were, fortunately, very much what interested Bowlby most.

Each of us, including that instigator of paradigms, John Bowlby, is bound to be influenced by the political and economic milieu in which he lives. The same can be said of Freud (Fear, 2015, pp. 11–22), who, despite the paradigmatic shifts he set in motion, evidenced within his theories that he could not avoid being influenced by the *Zeitgeist* of his era. I write in *The Oedipus Complex* (Fear, 2015) of the way in which Freud was intrinsically affected by being a part of the paternalistic and patriarchal society in which he lived.

No doubt because of the hostility he encountered, Bowlby spent little time in the Psychoanalytical Society after the mid-1960s, and he devoted his time from 1964 to 1979 to writing his well-known trilogy: *Attachment* (1969), *Separation* (1973), and *Loss* (1980). These books have all been bestsellers, selling between 45,000 and 100,000 volumes each (Holmes, 1993, p. 29). In 1980, he was made Freud Memorial Professor of Psychoanalysis at University College London, and, during this time, he undertook a number of lecture tours, from which we are lucky enough to have the collection of lectures found in *The Making and Breaking of Affectional Bonds* (1979a) and *A Secure Base* (1988). His wide range of both papers and books are well known, his last book being a psychobiography of Charles Darwin (Bowlby, 1990) published a few months before his death at the age of eighty-three, on 2 September 1990. A simple Skye funeral was held, as he had wanted, on the island that had become his second home—remote and simple, reflecting as it did the man himself, in spite of his high intelligence and fervour for his cause.

It is noteworthy that John Bowlby was somewhat rebellious, wanting from the outset to carry on his life a little differently from the norm. Thus, despite the fact that he decided on a career in medicine (perhaps so as to please his emotionally distant but revered father), he did not steer an obvious course through medicine. He took full advantage of that chance meeting with John Alford, and applied himself to the formidable task of training as a psychoanalyst. Never deterred by hard work or the need to engage fully at an intellectual level, he buckled down to the arduous training of becoming an analyst and succeeded. However, he was not wont to accept blindly the dogma that was laid before him. He questioned the dominant value systems of the time, and put his own particular spin on psychoanalytic theory. Not for him the primacy of what went on within the individual's mind; he believed that the answer lies in the effect of environment. Maybe it is true that his view is a little too simplistic: does the answer not lie somewhere that incorporates environment and intrapsychic conflict?

Second, I would like to point to another character trait of John Bowlby that I find entrancing. Despite his seeming self-confidence, his "inner calm" (Phelps Brown, 1992, quoted in Holmes, 1993, p. 16), and his undoubtedly high intellect, it was not until later maturity that Bowlby felt confident enough to publically challenge the *status quo* and to produce his trilogy. He was in his sixty-second year when *Attachment* was published.

Despite the fact that he wrote a lot about the feelings of loss, separation, and grief in others, he remained somewhat enigmatic in his own feelings. He was, reportedly, a distant father who left the upbringing of his four children to his wife, Ursula. However, interestingly, perhaps because he regretted that he "had not done a good job" as a father (his children questioned his absence by asking if he were a burglar, because he only came home late at night!), he was "a brilliant grandfather", in the words of his daughter Mary. His interest in bringing the role of women to the fore in post-war Britain is possibly because of his disappointment with his mother, who did not provide him with the love and attention he craved, and who displayed favouritism towards his brother, Tony. The rebellious streak in his personality is again perhaps the result of his being a hurt and neglected child, just like the "affectionless characters" of whom he talked in "Forty-four juvenile thieves" (1944), but in a less obvious way. This hurt motivated the indefatiguable energy to continually fight to repair the ravages of neglect that he recognised in those who had suffered, and with whom he empathised.

The central concepts of Bowlby's attachment theory

Maternal deprivation: the concept as it appeared in Child Care and the Growth of Maternal Love *(1953)*

Bowlby was at the heart of the "moral panic" that ensued following the Second World War, with its attendant emphasis on loss, separation, and trauma. Politically, there was extended moral debate about the effects of loss, as children and their mothers suffered the loss of fathers and husbands who did not return from war. During the war, mothers had been forced to take the jobs hitherto filled by their menfolk, who had gone to war. In consequence, there had been a temporary increase in state provision of childcare, and a cessation of it on the men's return from war. Although I realise it is cynical, it is, none the less, true that it best suited the state in the post-war era of "making a land fit for heroes" if women were to stay at home, raising the children and keeping house, so that men, returning from the war, could take back the jobs that had been filled by women during the years at war. This policy avoided the mass unemployment that otherwise would have been the consequence. Thus, Bowlby's findings in his WHO report fell on fertile soil, and were well received. This is not to say that I disagree with the tenets of his argument, but I think it was economically and politically expedient for a government that needed to find jobs for a prospective male workforce.

It is also worthy of note that Bowlby argued that women in their domestic environment should be the nurturers and carers of the young, because those children who are brought up in institutions are more likely to be physically smaller, less verbally proficient, and less able to establish stable relationships as they reached adulthood. Indeed, Ainsworth discovered that attachment to the mother dominates by the age of thirty months (Ainsworth et al., 1978). I wholly agree with the view that children blossom most prolifically, mentally, emotionally, and physically under parental care. There is, however, a corollary to this view.

I would argue that children *are* best suited to an experience of living with two parents, for unless this occurs the child cannot work through the Oedipus complex, during which he at first wants to separate his parents, one from the other, and eventually learns with relief that he has been unable to achieve this ideal, which would actually have caused heartbreak. I think that it will be apparent that I believe that this period of intrapsychic conflict is seminal in the child's development.

Additionally, children are best suited to living in homes with their parents, or at least with a "significant other" (perhaps a grandmother, for example) that they can call their own. This helps to provide what Bowlby came to call "a secure base". He went on to realise that attachment behaviour involves a need to keep proximity to one's attachment figure. He said, "All of us, from the cradle to the grave, are happiest when life is organised as a series of excursions, long and short, from the secure base provided by our attachment figures" (Bowlby, 1988, p. 62).

Essentially, attachment theory is a spatial theory, involving the need to keep the attachment figure at a distance that the individual finds comfortable. This might mean a literal distance, or, as Holmes designates it, an invisible "Maginot line" (Holmes, 1993, p. 70) as can be seen in the child at playgroup who plays with his chums, somewhat in parallel play, a few feet away from mum, and regularly comes back to check her out, and tug on her skirts in order to gain reassurance. Alternatively, it might mean proximity in a more sophisticated and abstract form, where a photograph of a loved one suffices, or even the holding on to a transitional object. I have known clients of mine, deep in a dependent transference, keep by their sides a book that I might have lent them, or even go to sleep at night with one of my business cards clutched in their hand.

I would wish, however, to take issue with Bowlby's dictum that living with two parents is always best. Living with two parents *is best if the parents are enjoying a close relationship.* Sadly, this is not always the case. I have borne witness to many clients' complaints that they wished their parents had divorced earlier because they suffered the effects of seemingly interminable aggressive conduct (both emotional and physical). I took issue with a BBC Panorama programme, the tenet of which was, unsurprisingly, that living with two parents was preferable for a child's development. Yes, this is so, but with one proviso: *only if* the parents are habitually happy together. Living in an atmosphere of constant conflict can be most unsettling, and sets a precedent in which conflictual relationships can grow to seem to be the norm. It is true that parents should show that conflict can be expressed and tolerated, and not hidden and avoided, but constant aggression is destructive.

I want to touch on the argument promulgated by the feminist critique. I agree that females should not be tied to the kitchen sink, and neither should they be unpaid slaves to men. For an exposition of the feminist perspective on this point, or the whole of feminist theory, I refer you to Chodorow (1978) and Oakley (1981). It is outside the remit of this book to look at these issues in detail. However, while it seems to me that it is impractical to pay women officially for housework, as some feminists have suggested, none the less it is an emotional burden which is too great for some women to bring up children, isolated from other adult contact, with no other stimulation. My sister needed, for her psychological wellbeing, to return to work when each of her infants was aged one, and to find an alternative means of childcare, in order to avoid debilitating depression. Similarly, there are millions of women in today's society who need to work for pressing financial reasons because they are either single parents or need to augment or supply the family income. Given the dictates of economic expediency, the present Conservative government is raising the level of benefits payable to mothers (of three- and four-year-olds) who work in excess of fifteen hours a week. Times clearly change—no longer that post-war idea of a cosy and caring matriarchy!

The reality is that children *do* show attachment behaviour. However, while attachment is monotropic (that is, to one figure rather than to many), Bowlby failed to recognise that most children can cope with a hierarchy of attachment figures. Thus, the little boy may have a primary attachment to mum, plus a secondary attachment to father, and a tertiary attachment to a key worker at his nursery.

At the heart of the feminist argument against Bowlby lies his assumption that anatomy is destiny: that mother is the only sex that is capable of giving birth, so children must form primary attachments to a female. In this, Bowlby took a view surprisingly similar to that of Freud, though perhaps this is not surprising, given his upper-middle-class background where mother did not work outside the home and patriarchal values were wont to flourish. Children do not only form attachment to females; males can just as readily become attachment figures (though, unfortunately, there is little research of attachment relationships between fathers and children). Bowlby's ideas, perhaps, are the result of his disappointment with a mother who possibly did not give him what he most craved and his resentment towards her due to her favouritism of his brother, Tony. Maybe his belief that women should be the carers was the result of an idealised view of reality.

Bowlby saw the emotional bond between carer and child as being psychological in origin, rather than the result of a need for sustenance or infant sexual desire (Kleinian and Freudian concepts in their turn). He stated that the child's primary motivational need was for the proximity of his mother to keep him safe, in contrast to Freud's belief that physiological needs were paramount.

Marcel Proust, in 1913, was consciously aware of the precious nature of his own mother's love, and expresses in the following paragraph his own insecure attachment, perhaps borne of mother giving too little. He wrote, in *À La Recherche Du Temps Perdu*:

> My sole consolation when I went upstairs for the night was that Mamma would come in and kiss me after I was in bed. But this moment lasted for so short a time, she went down again so soon, that the moment in which I heard her climb the stairs, and then caught the sound of her garden dress, from which hung little tassels of plaited straw, rustling along the double-doored corridor, was for me a moment of utmost pain: for it heralded the moment that was to follow it, when she would have left me and gone downstairs again. So much so that I reached the point of hoping that this good night which I loved so much would come as late as possible, so as the prolong the time of respite during which Mamma would not yet have appeared. Sometimes, after kissing me, she opened the door to go, I longed to call her back, to say to her "Kiss me just once more", but I knew that she would at once look displeased, for the concession which she made to my wretchedness and agitation in coming up to give me this kiss always annoyed my father, who thought such rituals absurd. (Proust, 1995, pp. 14–15)

Bowlby's ideas grew not from reading Proust, but from ethology. For example, he was much affected by the following experiment concerning monkeys' attachment behaviour. Harlow's (1958) well-known experiment focused on baby monkeys' relationships with wire-framed "monkeys" who had feeding bottles holding milk attached to them as opposed to some cloth-covered, cuddly "monkeys" who had no milk supply. Harlow found that the baby monkeys preferred to cling to the cuddly, cloth-covered monkey-mothers rather than the feeding monkey-mothers, indicating that they preferred proximity to warmth and tenderness rather than sustenance.

However, the monkey experiment failed to give weight to another facet of what Bowlby saw as attachment behaviour. In addition to seeking proximity to the attachment figure, the child actually gains a sense of mutual reciprocity with his "secure base". In other words, just as he likes to keep mother (shall we say) nearby, so does mother prefer proximity to the little one that she cares for. Thus, we can observe that mothers who work in paid employment frequently miss their young children during the course of the working day, pine for them, and think of them, even telephoning the nursery or childminder to find out if they are all right. Most working mothers also talk of continuously suffering a gnawing sense of guilt, though they might appreciate that this is not rational.

Another facet of attachment behaviour as defined by Bowlby is that of separation protest. Protest is thought to be made in order to attempt to stop the secure base from leaving, or in the hope that it will cause the person to return. Of course, it is also an outlet for emotional release. At the base of protest lies the concept of maternal responsiveness. Here, we are reminded of Winnicott's concept of maternal attunement and the mirroring with which mother intuitively responds to the baby's cues: for example, the "oohs" and "aahs", the peek-a-boos, the return of a smile, the chuck under the chin. All of these actions are dialogic—it is as if mother and baby are having a conversation while magically attuned. In fact, this dialogue provides the baby with a sense of agency—that he can alter or affect the mother's behaviour. "Power" is defined as "the capacity for producing an effect; energy; right to command authority" (*Chambers Dictionary*). The baby has power during the mirroring sequence between mother and baby.

The difference between pathological attachment and normal attachment

Secure attachment

Bowlby came to realise that if the child grew up in an atmosphere where mother or father were reliably available, both emotionally and physically, then the child grew to feel he possessed a "secure base" (Bowlby, 1988). For the child to experience emotional availability, the carer must be emotionally attuned, reliably and consistently available, and consistent in her level of care and in the manner in which she responds to his needs. While she might not be physically available all of the time, he must be told when and under what circumstances she will not be available, and prolonged separations are to be avoided. If there is a case of, say, hospital admission, visiting should be frequent. I was hospitalised for three months before the birth of my second child because of a diagnosis of placenta praevia, but the emotional toll of this unavoidable separation for my elder daughter was minimised by arranging for her to visit me daily.

Parents, therefore, need to encourage the infant and the developing child to express any negative affect, not in a violent manner, but by recourse to words to express his dissatisfaction verbally. Similarly, it is normal for mother or father to be angry with the child at times, but anger needs to be expressed verbally, in a calm, positive, and measured way, without aggression. When the child is angry, it is important that the carer does not retaliate with aggressive behaviour.

Insecure–ambivalent attachment

There are several reasons that lead to the child adopting an insecure–ambivalent attachment pattern of relating. This happens when the carer is not reliably emotionally and/or physically available, or she might be inconsistent in the way she responds. In other words, at times she might be patient and interested, while, on other occasions, she might be impatient, unwilling to wait, desirous to "get on" with the day, disinterested in what her little one wants to tell her. For example, I feel very strongly that, in these days where social media is so integral to many mothers' lives, that mothers need to put aside the mobile phone and the Facebook messages while their children want their attention, and make time for their personal pleasures when the children are asleep, or at nursery or school. In similar vein, a mother who might sometimes tolerate anger from the child, while at others being openly rejecting of his demeanour, is acting in such a way as to construct insecure attachment in her youngster.

Mother might seem preoccupied when playing with the child or baby, or just not be able to be attuned (Stern, 1985) and responsive to him. It is the *quality* of the interaction rather than the quantity that matters. Passive contact does not necessarily promote secure attachment (see Gerhardt's (2014) case study of Kirstie and Millie in Odgers, 2014, pp. 16–22).

As a result of finding it difficult and indefinite whether he will "catch" mum's attention, the child could develop an overall presentation of "weakness" or frequent illness. The child hopes that if he makes enough fuss, then mother might well give him the attention he otherwise lacks. It is wise to avoid this scenario, for it can be responsible for the child developing psychosomatic illnesses in later life.

A similar set of circumstances could possibly develop when mother is suffering from depressive illness and, therefore, is not emotionally available to the child for a protracted period of time. It is possible to observe the effect of this in three of the case studies in Part IV. While the mother is most probably physically present; she is not emotionally available, much as she might like to be. This can be a very real cause of regret for many mothers during later years of their lives. The child, meanwhile, experiences the mother as withdrawn, preoccupied with her own internal world, and having no availability for his needs and wants. He feels isolated. "on his own". This can lead to the child developing one of the less than ideal patterns of attachment: either an insecure–ambivalent or an insecure–avoidant style of relating. Both these attachment styles are pathological, though, in my experience, insecure–ambivalent attachment can more easily be rectified through long-term therapy than insecure–avoidant attachment.

I would direct you to the case studies in *The Oedipus Complex: Solutions or Resolutions?* (Fear, 2015, pp. 49–120). One can then compare how the work in the transference with six different individuals seemed to be more successful in healing the pathological style of attachment of each of the clients who initially had presented in therapy suffering an ambivalent style of relating rather than an avoidant style.

Mikulincer and Shaver (2008) have pointed out, quite correctly, that many individuals' attachment schema are somewhere along a continuum that stretches from insecure–ambivalent to insecure–avoidant. In fact, they have recently devised a different typology for these insecure patterns, naming them hyperactivating (insecure–ambivalent) and deactivating (insecure–avoidant).

insecure–avoidant attachment

There are other situations in which the mother might be physically available, but emotionally out of tune with the child, for one of many reasons, sometimes with dire results. Perhaps mother did not want this child because the child is the product of rape and involuntary pregnancy. Perhaps the mother is suffering from abuse (domestic, physical, or emotional) or addiction, and is frequently under the influence of intoxicating substances. Perhaps she suffers from a mental health problem, such as psychosis or borderline personality disorder; this could mean that she is so wrapped up in her internal reality that she is unable to give her time, energy, and consideration to her child. Likewise, the cycle of deprivation might play its part—that is, the mother's own experience of maternal deprivation under which she might have suffered could mean she is unversed in knowing how to behave as a consistent, available mother. Maybe the poverty in which she lives is so severe that she is constantly preoccupied with the problem of paying the rent and putting food on the table. There are many and varied reasons that a mother cannot be consistently available to her child. If a carer is dismissive and not emotionally or physically available (say, leaving the child alone for periods of time), then the child is likely to grow up with an insecure–avoidant attachment style. This might result in the young adult acting out with delinquent or rebellious behaviour as he "identifies with the aggressor" and becomes "a bully" at school or in the workplace.

Less obviously, though far more commonly seen in our consulting rooms, is evidence of the individual unwilling and unable to allow anyone to get close to him at an emotional level. He may well crave intimacy, but when favourable circumstances present themselves, he will take avoidant action. For example, he might deliberately start arguments with his adult partner, as in the film *Who's Afraid of Virginia*

Woolf? (Albee, 1966). This enables a level of intimacy to be unconsciously regulated by frequent arguments in order to keep the other at a distance. Another mechanism that is frequently unconsciously employed by an individual is to repeatedly choose unavailable partners—lovers, for instance, who are married to another person, and, therefore, not fully committed to the relationship, or by making a relationship with men whose career in the armed forces frequently takes them away from home.

Bowlby's succinct definition clearly identifies the nature of the insecure–avoidant syndrome. He speaks of how the individual shows

> The determination at all costs not to risk again the disappointment and resulting rages and longings which wanting someone very much and not getting them involves. A policy of self-protection against the slings and arrows of their own turbulent feelings. (Bowlby, 1944, p. 57)

This statement applies to so many of my past clients; clients who have innovatively employed numerous defence mechanisms in order to keep "the other" at a distance (sometimes this being me in the consulting room). I have found that by gently employing the use of this evocative quotation, and explaining what it means, while gesticulating with my hands in a "Keep your hands off" gesture as if to ward off danger and unwanted "attack", some motivation to change attachment style is gradually discovered. It also, however, requires that I act as a secure base for that individual for quite some protracted period of time. It is, as we shall see in Part IV of the book, the work in therapy, in the transference, that achieves the most priceless psychic change and sometimes healing of the pathology.

An insecure–avoidant style of relating can be the result of either an unresponsive mother, an unattuned parent, or, at the other end of the continuum, an intrusive parent. Thus, the behaviour of physically abusive parents, sexually abusive parents, or even emotionally abusive parents who continuously rant at their children and allow them little sense of peace, can result in the child becoming an adult who resolves never again to let anyone in close. In similar vein, a parent can be intrusive by crowding the growing child or adolescent, continually accompanying him wherever he goes, not allowing him out of her sight, or by emotional intrusiveness that leads to a feeling of suffocation.

Insecure–disorganised attachment

A very small percentage of individuals suffer from an insecure–disorganised attachment style. The figure is small and used to be thought to be statistically insignificant. It was usually only noted among clinical groups. However, later research by Main (1990) found that when she identified this fourth attachment style, a number of the adults in the AAI who had formerly been classified as securely attached should, in fact, have been recorded as belonging to the disorganised category. This is due to the fact that the children in question were diagnosed as being unaffected by their mother's absence and, thus, they were thought to be securely attached, when in reality they were displaying the "signs of watchful attention from a distance" which, instead, indicated that they were avoidant attachers. This miscalculation actually accounted for approximately 14–15% of the 69% previously recorded as securely attached. This reduces the secure group to 54%. It is noted with horror that this means that only just over half the population can be classified as secure.

This attachment style was first identified by Margaret Main, who was a doctorate student of Mary Ainsworth, in her work on developing the adult attachment interview (AAI) and the associated research samples. The following characteristics are evidenced: the individual displays a disorganised, chaotic attitude towards his attachment figure. There is alternating pulling towards (wanting the person) and pushing away of the carer. The carer tends to feel very confused: not knowing whether they are wanted or not, or how to behave. If they approach and come close, they are rejected, but if they stay away, they are punished. There might be other examples of chaotic behaviour, such as hair-pulling, rocking, "freezing", and head-banging. It is now thought that such behaviour represents an attempt to self-soothe as a result of a vicious circle: the child feels insecure and, consequently, sets off to search all the more avidly for a secure base, and finding none, then becomes progressively more anxious. Frequently, it is the case that the individual with a disorganised attachment style was raised by a carer who herself had a disorganised style of attachment, and could not tolerate any considered and consistent show of affection. The individual also tends to display a level of aggression not commonly seen in the other attachment styles.

When one meets with someone with this style of relating, one ends up, as an observer, feeling utterly confused and muddled. I admit that I have frequently suffered with a splitting headache as a result of observing this behaviour. I found this perplexing until I read a book entitled *The Psychotic Wavelength*, by Richard Lucas (2013). He echoed for me the feelings that I had endured week after week, but had been unable to articulate until I read his book. He, too, speaks of suffering from headaches in the company of such chaotic attachment styles. It was not only my head that was "splitting".

It is fairly accurate to say that many of us will not encounter this attachment style in our professional lives, unless we work in psychiatric hospitals or with psychotic patients and their families. If we do, it is likely (though not inevitable) that these clients either have a psychotic parent or are themselves suffering from psychosis. It is very rare for such individuals to manage to retain personal relationships over a sustained period of time.

Van IJzendoorn and Kroonenberg (1988) originally calculated that the percentage of individuals suffering from this attachment style is 0.1%, and that individuals are usually only found in clinical psychiatric settings. However, later research by this dyad concluded that if one statistically assesses a group of patients where the family system is under severe psychological trauma, the percentage of those who can be classified as insecure disorganised can rise to 70% (Van IJzendoorn & Sagi-Schwartz, 2008).

Van IJzendoorn and Kroonenberg (1988) also report that the incidence of the other attachment styles is as follows:

Secure attachment	66%
insecure–ambivalent attachment	8%
insecure–avoidant attachment	26%

These figures are valid for the inhabitants of Western Europe. Figures vary for other parts of the world.

It needs to be said that the first three categories of the above four-part typology of attachment styles were not actually developed by John Bowlby, but by his colleague, Mary Ainsworth. She is responsible for identifying the three attachment schemas that are more often encountered. She did this during her work in establishing the strange situation test in Baltimore. It is to this test that we shall turn in the next chapter.

However, the concept of what constitutes normal attachment, and what conditions lead to abnormal ways of relating, was, in essence, born because of the life work of Bowlby.

Mary Ainsworth is known as the co-founder of attachment theory, and to her we owe the debt of the establishment of the three-part typology. The fourth sector of the typology, insecure disorganised attachment, was added separately by Main and Solomon in 1990.

Conclusion

It is to the work of Mary Ainsworth regarding her strange situation test, and to the work of Mary Main and her collaborators (adult attachment interview), that I turn in the next chapter.

CHAPTER TWO

Attachment theory post Bowlby

Introduction

Since Bowlby's death in 1990, a number of different individuals have come to prominence in the field of attachment theory, as both theorists and researchers. Mary Ainsworth had worked alongside John Bowlby during the early days before going to Uganda and later to Baltimore, where she developed her seminal strange situation test. Her research has eventually led to the adoption of a four-part typology of attachment schemas that has been widely adopted throughout the Western world.

Later in this chapter, some of the post-Bowlbian developments in attachment theory are described, although it is beyond the remit of this book to make an exhaustive study of the literature on the subject.

Mary Ainsworth and the strange situation test

Bretherton (1991) has described Mary Ainsworth's "strange situation" as "a miniature drama in eight parts"—a drama that unfolds during a twenty-minute period while the three participants are observed.

Ainsworth wanted to devise a standardised test that would assess the attachment relationship between mother and child in a reliable, naturalistic way.

The strange situation (Ainsworth et al., 1978) consists of a session in a room with mother, her one-year-old, and an experimenter, who are, at first, all present together. The mother then leaves the room for three minutes; she returns, and then, shortly afterwards, both she and the experimenter leave the child in the room alone for three minutes. The whole sequence of events in the room is filmed, and then the session is assessed, taking particular note of how the child responds to the stress of separation and subsequent reunion with mother.

Initially, Ainsworth detected three patterns of response, labelling these as secure, insecure–ambivalent, and insecure–avoidant. The three-part typology of attachment schemas was born. Later, Main and Goldwyn (1984) and Main and Solomon (1990) added a fourth style of relating: that of insecure–disorganised. This has led to the following typology, which is still used today.

- Secure attachment: these infants are usually, but not always, distressed on separation. They tend to welcome the mother back at reunion, and then quickly resume contented play.
- Insecure–avoidant: these infants show few overt signs of missing mother when she either leaves or returns to the room, showing neither overt signs of distress nor pleasure. However, this seeming disinterest is belied by the fact that they remain watchful when mother returns and seem preoccupied. They go on to play with toys in a distracted fashion, constantly looking across at mother to check whether she is still there. They appear to want to avoid betraying any emotion. Such an individual's behaviour reminds me of Schopenhauer's "Dance of the porcupines" (quoted in Melges & Swartz, 1989, cited in Holmes, 1993, p. 175), in which he describes the behaviour of a group of porcupines on a dark, cold night. They draw close together, but then their quills stick into each other, so they move apart, but then they become chilly, so they draw closer together again. They then continually repeat this pattern of behaviour. They cannot find an optimal level of intimacy with which they are comfortable. In this way, a similar pattern of behaviour is displayed by insecure–avoidant children.

- Insecure–ambivalent: these infants are very distressed on separation and mother finds it hard to pacify them when she returns. They seek contact, but then cannot settle to it; instead, they may resort to biting, kicking, screaming, or clinging behaviour towards mother. Of all the groups, they are the hardest to pacify, and take the longest time to settle back into play.
- Insecure–disorganised: this statistically small group show a diverse range of confused, chaotic, bizarre behaviours; this includes "freezing", head-banging, and stereotypical, repetitive movements. The child tends to approach mother, then as he comes close, he veers off, and displays a wish to get away quite aggressively (to kick/scream/push/shove). I summarise such behaviour with the phrase: "Approach–avoidance with distinctive display of aggression".

The child both appears to want intimacy but, at the same time, is repelled by it when he comes within reach of its actuality.

In the original Ainsworth sample, the following percentages applied to each group:

- secure: 66%;
- insecure–avoidant: 20%;
- insecure–ambivalent: 12%.

Since then, many other researchers have carried out tests. The results vary according to cultural mix. It has been discovered that in Western Europe and the USA, the percentage of avoidant classification is greater; in Israel and Japan the percentage of ambivalent category is higher.

I would postulate the notion that if this test were carried out in an African country, such as Nigeria, where the indigenous population still tend to raise their children utilising the extended family structure, and where polygamy is regarded as normal, the test would result in a very different analysis. It is common for attachment not to be pronounced towards mother or any one member of the family: that is, it is not monotropic. My brother-in-law is Nigerian, and his marriage to my sister has sustained for over fifty years. In contrast, the majority of my sister's friends, who were non-Nigerians married to Nigerians, have experienced marriages that have ended in separation and divorce. I believe that the reason my sister's marriage has endured is that her husband, unlike his fellow countrymen, was brought up purely by his paternal grandfather, and, therefore, he formed a secure attachment to a single person from age one to age eighteen. Had he been raised in the typical Nigerian extended family structure, I dare to hypothesise that their marriage would have broken down long ago because he could not have made a secure and lasting adult intimate attachment to a single individual.

The incidence of aggression in different attachment types

Aggression tends to be overt in the behaviour of infants and children who have an insecure–ambivalent attachment schema. This seems to replicate with their life partners when they reach adulthood. In contrast, insecure–avoidant children tend to disguise their feelings of aggression; perhaps this is because they are so unsure of the "crumbs of love" they do receive, rather than being free to feast on the "whole cake", that, in consequence, they do not risk scaring the carer away for fear of being abandoned/"not fed" at all.

A client with whom I worked in long-term therapy (whom I refer to as Emma in the case studies) proved to have an insecure–avoidant schema, as a result of her mother repeatedly threatening her during childhood that she would arrange for Social Services to take my client and her siblings into care. She was one of those to whom Bowlby's evocative words apply about the determination to avoid feelings of "desperate rage and longing" ever again (as quoted in the Chapter One).

In the first four years of therapy, Emma was so consumed with anger and aggressive feelings that she ranted at me frequently in sessions. I could do nothing right. I grew to understand what it is to withstand the negative transference in all its force, and not to retaliate. However, while she did display verbal anger (contrary to the dictum above), she was compliant in terms of always appearing for her sessions (three a week) on time. In more recent years, coming to therapy now once weekly, her anger is still evident on specific occasions but is far more muted. She rarely complains about me or is consciously angry, but she does arrive late for her sessions repeatedly nowadays. While this might seem paradoxical, I think that the fact that she dares not to comply any longer in so subtle a way says that she believes I care for her and that my love of her will not disappear if she is rebellious. It is my speculation that she no longer needs to be "good".

Further research after Ainsworth's strange situation research: the adult attachment interview (AAI)

Ainsworth had a host of doctoral students and a whole generation of attachment researchers was born, including, among others, Silvia Bell, Mary Main, Robert Marvin, Mary Blehar, Inge Bretherton, and Everett Waters.

Some years after the strange situation test was devised, a semi-structured interview was designed to study adults' attachment schemas. This "adult attachment interview" (AAI) was initially developed by Carol George (George et al., 1985) as a part of her doctoral research. Her analysis of the questions was not successful in proving any grand hypothesis, but then Main and Goldwyn (1984) employed discourse analysis regarding the way in which the mothers discussed their experiences of their own childhood. This qualitative method of research found a strong positive correlation between the analysis of mothers' attachment styles and their infants' behaviour in a subsequent strange situation test (carried out at age one year). What has become known as the AAI was born.

On the basis of an evaluation developed by Main and Goldwyn (1984), and continued by Main and Solomon (1990), the responses to adult attachment interviews can be classified into four categories. These are the following:

- secure or free–autonomous;
- dismissing;
- preoccupied;
- unresolved (Main & Goldwyn, 1984).

The AAI evaluations require extensive training, because the interviewers are trained to look for the ways in which the discourse is peppered with inconsistencies; irrelevance; understanding or lack of it; with order or chaos; with detail or generality; saturated with emotion or evidence of self-regulation; whether there is supporting evidence for statements or lack of reinforcement. I remember asking Helen (in the case studies in Part IV) if she could give me an example of her mother showing the love that my client professed she received, and the only instance she could offer consisted of the following: "She did a lot of needlework for us. She made a lot of my dresses."

Interviewers frequently find that the sessions with the preoccupied or entangled individuals seem to be interminable—it is as if the session will just go on and on, because the individual's story becomes oversaturated with detail and unprocessed emotion, none of which provides any reinforcement or adds meaning.

Again, as I stated before, the interviewer is looking for a sense of autobiographical competence which is generally only found in those individuals who have a secure schema.

Fonagy and colleagues continued to carry out more research and developments in the field of the AAI by using it to compare the mother's attachment schema directly before the birth of her baby with the attachment schema (diagnosed by the strange situation test) of the infant when he or she reached the age of one. These researchers came to the conclusion that the degree to which the mother possessed a reflexive function (RF) made a great deal of difference for the infant regarding the attachment schema he developed. If the mother was reflexive, the child was likely to develop a secure attachment; if the mother did not possess a reflexive skill, then the child was more likely to become insecurely attached.

It is the ability to have developed a reflexive skill despite having endured some of life's traumas that Jeremy Holmes defines as the individual having earned security (Holmes, 2010, p. 25). This does not align itself precisely with my interpretation of learned security. I believe that learned security exists when the client is able to attain a psychic position where he feels that he has gained a secure base of his own, to which he can return in times of anxiety and stress, whereas, previously in life, he has not experienced this sense of security as a result of some traumatological experience. This learned security is arrived at as the result of a strong, sustained, and emotionally intimate relationship (usually) with a therapist or, possibly, with a close friend or life partner. It is the secure-base experience rather than the possession of a reflexive function that leads me to define a state of learned security. It might well be that, as a result of the secure-base experience, one develops a reflexive function, but I do not see the latter as being the defining element. This is yet another reason why I have named the concept differently from earned security, because it involves a discretely different concept.

A certain amount of research has been carried out to study the relationship and differences between what the researchers (particularly in the USA) refer to as "continuous-secures" and "earned-secures". Continuous-secures refers to those individuals who have always felt secure in their attachments because of a nurturing, consistent relationship with a parental figure. Continuous-secures can provide a coherent narrative of their childhood, unsaturated with emotional overload. Earned-secures, by contrast, are defined as those individuals who have been raised in a family or institutional setting where they have suffered some lack of continuous loving care, but they appear to have gone through a reparative process during adulthood, where they have attained a secure way of relating, and are able to talk about their childhood dispassionately. As a consequence, they are able to transfer this secure way of relating to their children. However, whereas both categories of people are successful in caring for their children, offering secure attachment, research implies that there appears to be a positive correlation between the earned–secures and their propensity to suffer some periods of depression in adult life. The question is then posed as to whether the earned-secures *did* have a difficult childhood, or whether they interpreted it this way because of their propensity to depression/pessimism/negative attitude to life/belief in an external locus of control.

It can be seen, therefore, that the term earned–secure has been in relatively common parlance among the attachment fraternity for the past decade. While I think it is useful to point out this research field, I am not convinced that the researchers are referring to the same concept in using the term earned security as I refer to by use of my term, learned security.

Another aspect of research carried out in the era post-Bowlby is that carried out by Lyons-Ruth and Jacobvitz (2008), which concerns another aspect of the infant–mother communication. Their measure has explored the mother's ability to repair ruptures in her relationship with her little one. Is she able to be sensitive enough to discern when there is a rupture, not to see it as wilful or "naughty", or of no consequence, and does she also have sufficient confidence in her own abilities to set about repairing the rupture? This measure is known, in recent attachment research, as AMBIANCE.

Further to this, the PDI (parent development interview) was developed as a spin-off from AMBIANCE. It was developed in order to assess the correlation between maternal reflexive function (RF), and the score the mother achieved regarding AMBIANCE. It seems as if the capacity to mentalize, or otherwise, is very important with regard to one's ability to detect, appreciate, and then repair ruptures with one's child.

The concept of mentalization is associated with all the measures discussed above: this concept effectively makes use of one's reflexive skills. Mentalization has been developed by Peter Fonagy and his collaborators (Fonagy et al., 2002). Possessing a reflexive function (RF) essentially enables the individual to be able to stand back and be aware of what she was thinking about, and to have an awareness that others might be thinking differently. Thus, a mother with a reflexive function is likely to employ this capacity in order to empathise effectively with her infant. It is to this topic that I turn in the next chapter.

CHAPTER THREE

Mentalizing: a development in attachment theory post Bowlby

Introduction

As I stated in the previous chapter, the third phase of attachment theory has emerged the 1990s, with a series of experimental, theoretical, and clinical studies by Peter Fonagy, Miriam Steele, and Howard Steele at University College London, and Mary Main and colleagues in the USA. They have developed and used the adult attachment interview (AAI) to categorise the state of mind of parents-to-be regarding the ways in which they tend to make and sustain important attachments in their lives. They have then used this to compare the subsequent attachment classification of the infant born to them, by classifying that infant's attachment schema using the strange situation test that Mary Ainsworth first devised (Fonagy et al., 2002).

This research relied upon the carers' ability to think about thinking: that is, to consider their thoughts and those of their infants as perceptions, rather than "facts" or "reality", and to appreciate that others are sentient beings. This, in short, has come to be known as the possession of a reflexive function (RF).

These researchers have found that RF and security of attachment, or, conversely, insecurity, tends to be transmitted from generation to generation. This is in line with Holmes' definition of earned security that I spoke of in the previous chapter. It is true, as Holmes says, that "anxiety is the enemy of mentalisation" (Holmes, 2010, p. 24). The root of this belief lies in the fact that an individual is too preoccupied, when anxious, to be able to think clearly, or, more pertinently, to be aware of herself thinking and to stand back and analyse her thinking. Psychoanalysis or psychoanalytic psychotherapy enables the client to give voice to thoughts, some of which have always been conscious, some (until the therapist's intervention) which have been unconscious until recently. Thus, in this way, psychoanalytic psychotherapy helps to give birth to the process of mentalization for many of us.

The term "reflexive function" became the guiding principle of Fonagy's group, who have developed the concept of mentalizing, along with Allen (Allen & Fonagy, 2006; Allen et al., 2008) and others (Bateman & Fonagy, 2004). It is the work of Fonagy, Target, Gergely, and Bateman that has brought the word mentalization into being. In short, it refers to the process of "thinking about feelings and feeling about thinking".

I find Jeremy Holmes' definition of mentalization particularly useful. He says that mentalization is "mind-mindedness", the ability to see ourselves as others see us, and others as they see themselves. In addition, it allows us to appreciate that all human experience is filtered through the mind and, therefore, that all perceptions, desires, and theories are necessarily provisional (see www.wardipedia.org/7-mentalising/).

The main rationale of the Fonagy group in developing the technique of mentalizing has been in the hope that it would help those clients who suffer from borderline personality disorder (BPD). This categorises those individuals with a mental illness who have, until now, been very difficult to treat and for whom standard treatments (both medication and talking therapies) have only achieved a modicum of success. It is thought that if we can improve the mentalizing capacities of those suffering from BPD, then they may well be able to function a lot better in the external world. As I have indicated above, research shows that individuals with BPD tend to have developed very limited capacities of mentalizing, perhaps because they had parents who were unable to mentalize in their turn, or to think beyond their own self-experience because of their own difficulties, traumas, and dissociated attachment schemas.

However, I would like to point out that increasing the capacity to mentalize is important for all of us, especially those of us who use the skill of empathy in our everyday lives. It is also important for our clients who, through mentalization, can start, for the first time in their lives, to hold us in mind when they are physically separated from us. This skill helps to heal the deficits that they have suffered as a result of not having experienced a secure base during their developmental process.

An introduction to mentalizing

Mentalizing involves the individual in a three stage process:

1. Thinking accompanied by *feeling*.
2. An *awareness* of what one is thinking and feeling.
3. Thinking about what one has caught oneself thinking about.

Holmes (2010, p. 12) describes us as needing to apply a five-stage model to mentalizing, and I find this model very useful:

1. *Self-mentalizing*: being aware of one's own feelings.
2. *Other-mentalizing*: being aware of what the other might be feeling.
3. *Self-with-other-mentalizing*: being aware what one might be feeling towards the other.
4. *Other-with-self-mentalizing*: being aware what the other might be feeling towards oneself.
5. *Self-and-other-mentalizing*: being aware of the interaction between the two of you from a neutral standpoint.

Below I give you an example from my own life of my process of mentalizing when I first heard that my mother had died.

One December evening, my sister rang me while I was on holiday in Tenerife to tell me, in a somewhat disjointed fashion, that she thought that it was possible that our mother was dead. She was not sure, because she could not get confirmation of this "fact" from the police, but had been told by a friend that our mother had died in a taxi on her way home from lunch out at a hotel.

Stage 1: *Self-mentalizing*: I was aware of feeling shocked and sad, and very confused, and a bit angry because of the confusing circumstances around the way the information had been related.

Stage 2: *Other-mentalizing*: in the next few hours, before my sister telephoned again the next morning, I became aware that my sister might become deeply distressed owing to her being, at that time, the principal carer of my mother, our father having died only eleven weeks prior to this. She was also on the scene, unlike myself, and would doubtless be feeling responsible.

Stage 3: *Self-with-other-mentalizing*: I was aware, when I spoke to my sister the next morning, that I felt sorry for her because the police had been unhelpful and unwilling to confirm that it was true that our mother had died, and had been remiss in availing my sister of any help; as a consequence, she had been unable to find out whether our mother was dead for some twenty-four hours. I was also annoyed on her behalf at the way it had been handled.

Stage 4: *Other-with-self-mentalizing*: I became aware that my sister had felt abandoned by me in her hour of need. I, who according to family myth, had historically held everything together, was unavailable at this time because I was over 2,000 miles away.

Stage 5: *Self-and-other-mentalizing*: I wondered if each of us had become isolated in our own pockets of grief for a while. This was as a result, I believe, of the geographical divide, and the way this had led us to experience our mother's death in different ways. When our mother's funeral took place (interestingly, after another long gap because of the Christmas and the New Year break), the vicar leading the service made a mistake during the funeral service in that he forgot to read the eulogy that we had composed. This oversight served to unite us again with a common experience of exasperation, disappointment, and regret.

The capacity of the therapist to mentalize

It becomes normal for most of us as therapists to be able to put our own problems and issues to one side and to think beyond them, and instead to focus upon the client's world while we are in our consulting rooms. In summary, we are able, during our time with our clients, to think about thinking: to be aware of our own thoughts, our own feelings about our thoughts, and to be aware of what our clients may be feeling, and may be feeling towards and about us. We can usually monitor, as if hovering above, how we are interacting as a dyad.

None the less, on a bad day, or maybe when we get hooked up in a countertransference response to our client's transference, we can get caught up in our own material. We then find it difficult, or even impossible, to think beyond our own thoughts, or to settle on the perspective of "the other".

An example of this occurred, I believe, in my own therapy many years ago, and my therapist and I have returned to the episode and both learned from it since. I was describing an event at my younger daughter's rental property in her university town, when my husband had been particularly lacking in empathy concerning the mental difficulties that our daughter was encountering at the time. Our daughter was quite ill at the time. I sensed it was my role to act as a bridge between my husband and daughter, not dissimilar to the eponymous central character of L. P. Hartley's brilliant exploration of this role in the novel, *The Go-Between* (1953). I wanted some succour from my therapist for my position in this role, trying to make peace between the two warring parties: my daughter and her father. Admittedly, I spoke to my therapist about my husband's relationship with our daughter; they were experiencing a very difficult, conflictual period. My narrative set off a transference response in my therapist; I suspect in connection with his own protective feelings towards his own daughter or stepdaughter, and his response was to reply empathically concerning my daughter, entirely ignoring my feelings in this situation. His own countertransference response, originating in the feelings he had about his own life, had taken him unawares, and temporarily prevented him from mentalizing. In contrast, he was able to say to me recently, about another event, "You are my concern, not your husband or your daughter."

He learnt a lesson that day, just as Patrick Casement says in his enlightening book, *On Learning from the Patient* (1985, pp. 57–71). It is through processing our mistakes, often in the company of our clients, and by being prepared to admit our mistakes, that we learn the most valuable lessons. I am pointing out that my therapist learnt a lesson, as I did, too. I also accept that any of us, as therapists, are just as likely to make this "mistake" again, caught up as we are wont to become from time to time in powerful countertransference.

The possibility of partial mentalizing

Partial mentalizing is something that occurs to those individuals who have been subject at an earlier part of their life to severe emotional, physical, or sexual abuse. As a consequence of this early abuse, it is possible—possible but not automatic—that one might suffer from what I term hyper-arousal.

Hyper-arousal occurs when one has a tendency to lack the capacity to differentiate between imagined reality and actual reality. By this, I mean that there might be a tendency for the therapist to imagine that the possible event a client is describing has actually occurred, and make of it a tragedy. In this way, there is a tendency for the individual to suffer from "equivalence". This means, in fact, that the individual sees two things as meaning the same; there is no awareness of the "as if". I will give an example from my casework. One of my clients was furious with me when she declared, "The flowers in your consulting room are dead!" This mattered to her because, if the flowers were dying, she felt this was equivalent to me allowing her to die while she was in my care. She was not able to see that the dying flowers were only symbolic of a dread that she was suffering. As a consequence of equivalence, there is a tendency to "catastrophise". This tendency to perceive things as actually having occurred, and to have lost the "as if" quality, is, if analysed, often found to be accompanied with a certain amount of covert excitation. This can be traced back, through a process of analysis, to the excitation associated with the original abuse, about which the person might well have felt extremely guilty. He probably has never been able to verbalise this guilt to anyone but his therapist.

There is a way in which this hyper-arousal can be controlled. It requires the person who has been the victim of abusive behaviour to undergo an experience in therapy where he finds a secure base or intimate partner. This "partner" will soothe the individual and, thus, enable the hyper-arousal to be controlled. Gradually, the tendency to conflate events will tend to stop, as the addiction to the associated drama is assuaged.

One needs to be aware that one is on very dangerous ground whenever one hears oneself say, "It *must have been* such and such!" or one uses similarly dramatic paraphrasing. It may indicate that one is catastrophising.

Conditions for mentalizing

It is difficult to employ the process of mentalization on a consistent basis, as therapists try to do. Most people use mentalizing skills instinctively some of the time and, because they are employing these skills unconsciously, they are unaware of the actual process they are using. They do not consciously think to themselves, for instance, "What is it about my friend that I am feeling irritated with this morning, and might she be feeling annoyed with me?" They are often guided by intuition. They decide using gut instinct, for instance, whether to trust a friend and lend him some money, or whether that would be an unwise course of action.

Counsellors and psychotherapists, however, employ mentalizing skills in an ordered, conscious way (although they might well not name this process as such). They use it as a way of augmenting their empathic response to the difficulties and dilemmas that their clients are facing. In my experience, it is not just a case of how it might be to stand in someone else's shoes; it is also a case of being aware of how that person might be feeling towards me as her therapist and what effect(s) I might be having upon that person.

Mentalizing becomes particularly difficult when one is in a highly aroused emotional state. For example, I found it hard to empathise with my clients' difficulties and the situations they were experiencing when my daughter (some years ago) was so ill that I thought she was dying. I was so overcome with anxiety that it was difficult to find a way to focus my thoughts and feelings on others' difficulties, and I took a short break from my work as a therapist. This is one of the reasons that the BACP Code of Ethics cautions us as therapists to continuously monitor our fitness to practise at an emotional and physical level. We are advised to discontinue our work for an appropriate period of time if we feel mentally or physically incapable of prioritising the other's needs.

There are many instances in which one might lose one's capacity to mentalize for a while. I have noticed myself, while working in a psychiatric setting, that nurses and doctors working with patients with borderline personality disorder can tend to lose their capacity to mentalize. This temporary loss of ability to mentalize is well documented in various journals and on various websites (see, for example, www.wardipedia.org/7-mentalising/).

How do Bion's theories fit in with mentalizing?

One of Bion's principal concepts concerned alpha and beta elements. Bion differentiated between thoughts and the apparatus that enables us to think. He called the capacity to think thoughts "alpha function". "Beta elements", on the other hand, are "thoughts without a thinker". Alpha function can, therefore, transform beta elements into alpha elements, which are then available for being thought about.

What is the role of the therapist in this? Essentially, therapists help the client to express "beta elements" which are often located around loss, frustration, rejection, abandonment, suffering, guilt, shame, and remorse. In putting those feelings into words in a containing environment, they become detoxified, and are changed into alpha elements. Like Winnicott's mother, who holds the baby, introjects his intolerable feelings, and then returns them to him in an acceptable, manageable form, we, as therapists, put the feelings of the client into words in a digestible form that can be accepted, in a containing environment, thus circumventing the involuntary urge in the client to run away or act them out.

A further link between Bion's ideas and mentalization is drawn by Holmes (2010, p. 18–19) regarding Bion's concepts of "K" and "minus K". "K" represents knowing and knowledge, "minus K" not knowing. Bion sees this "not knowing" as arising from "attacks on linking" (his version of the oedipal child's resentment of parental intercourse). Exploration is then seen as being brought to a halt by acute anxiety. Thus, it is the therapist's job to identify when fear takes over (that is, as a result of anxiety) and to diminish it, and to enable exploration to continue unabated.

The process of mentalization, and, indeed, the acquisition of alpha elements, enables us to bring the loved one to mind—to think about him or her, in our "image-ination". The client who is deep in the transference relationship with the therapist finds, during a break, that there is no therapist, so instead he imagines the therapist: the process of mentalizing enables him to hold her in mind, to think about her, and to think about her thinking about him, and to think about them interacting together, and how that might be and feel. We shall see how this plays out in practice in the case studies of Nick, Emma, Jane, and Helen. All of them are able now to hold me (their therapist) in mind during breaks and week-ends, while, in the early years of therapy, they found difficulty in this.

We can draw a parallel between this process and the process of internalisation (using different language), or what my therapist terms, "Having an internalised version of me inside you". By the end of long-term therapy, the client no longer needs the therapist to act as a secure base in everyday life. This is brought about by the therapist having facilitated the very precious process of internalisation. The client has an internal representation of the therapist in his mind, and can imagine having a discussion with the therapist, and intuitively knows, by this stage, what her answer will be. When we have reached this stage, it is appropriate to end therapy, for the client no longer needs a life-sized, concrete representation of a secure base.

I feel also that it is a significant function of therapists to help our clients to develop their capacities to mentalize. It is not, in my opinion, the preserve only of those with BPD to have difficulties in mentalizing. I currently have a new client who brought to me last week a difficulty she was experiencing in a relatively new relationship. Recently, her boyfriend had found himself walking from his house to her house, somewhat on automatic pilot, and, in a dream-like state, had refused anything she offered him to eat but had blurted out thoughts about enrolling as a mature student in order to embark upon a career change. She expressed to me complete puzzlement about his behaviour and the thoughts he expressed because they were so new to her, and had appeared as if from nowhere. She expressed overt anxiety that maybe he had turned up at her house in order to terminate the relationship; that is, she was deeply involved in her own frame of reference as a result of her own anxieties. This had prevented her from mentalizing, from being able to put herself in his shoes, and to think of the two of them communing together from a neutral standpoint. I helped her to analyse the situation by calming her anxiety, and she was then able to see that the fact that he made his way to her house when in distress was an indication that he was beginning to perceive her as his secure base, quite the opposite of her fears that he had come to terminate their relationship. Indeed, he had come to discuss his future with her—quite a compliment. Her anxiety had taken away temporarily any mentalizing facilities that she usually possessed.

The idea of mentalization is neologistic (that is, the use of a word or words that only has meaning to the person who uses them; a new word that has only just come into operation) in Britain. However, the concept known as *pensée opératoire* (operational, robot-like thinking, devoid of affect) has been known in France for a long time. This represents the converse of mentalization. Being alexithymic (the inability to put feeling into words) is the English equivalent of not being able to mentalize. For example, we are alexithymic when we are infants (the word infans = without speech), or when we are in shock, and often when we are in the first stages of bereavement. In consequence of this inability to put our feelings into words, we tend instead to act out, which can be regarded as a sort of remembering and repeating (Freud, 1917e). For example, a young woman who was one of my first clients twenty-five years ago presented because she was in a vicious circle of repeating highly sexualised, short-term relationships from which she found no reward or succour, but to which she felt addicted. After a relatively short piece of psychodynamic work, it emerged that she had been sexually abused as an adolescent, and, as a consequence, viewed herself purely as a sexual object, to be used and then discarded. She was, therefore, unconsciously remembering and repeating a pattern of behaviour, in a way hoping for a different outcome; perhaps she hoped that a fairy prince on a white charger would gallop in and rescue her. But he never came. We found a different solution together: we formulated a different way of living for her to adopt. We worked on creating a different image for her: one of a sentient being who could decide her own destiny. By the time she left therapy, she described herself as "a butterfly emerging from a chrysalis: ready to meet the rest of my life head-on!" I shall never forget that client; I have much for which to thank her.

Conclusion

I hope that this chapter has communicated the importance that one should place upon helping clients to increase their capacity to mentalize. It helps those of us who utilise the skill of empathy in our daily work to increase our understanding of "the other's" point of view, and, thus, it supplements our ability to work together with the client—collaboratively—in order to aid our comprehension of the client's experience. Mentalization helps our clients to hold us in mind, in order that they can bring to mind the therapist when she is not physically present.

I shall move on in the next chapter to another concept that has started to be described within attachment theory over the past ten years. I have already mentioned this in some detail with regard to recent research in the attachment fraternity. The concepts "earned security" and "learned security" provided me with the impetus to write this book. In fact, the remainder of the book is devoted to the ideas that I have developed in consequence of the concept of security.

CHAPTER FOUR

The concepts of earned security and learned security

An emerging concept: earned security

I have kept a watchful eye on the attachment theory literature and attachment therapy seminars in vogue throughout my career, but especially during the past decade. The recent concept that has both attracted and fascinated me has been the idea of earned security (Holmes, 2010; Odgers, 2014), as discussed briefly in Chapter Two. It has been announced very modestly, without any banging of drums: it is still slowly evolving. Indeed, as I write, I find an evening seminar has been announced (by nscience), to be run by Jeremy Holmes, on the subject of earned security and other major tenets of attachment theory.

I became interested in this concept a few years ago because, in essence, it "spoke" to me. The phrase seems to have derived from the research that I have described in Chapter Two regarding the differences between those respondents who were classified as either "continuous-secures" or "earned-secures". When I first met the concept, I began to formulate that, to me, earned security expresses to some degree the way in which I have been trying to help my own clients achieve a seminal change in their internal working models (Bowlby, 1988) or organisational structures (Stolorow et al., 1995) through their work in psychotherapy with me. It was just, until I read of this term, "earned security", I had not thought of giving a *label* to it.

How are we, as therapists, to create the feeling of earned security?

The answer to this question is at the heart of this most recent development in attachment theory and therapy. To my dismay, while I could find quite a number of brief references to earned security, I could find very little detail of the process one should engage with in order to help the client achieve a sense of earned security except in two texts that I will discuss shortly.

However, first, I think it is pertinent that I have attempted to research the derivation of the term "earned security". The first chronological reference to it that I could find is dated 2002. It seems to have derived from a number of pieces of research that aimed to investigate the differences between those individuals who were either continuous-secures or earned-secures. As I have described in Chapter Two, continuous-secure individuals are those who have a secure attachment schema as a result of having been raised by parents who provided a secure base, and they are, thus, able to raise their children in a secure environment. Earned-secure individuals, in contrast, are those individuals who describe having suffered some developmental deficits during their growing-up years. However, such individuals have developed a way of being capable of providing a secure attachment experience to their children. It is not stated clearly how this may have been achieved, but it certainly does not specifically state that this is as a result of work in therapy (as does my theory). It might be that Jeremy Holmes goes some way towards an explanation for earned security by focusing upon the way in which such individuals have achieved a reflexive function, though Holmes is not saying that such a reflexive function is the direct result of being in long-term therapy.

The best case examples of therapy associated with the gaining of earned security are given in the book edited by Andrew Odgers (2014), *From Broken Attachments to Earned Security: the Role of Empathy in Therapeutic Change*. This is a book which was compiled as a monograph of the Annual John Bowlby Memorial Conference, and it consists of papers that were presented by various psychoanalysts and psychoanalytic psychotherapists. I found the chapters by Jane Haynes and her client, Harry Whitehead, and by therapists Eleanor Richards and Anastasia Patrikiou to be of particular interest. Each of these three chapters describes the interaction between the therapist and her client. I assume, from the choice of clinical material, that the processes described aim to give the reader an insight into the way in which a client may—or may not—gain a sense of earned security.

The second text that speaks of earned security has been written by Jeremy Holmes, entitled *Exploring in Security: Towards an Attachment-Informed Psychoanalytic Psychotherapy* (Holmes, 2010). This book also highlights some of the processes involved in enabling clients to gain a sense of earned security. For example, Holmes stresses the need to develop "the dyadic idiolect" (Holmes, 2010, pp. 87–88). An idiolect (Lear, 1993) is a language that is private and particular to the individual therapist and her client, so that they grow to be able to communicate in their own particular form of shorthand. This helps to form an emotional connectedness, which I feel is at the heart of earned security. An example of an idiolect is the way that I refer, with one of my clients, to his feeling of vulnerability upon occasions, say about his feelings of shame or guilt: we call it "a moment when he is contentedly walking down the High Street, when suddenly he realises he has no clothes on underneath his cashmere overcoat". This is a metaphor that we have privately evolved in order to enable him to get in touch with a difficult emotion. Metaphors often have this power, because of their "as if" quality. The "no clothes on" metaphor is part of our dyadic idiolect, and it would not have the same communicative implications for anyone other than the two of us.

Holmes (2010) talks in his book about the process by which the client attaches to the therapist and, in a chapter of another publication, he describes a way of working collaboratively that enables the therapist and client together to reach a sense of "autobiographical competence" (Holmes, 1993, p. 182). He points out, interestingly, that the therapist's real power lies in her ability to provide an experience of secure attachment (Holmes, 2010, p. 71). In speaking of the need for emotional attunement, he talks about what he sees as inevitable periods of "rupture" (Safran & Muran, 2000). Holmes makes the very relevant point, as do Safran and Muran (2000), that what matters is that the ruptures—however caused—are repaired. This needs to be managed non-defensively by the therapist.

An example of rupture can be described by referring to my own experience in therapy. My therapist responded to a telephone message left by me during his break between two clients. I found his answer to my plea for succour highly unsatisfactory, and, in consequence, I was very disturbed at his lack of appreciation and emotional connectedness with me regarding my feelings of rejection and abject loss. This caused a rupture in our relationship and I was very angry in the following session when I complained about his response to me the previous day. He was slightly defensive at first, in that he rationalised his behaviour by saying that he needed to have these minutes to himself between clients in order to process the material raised in a session. I pointed out to him that, in that case, he would be better not to answer the telephone during breaks between clients, but to answer messages at some other time. He could readily see that this would be more advisable, and said that he had learnt from the event: he was now non-defensive, and we both learnt from the mistake, just as Casement advises us to do. I do not telephone him during his breaks, and he does not make or take calls at these times.

As described above, Holmes' book eloquently brings together some of the concepts that are associated with earned security. For me, the book adds some theoretical reinforcement to the case studies that are put forward in the monograph edited by Odgers. However, I found that generally there is a dearth of literature on the subject of how one should work clinically in the consulting room in order to help the client achieve a state of earned security. Thus, I have been motivated to write a book that I hope will give you a clear idea of how to achieve this. I will present (in Chapter Twelve) a detailed description of how *I think* that the therapist should behave, and what skills she particularly needs to employ, in order to promote the growth of learned security in the client.

A new name for a related concept: "learned security"

You might have noticed in the previous sentence, I have given the process that I describe a significantly different term: that of learned security. This is for a specific number of reasons. Most importantly, there are various differences between the concept of earned security and my concept of learned security. Both concepts, in any case, are still evolving. This is not to say that I do not acknowledge that the birth of the concept of learned security arose as a result of the seminal ideas about those who are "earned-secures". However, I have moved on from the way that Holmes (2010) and Odgers (2014) discuss the concept. As discussed earlier, Holmes sees earned security as being gained when one has developed a reflexive function, despite the individual having undergone "unpropitious developmental circumstances" (Holmes, 2010, p. 25) during childhood. The first reason that I have changed the label is that I do not see learned security as resulting purely as a consequence of the individual developing a reflexive function.

There are a number of other reasons for this change of name. First, and simply, I feel that learned security is a more appropriate label, because I believe that the client's achievement of a sense of a secure base essentially involves an unlearning of old ways of thinking, behaving, and feeling, plus an experiential relearning of what has been a dominant attachment schema if he is to enjoy an experience of learned security. It is, essentially, a *learning* process. The word "earned" implies, rightly, that the client undergoes a change by being able to mentalize, but the adjective "earned" implies that one person deserves a reward for entering into the process, but, maybe, that others have not tried as hard, and are not worthy of reward. It seems to me to involve a deficit comparison. I might be unduly harsh with regard to this. In comparison, the process of gaining a sense of learned security does, indeed, involve a conscious effort in the individual being committed enough to come to therapy for an extended period of time, but it does not necessarily mean that the two parties have verbalised the process that they have engaged upon. As I have just testified, it is also true that the term "learned security" implies that *two* individuals have been involved in the process—that there is a "teacher" (albeit an informal, experientially based one in the person of the therapist) and a "learner" (the client).

Even more importantly, the theory of learned security is essentially different because it is an integrative theory which encompasses all the elements that I think make it an accomplished method of working. As can be seen in Part III of the book, I have sought to achieve an integration of three different theories, rather than classing it purely as a development within attachment theory. I describe later the essential concepts of the other two theories that combine with attachment theory in order to create an integrative theory. The two theories—both also from relational psychoanalysis—are Kohut's psychology of the self (1971, 1977) and Stolorow and colleagues' intersubjective perspective (1983, 1995). Having presented the essential points that underpin each of these two theories, I have proceeded to devise an integration of these two theories along with that of attachment theory. For example, it is primarily from the theory of the intersubjective perspective that I draw the concept of collaboration and co-construction that I believe is integral to the process of gaining a sense of learned security.

So, what is the essential meaning of providing therapy that leads to learned security? We shall see in Parts III and IV that I posit a way of offering therapy where attachment theory forms the bedrock of every one of my sessions. In short, I put forward the notion that the most important thing for us as therapists to achieve in the course of an individual's therapy is to enable the client to enjoy a relationship where, for the first time in his life, the client can learn (experientially) how it feels to have a secure base. For this to occur, I believe that the therapy has to be relatively long-term—three years plus. The therapist must model a relationship where she is utterly dependable, reliable, consistent, honest, open-minded, and empathic. When I say "utterly dependable", I do not mean that she cannot take breaks, but such breaks should always be discussed with sufficient notice, and information given about ways of contacting her in an emergency, or alternative arrangements made if she is out of contact entirely. Breaks and the effects of them should be talked about, and be part of the rhythm of sessions. Sessions should start on time, and end on time, so that the client understands what constitutes "his time". The therapist should keep to the same session time or times each week, except in extenuating circumstances. Consistency concerns not only session times and length of session, but also the manner in which she greets her clients, her mood and demeanour. She should also take care that she gives her full attention to the content the client brings to each session, whether she finds it riveting or not. The therapist must give the material due respect because if the client is devoting session time to the matter in hand, it must be of importance to him. With regard to willingness to engage, I think it is necessary to point out that one cannot afford, as a therapist, to be a little (or greatly) preoccupied in some sessions. One should monitor one's capacity to work, and if one is truly preoccupied with personal difficulties or internal conflicts, then one should consider calling the client to discontinue working for a short time. An empathic stance is the *sine qua non*. The therapist should always aim to understand how it feels to stand in the client's shoes, and to remember that even if similar circumstances have occurred in her life, she might well have been affected very differently. Finally, I just want to stress here that the therapist must aim to be emotionally attuned consistently to the client in order that he gains a deep sense of emotional connectedness, and she needs to work to create an atmosphere of "companionable interaction" (Heard & Lake, 1997).

Research has shown that it is not enough for the therapist to be aware of the client's affect and to communicate this understanding to the client. She must also be able to help him to learn to self-regulate his affect by, in the first instance, regulating his feelings on his behalf. The therapist needs to work to help the client gain a sense of emotional autonomy. Autonomy refers to the way in which the individual should aim to take control of his life—and not that this should lead to isolation or the avoidance of dependency.

In order that the client can gain emotional autonomy and self-regulation, the therapist must convey a sense of mastery (Slade, 2005). By this, I mean that the therapist provides evidence that *whatever is thrown at her, she is able to cope*, and will continue to be able to provide a secure base for the client.

It has also been discovered that a satisfactory outcome for the client (knowing he has a secure base through a constant sense of emotional connectedness) is only achieved by the therapist having the capacity to repair ruptures as they inevitably occur within the therapeutic relationship. This has been discussed previously.

I believe that a good experience in therapy enables the client gradually to learn how to self-regulate his affect. The securely attached individual learns this in stages during childhood through interaction with mother. He learns how to cope with difficult emotions, whether these are the positive, yet overwhelming, emotions of excitement, or the powerful sad and angry affects that follow loss. He gradually learns to assimilate these emotions without being overcome by them, or unable to function and carry on normal day-to-day living. He does this through his ability to affect his mother's feelings and reactions: for example, by her response to his smile with a look of pleasure and an affirmatory smile, the child learns a sense of agency—that is, that he has some control over his environment, that he is capable of influencing how events proceed. He learns also, through interaction with mother, that she can cope with whatever he throws at her, and she still survives. As Winnicott said, "the mother's face is the mirror in which the child first begins to find himself" (Winnicott, 1971, p. 51).

Clients who come to therapy without the comfort of a secure base need to gain this capacity through the therapeutic relationship. The insecure–avoidant or insecure–ambivalent individual frequently comes to therapy without these skills. He might find anger too hard to dare to voice in its raw form, and so it evidences itself in covert ways—for example, by the client cancelling sessions after a therapist's return from a break, or by arriving late, or walking out on a session, or by delaying payment.

For other clients, it is possible that they might even be so angry that their aggression is displayed in physical form in the consulting room—by the throwing of objects, pacing the floor, or swearing at the therapist. In my career, I have twice experienced physical violence against my person in the consulting room while I was working as a Relate counsellor. In past attachments of the client, it is likely that anger would not have been tolerated, or, at the other end of the continuum, anger might have been the only expressed emotion in the home. I have referred before to the content of the play, *Who's Afraid of Virginia Woolf?* (Albee, 1966). We can use this play to see an example of anger as the only expressed emotion. It was played so well by that famous couple (both on and off screen), Elizabeth Taylor and Richard Burton, who seemed only to be able to communicate through argument and continual displays of bickering. Whether suffering from covert or overt displays of anger, clients can learn, through the relationship with the therapist, to be able to process negative affect in a positive manner, rather than to find it impossible to express the full range of their feelings in an acceptable form.

The same argument can be used for the negative affect of sadness. Tears might either have been used repeatedly as a defence, or never succumbed to. Some clients cry so regularly that there could be tears in every session for years, but, as a therapist, one might feel unmoved. If this is so, one needs to challenge the client by commenting (kindly and compassionately, offering the challenge as a gift) that it is strange that, as the therapist bearing witness to the tears, one feels unable to connect with the sadness. This might give rise to some interesting work, and some movement, as the client comes to recognise how he is using tears as a defensive weapon.

It is the attachment therapist's role to help the client gradually to build up and gain, by the end of therapeutic relationship, a sense of "autobiographical competence" (Holmes, 1993, pp. 122, 182). The client usually comes to therapy with a narrative of his life that is fragmented; it does not join together all the disparate incidents and differing feelings he has encountered throughout his life to date. Such life stories might either be rambling and disjointed, confusing and muddled, and overladen with affect, or, conversely, they might be brief and banal. For example, when asked about his childhood, I remember one client saying, "I had a perfect childhood. My mother was wonderful." Yet, he could offer no more in the way of elaboration and was not able to provide any supporting evidence for this statement. Sometimes, in such cases, there might prove to be a temporary stumbling block in persuading the client that there is more to be said. Sessions at first might be stilted and full of silences. This is resistance in all its glory. By the end of therapy, the client will be able, if the therapist has worked in companionable co-construction, to own his life history, and to tell the tale without becoming immersed in a rambling, tangled mess of memories and oversaturated feelings. He will be able to give one a synopsis of his childhood, how it affected him, and what was important to him. Of course, it will still be a subjective story, but it will no longer be laden with unprocessed emotions and events that have no significant place in his history. It is this capacity that Main and colleagues were searching for in their AAI, if they were to classify the individual as "secure-autonomous".

It is pertinent here to mention that the word "narrative" is derived from the Greek word, "gnathos" meaning "to know oneself". It is to be hoped that we, as therapists, help clients to get to know themselves. Holmes (1993, p. 150) reminds us that psychotherapy is based upon the Delphic injunction of "know thyself", and that autobiographical competence is one of the important purposes of psychotherapy. Certainly, this is one of the ways in which a client gains a sense of learned security. However, I write more about this in further chapters in which I present the theory of learned security and then go on to explain in more detail how the therapist applies this theory in the clinical setting of the consulting room.

PART II

PROBLEMS THAT LEAD TO INSECURE ATTACHMENT

CHAPTER FIVE

Maternal deprivation

Introduction

The question has been posed: should the phrase be "maternal deprivation" or "maternal privation"? I think that the defining point concerns whether the child has ever experienced the full benefit of mother's love during his childhood and adolescence. Deprivation is surely, by definition, the removal or loss of a quality that one had once enjoyed. Can it, therefore, qualify as "deprivation" if the individual was never fortunate enough to enjoy the full extent of motherly love, affection, "attunement" (Stern, 1985) or "holding" (Winnicott, 1965) that securely attached children accept as normal during their childhood? This chapter seeks to answer the question: what exactly do we mean by the term "maternal deprivation"?

Bowlby stated directly in 1951 that "mother love in infancy and childhood is as important for mental health as are vitamins and proteins for physical health" (Bowlby, 1951). Bowlby went to an extreme by saying that he believed that all psychiatric disorder had, at its root, some degree of maternal deprivation. Here, in consequence, I proffer my second criticism of Bowlby: for such a genius, I find that he was wont to make sweeping statements at times, with a proclivity towards thinking in black and white rather than in shades of grey. Upon reflection about this quality in individuals, it has occurred to me that the innovators and instigators of radically new ideas tend very often to be unduly certain in their thinking. Possibly this is due to the fact that they are so embroiled in the creation of a new paradigm (Kuhn, 1962) and exposition of their novel theses, that in order to be heard and "to mark their territory" they consequently promulgate their theses in very definite terms. Perhaps some of you will accuse me of the same fault with regard to my promulgation of the theory of learned security.

Let us look, then, at Bowlby's statement that all psychiatric disorders have as their root cause a case of maternal deprivation. Current evidence clearly supports the notion that this is not the case. There are proved biological and genetic factors and organic brain damage that lead individuals to suffer from mental illness, albeit that environmental factors can cause, or be the catalyst that leads to, a diagnosis of mental illness. In this section of the book, space permits that we focus upon the environmental factors to which psychological disturbance can be connected.

What qualities of maternal care are needed for normal development?

First, the infant and then the child needs a continuous relationship with one person, be that mother or father or even grandparent. Bowlby coined the term "monotropy" for this: attachment to one particular figure that he believed should be mother. Second, this relationship needs to be loving. By this, I mean that there must be warmth and comfort provided by the carer. My definition is that love exists when the individual feels that the other's welfare is as important, or more important, than her own. I say "as important" because I sincerely believe that in order to provide love to someone else, one needs to care for oneself and to value oneself and one's welfare.

Third, *the affectional bond needs to constitute an attachment*. Attachment is usually asymmetrical: the relationship is not characterised by an equality of mutual reciprocity. In terms of dependence in attachment relationships, one person is more reliant upon the other than *vice versa*. In fact, parentification (that is, where the parent is dependent upon the child) is detrimental to the youngster, and always points to some level of dysfunctionality. The intensity of the relationship is important—the mother needs to provide stimulation, and to be regularly and consistently available. It is not enough to be physically on hand but to lack emotional availability, and we shall see this does occur (in the next chapter) in certain circumstances, as when mother is suffering from severe depression. Moreover, Ainsworth pointed out that mother needs to be sensitive to the infant or child's cues or signals. Bowlby was very aware that it is not necessarily the quantity of time that mother spends with her child but the quality of the relationship that counts. As an example of this, research has concluded that children who live in *kibbutzim* usually remain closest to their mothers rather than to the metapelets who look after them during the day. Also, not surprisingly, children raised in orphanages or institutional care rarely receive the same degree of stimulation as those brought up in family homes, and this, too, can lead to underdeveloped linguistic and motor difficulties, and accompanying alexithymia as a result of a deficit during childhood.

It is important for mother to share and informally teach her child language, not only grammar and vocabulary as he grows older, but also other, more subtle linguistic skills, such as how to engage in the turn-taking and the ebb and flow of two-way interaction. Children whose mothers have not talked to them, either because of organic failure or mental illness, tend to suffer from speech difficulties. While these difficulties can persist for a lifetime if the child has some organic problem, it is more often the case that possible global developmental delay can be accommodated by therapy and the effects of the deprivation reversed. It is also important that the child develops some sort of private idiolect with his attachment figure. For instance, my therapist and I, over the years, have developed a shared idiolect where, for instance, the words "as in the beach-hut experience" have a mass of connotations for us both, which no one else would appreciate because they lack the associations to the words, which in themselves might seem banal.

It is also true that play is vital between mother and child; not only can language skills be informally taught during play, but also the atmosphere is stimulating and mutually reciprocal. The child feels that mother is interested in him and his world, that he matters, that he is worth the time. This leads to the development of a sense of agency:

a sense that the individual has the capacity to act in any given situation and to have some effect on his or her environment.

Short-term and long-term effects of maternal deprivation

Bowlby delineated three stages through which the child progresses upon separation or loss of the attachment figure: these are protest, despair, and detachment. I have described these stages in Chapter One on the origins of attachment theory.

The following is an example of the effect of a prolonged period of separation leading to the individual developing an insecure–avoidant attachment schema. A client of mine was in hospital as a very young child for fifteen months during toddlerhood. She was kept in an isolation hospital, as was usual practice during that era when one had a disease such as tuberculosis or rheumatic fever, because of the lack of effective treatment and the high possibility of contamination. My client did not have any contact with any of her family for the whole duration of her stay in hospital. When she was finally allowed to go home, she remembers that she did not recognise her mother, and felt as if she was with strangers. It is questionable whether her attachment schema will ever fully recover from the insecure–avoidant style of relating that developed as a result of this early trauma. In such a situation, the individual needs some extended experience of a secure base from the therapist. This can sometimes be provided through a therapeutic relationship, but it depends whether the client is sufficiently trusting of the therapist to "let her in" and adopt her as an attachment object on which she can dare to try out new ways of behaving and feeling. Using the skills and generosity of spirit that I describe in Chapter Twelve, the therapist is able to provide an experience of learned security. The client, through his interaction with the therapist, learns in an informal environment (that is, not in the formal places of learning, such as at school, college, or university) what it means to feel secure.

Factors that modify the experience of separation

The various factors are listed below with some comments.

1. Age of child: infants separated from mothers under the age of six months do not seem to be badly affected by separation. One of my own grandchildren was hospitalised for ten days following open-heart surgery at five months of age. The effects of this separation were minimised by her age plus her parents' close proximity. My daughter was given the opportunity to stay within touching distance of her daughter the whole time, and at first slept in a chair by the bed. Later on, she was provided with the facility to sleep in a special parents' unit nearby.
2. Temperament of child: children who are extrovert—outgoing, and popular with their peers—seem to be less affected by separation than do introverted, shy, or aggressive children. This is probably because the well-adjusted children who are socially well versed are more able to find support from peers and other adults in whose care they are left.
3. Duration of separation: not surprisingly, the longer the separation, the more deleterious the effect.
4. Previous mother–child bond: if mother and child have a good bond before separation, this appears to help to "insulate" the child against distress, especially if the separation is not prolonged.
5. Effect of environment: if the child is in an unfamiliar environment, then the effect of separation will be more pronounced than if he was familiar with the place, or it was his own home.
6. The nature of person left in charge: if the person with whom the child is left is known to the child, the effect of separation seems to be less pronounced. Thus, when the Robertsons (Bowlby & Robertson, 1952b) looked after two children temporarily separated from their parents in an experiment, it is felt that the effects were mitigated by two factors. First, the children had met the Robertsons briefly some time before coming to stay with them, and, second, Mr and Mrs Robertson took care to simulate parental care during their stay, and to continuously mention their parents in order to keep the idea of them alive. Adoption of these mechanisms is felt to be crucial.
7. Nature of events while in a strange environment: it is deemed helpful if routine is adhered to during a child's sojourn away from mother. My own experience of twenty-six days in hospital at age three is that, as well as seeing very little of my parents, I

was subjected to a number of procedures that make me think of the word torture when I recall them. It involved numerous barium meal X-rays, and, worse, the regular pumping of my stomach and administration of enemas, the latter two procedures being carried out in a public ward in front of other children. Unsurprisingly, it has resulted in a life-long phobia of vomiting (losing control of bodily functions) in public places.

8. Helpfulness and availability of a known companion: if a child is left in the company of a sibling, however young, then the effect of separation from the parent is ameliorated. It seems (as in the above point) that it is the retention of some degree of familiarity, rather than the replacement of a maternal relationship, that makes a crucial difference.

Finally, I feel it is pertinent to note that very little research has been carried out on the effect of separation from fathers. Some children do form their primary attachment bond to father rather than mother, although traditionally fathers have tended to be absent from the home in the pursuance of their careers more so than mothers during their children's younger years. If the primary attachment bond is to father, what, then, is the effect of a separation from him? Is the effect less pronounced if the child is left in the company of mother? Presumably, there is the same effect as I stated earlier: that of the child being less traumatised because he is left in a familiar environment, but it seems to me that the child will still suffer because of loss of proximity to his primary attachment figure.

However, I *do* question the prevalence of the research on the mother–child bond, and the lack of research on the father–child bond. Surely, mothers do not have magical properties. It seems that if it remains the received wisdom that only mothers can be effective nurturers, then it places an insupportable emotional burden upon women. It also places males in a "one-down position": they can never hope to achieve the recognition of being providers of emotional succour.

Effects of separation: long-term effects

It seems that disorders of conduct, personality, language, cognition and physical growth have all been found to occur in children with

> serious disturbances in their early family life, which have been included under the rather loose general heading of "maternal deprivation". (Rutter, 1981, p. 55)

This is the conclusion reached by Rutter in his classic text, *Maternal Deprivation Reassessed* (1981).

It will not be surprising to psychotherapists to hear that early life experiences are deemed to have a significant effect upon later functioning. Rutter (1981, pp. 56–58) tells us that the most convincing evidence for this comes from experiments and research with animals. He cites the work done with chimpanzees, mice, rats, geese, dogs, and nidifugous birds. Harlow's work (1958) with the cloth-mother "monkeys" as opposed to the lactating "monkeys" is well known and often quoted, as is Lorenz's work with greylag geese (1937).

Bowlby's 1951 monograph for the World Health Organization (WHO) has had a massive effect upon the world of institutional care. Standards of care have improved immeasurably as a consequence, and his report has been likened to that of Elizabeth Fry's in the nineteenth century concerning the insanitary conditions in the prisons at that time. In a similar way, Bowlby and Robertson's film (1952b) and the documentary evidence supporting it led to seminal changes in childcare; to extended parental visiting during periods of hospitalisation, for example. Similarly, Bowlby's paper "Forty-four juvenile thieves: their characters and home life" (1944) led to acceptance that there is a link between prolonged maternal separation and trauma in the home and the alienated behaviour of the "affectionless psychopath".

In short, as Rutter (1981) summarises, the following concepts are now taken for granted:

> The extensive evidence that many children admitted to hospital or to a residential nursery show an immediate reaction of acute distress; that many infants show developmental retardation following admission to a poor-quality institution and may exhibit intellectual impairment if they remain there for a long time; that there is an association between delinquency and broken homes; that affectionless psychopathy sometimes follows multiple separation experiences and institutional care in early childhood; and that dwarfism is particularly seen in children from rejecting and affectionless homes. (p. 123)

However, it is no longer considered that Bowlby was correct in his notion that a lack of primary and secure attachment to mother would *automatically* lead to difficulties in later life. Neither do we still subscribe to the notion that attachment is monotropic: that is, attachment is to one person only. Attachment now is generally seen to be to a hierarchy of figures; there may be a primary attachment, but other attachments are important—for example, to father or to mother-substitute in the child's nursery, or to a grandparent. Neither is Bowlby's idea that the primary attachment had to be to mother seen to be tenable any longer. It is now the received wisdom that the child can be just as securely attached to any figure that provides emotional and physical care on a regular, reliable, consistent basis. It is, therefore, a misrepresentation to promulgate the notion that the mother is some figure of mystical importance that alone can provide this magical and ethereal level of care. It is accepted that the attachment figure might not be biologically related to the child, and might not even be the most important person in the child's life, in terms of the quantity of time spent with the child.

In respect of the nature/nurture dichotomy, the more recent evidence shows that full explanation frequently relies upon recourse to both environment and biology/heredity. For instance, a child with Down's syndrome usually has a lower level of mental functioning than normal as a result of chromosomal differences, but the child will tend to develop better intellectually and in terms of verbal acuity if brought up in a private home providing a stimulating, inclusive environment, rather than if the child is left to grow up in institutional care. Similarly, educationalists support the idea that children with Down's syndrome should, preferably, be educated at least until senior level in mainstream schools, so that they can benefit from the interaction and stimulation that comes in harness with children who have no difficulties in verbal expression and understanding what constitutes appropriate social behaviour.

Factors that can modify the long-term effects of separation

Evidence in research samples has gradually proved that Bowlby was incorrect in his views that any institutional care or nursery provision of care for a child is detrimental. If nursery care is well provided, with plenty of toys and opportunities for play, with enough staff for the child to have readily available mother-substitutes to whom he can regularly and reliably relate, then it is thought now that there is little harm to the child. The original feminist argument that Bowlby, through attachment theory, was somehow attempting to force women back into the domestic sphere, from which they had escaped during the war years, no longer holds true. As I have stated elsewhere, the current government (2015) is extending the funding for help towards more than fifteen hours of nursery care for children to parents of three-year-olds, in order to promote the possibility of mothers being able to return to work. Part of the reason for this is political and economic: it suits the current government to increase the growth of the economy by helping women back into the labour force, as earners do tend to become acquisitive purchasers, and this fuels the economy. Also, the change of direction of policy is as a result of changing research into the benefits and disadvantages of institutional childcare. Consequently, repeated brief separations of the child from his attachment object for part of the day are no longer seen as deleterious.

None the less, transient separations (that is, separations of more than a month or so) are seen as sometimes detrimental to the child. Most studies show that children who have experienced separations from their parents for at least a month in the early years do have a slightly greater propensity towards experiencing anxiety upon separation over an extended period of time, plus there is an increased risk of psychological disturbance in later years. However, if one studies the evidence, it has been shown that the children who show a greater likelihood of psychological disturbance have actually experienced a disrupted home life over an extended period of time: for example, this might be a result of protracted marital discord, or domestic violence in the home. In these cases, the parents might both be physically available, but emotionally unattuned to the child. We need to ask whether such disturbance is due to disrupted home life, rather than to the one-month-plus separations. In fact, there is little evidence to suggest that children who have experienced a transient separation during childhood have later suffered anything more than maybe a slighter greater feeling of anxiety when placed in a strange situation, apart from their attachment object.

Prolonged separation or permanent separation, however, can have a significant effect. Children who have experienced permanent separation, as a consequence of the death of parent or divorce (or separation) of parents, tend to be affected at a permanent level. Evidence shows that children who have lost a parent as a result of parental divorce/separation are most likely to develop a neurosis in consequence. Certainly, in my twenty-seven years in practice, I have worked with a disproportionate number of clients whose parents split up when they were children. The clients who appear to be most severely affected are those who have completely lost contact with one parent, or where they, as the children, were used as pawns in a game of control played by the separated parents. I remember reading a book in the 1990s by Judith Wallerstein entitled *Second Chances: Men, Women and Children a Decade after Divorce* (Wallerstein, 2004), and she presented compelling evidence for the case that parental divorce was most deleterious for the children if their father, of his own volition, lost contact with them.

However, I am not arguing for parents to remain together at all costs. As Rutter states, neurosis commonly develops in adults who, as children, were subject to frequent and repeated parental bickering and disputes. This is not to say that every married and cohabiting couple are not expected to quarrel upon occasions, but protracted, year-in, year-out power struggles or arguments about infidelity, money, or alcohol consumption (to name but a few subjects of contention as examples) are not healthy for the child to be party to.

We now come to the question of whether the effects of deprivation can be reversed. Bowlby's initial conclusion was that mothering is almost useless if left until after the age of two and a half. We now paint a far more optimistic picture.

If a child is born into a very poor home, in terms of parents who are habitual addictive drug-takers and, therefore, unable to properly care for their child, then it may be appropriate to remove the child into fostering or adoption. It is possible and probable that the effects of such deprivation can be remedied, although it might well be an uphill struggle for the foster or adoptive parents for some years.

Evidence demonstrates that if children are removed early enough (prior to age two) from homes where it is felt by social workers that the parents' intellect is very poor, the children's intelligence quotient will rise by 20–30 points by the time they mature. It is questionable, however, in my opinion, whether it is morally acceptable for this judgement to be made by social workers.

Conclusion

This chapter has aimed to describe the problems that occur because of maternal deprivation, and has also tackled the contentious question of what exactly is meant by the phrase. I have attempted to look at ways in which the effect of separations can be minimised when, unfortunately, they are unavoidable.

Acknowledgement

For the insights and ideas identified here, I am indebted to Michael Rutter, the author of *Maternal Deprivation Reassessed* (1981).

CHAPTER SIX

The emotionally unavailable mother

Introduction

In this chapter, I address the effect of being an "under-mothered" adult: that is, growing up with the legacy of insufficient mothering as a result of one of a number of scenarios: mother being too preoccupied with drugs, alcohol, or poverty; catatonic as a result of suffocating depression; busy in the thrall of a demanding career; emotionally numb as a result of medication; preoccupied with her own sexual liaisons; under the dominance of an abusive partner; possibly seeing her child as the product of an unfortunate sexual encounter that she would rather forget. There are a variety of other contributory factors that have not been mentioned but, nevertheless, could account for the child being "under-mothered".

We shall look here at the effect of insufficient mothering upon the capacity of the individual to make and sustain his own relationships as he becomes an adult, and how therapy might be able to repair these ruptures. It is common for the individual to believe that the reason for the deficit lies within his own personality, whereas, in reality, the deficit can be traced back to a lack of emotional capability in mother; there is a tendency for the adult child to consider that he is essentially "bad" or unlovable. If the individual can grasp that the reason for his being under-mothered lies in the unwillingness and lack of capacity in mother to develop a loving relationship, the "under-mothered adult" may be released from feelings of guilt, and repair can commence. It is very hard for the individual to give up on the idea that he was not loved, at least to some extent, by a "normal" mother.

As Robert Karen eloquently stated in his doctoral paper, the (adult) child who is aware that he is in receipt of an abusive parental relationship, might, as a consequence, "Swear off his parents and deny that he has any love for them at all", but that, none the less, "the love is there, as is the longing to actively express it and to have it returned, hidden like a burning sun" (Karen, 1998, p. 230).

Possible reasons for mother's emotional unavailability

- Mother is preoccupied with grief as a result of personal loss.
- Mother has multiple children, all of whom naturally demand attention (Mother Hubbard comes to mind!).
- Mother had no role model herself for mothering because her mother, in her turn, was emotionally unavailable.
- Mother is ill/hospitalised/mentally ill.
- One child in the family is ill, or/and is hospitalised.
- Mother is taking care of a parent or prioritising the care of another sibling, who perhaps has special needs.
- Mother is addicted to illegal drugs, legal drugs, or alcohol.
- Child is the product of a sexual liaison that mother bitterly regrets, or was violent (that is, rape).
- Mother is head of household enduring severe poverty.
- Mother is too young to take on the responsibility of mothering.
- Mother has an abusive partner, who might or might not be the child's father.
- Mother has died, most probably, at her age, an untimely death.
- Mother is afraid to connect for fear of being hurt: this might lead to dissociative identity disorder.
- Mother is depressed, as André Green describes in "The dead mother".
- Mother was suffering from PTSD after some traumatic incident.

These are all valid reasons that could explain why it might not have been possible for mother to be emotionally available. The answer could lie in a combination of factors. The list is obviously not exhaustive, and I certainly accept that you might well be able to add more extremely valid reasons of your own.

Yet, it is a reality that many mothers *do try* to be emotionally available. We look next at how emotional availability presents itself.

The "good enough" mother (Winnicott, 1965)

Recent research by Fosha (2000) has produced evidence that the "good enough" mother needs only be attuned to her child 30% of the time in order to offer good enough parenting: that is, she needs to be in sync and available to her child, willingly, not reluctantly or carelessly, but wholeheartedly, *30% of the time*. Furthermore, Fosha goes on to say that it is important to remember that "What matters as much as (if not more than) the natural capacity to be in sync is *the capacity to repair out-of-syncness so as to re-establish optimal connection*" (Fosha, 2000, p. 64).

Mother needs to impart, subliminally, intuitively, to her child the following messages, and I also feel it is pertinent to point out the damage done if these messages are absent.

First, she needs to make it clear that she is glad that her child is here with her. Without this, the child is ever on guard, wary of the possibility of being abandoned. One of my clients lived with the constant spectre of this throughout her childhood, and it has wrought a severe cost on her attachment schema as a result, and taken years of therapy to mend. This features in the case studies in Part IV.

Second, mother needs to send the message that she "sees" her child and that he is "special" and that she likes him just as he is; if not, the child may get the message that he needs to adapt in order to be different in some way that will make him acceptable to mother. For instance, Helen (case studies) perceived that her mother wanted her to be "stronger" and more resilient, with an exhibitionist tendency, so that mother could admire her and feel captivated. Her sister showed these tendencies as a child, and, as a consequence, was favoured. Metaphorically, it is (in the case above) as if mother was holding up a mirror to her child and admired what she saw reflected if, and only if, the reflected qualities were those that she possessed or admired. It is important, therefore, that the child needs to know that she brightens her mother's heart, just by being her "true self" (Winnicott, 1965).

One of the fundamental messages the child needs to receive is a simple one: "I love you". Without this, the child feels ever insecure. All too often, the child perceives that she needs to do something in order to get that love. For instance, the sexually abused child might feel that being loved is conditional upon giving sexual favours; another child, in the grip of "parentification", might believe that she is loved if, and only if, she tends to mummy's needs. The message of being loved needs to run in tandem with the message "I respect you". The child who is not respected usually grows up to become too accommodating to others rather than knowing how to prioritise his own needs. One of my clients, though at the moment only thirty-four years of age and the youngest sibling, is, in actuality, "mummy of four": she has until now been living her life as a mother-figure to her own mother and three elder siblings. She has, for reasons that have been unconscious, taken on the responsibility for providing housing for them all, and helps them constantly to run their lives, at both a practical and an emotional level. However, when she reaches out for help, she finds there is little forthcoming.

Another associated important message that mother needs to impart is that her child's needs are important to her, and that she will always be there to satisfy them willingly and with love in her heart. It is detrimental to transmit such messages as: "I will help when I get round to it; oh—what a nuisance you are!"

Mother also needs to communicate another message as well: that she will keep the little one safe and that it makes her feel contented when the child rests and relaxes in her company—this too is at the heart of secure attachment. Without this, the child might feel constantly "on guard".

The roles of a good mother

Above all, mother needs to act as the primary attachment figure: to be the main source of nurturance, safety, protection, learning (the informal socialisation process where one learns norms, values, boundaries and roles as opposed to formal, subject-specific learning in school).

Additionally, she needs to be the main source of encouragement, bountiful admiration (again as Kohut describes in the "mirroring transference" (Siegel, 1996, pp. 89, 95–96)), and she also needs to teach the child how to self-regulate his feelings. This applies to both negative, painful emotions such as loss, and the positive feelings of excitement or a zealous sense of enthusiasm.

What happens when mother cannot supply these attributes?

There are a number of negative consequences of emotional unavailability. The next sections focus upon a number of these effects.

Loss of secure base

This is the most widespread and likely result, the almost inevitable consequence of mother being emotionally absent. Without a mother to run to, either physically, emotionally or both, in times of crisis, the child is likely to develop an ambivalent or avoidant attachment schema. His only saving grace may be if he has another close attachment figure in his inner circle, say a grandparent or aunt who lives physically close and whom he sees frequently. However, if one reads the case study of Allan in a previous book (Fear, 2015, pp. 101–113), one sees that even though he voluntarily visited his grandmother daily, and grew very attached to her, this did not prevent him from developing an attachment neurosis.

"The dead mother": the effect of a depressed mother

André Green (Green, 1983; Kohun, 1999) wrote a number of seminal texts on this topic that have been translated from the French. He coined the phrase "the dead mother" to describe the effect on the child of loss of mother at an emotional level when her mother is emotionally unavailable because the latter is mourning for a lost object. As Green says, in these cases "one finds the loss of a person dear to her: child, parent, close friend, or any other object strongly cathected by the mother" (Green, 2005, p. 149). But I have found in my practice that the mother's depression could have been triggered by a deception which inflicts a narcissistic wound: a change in fortune in the nuclear family or the family of origin; a liaison of the father, who then neglects his wife and causes her humiliation. In any event "the mother's sorrow and lessening of interest in her infant are in the foreground" (Green, 2005, p. 149).

The child discovers that, whereas until now the mother was authentically interested and enlivened by her child(ren) and their emotional lives, now she appears deadened, unaware of their feelings, even unaware of their physical presence at times. Green comments upon how frequently previous photographs testified to a rich and happy relationship; now all is dark and dismal. The child experiences this as a catastrophe; she cannot make sense of what has occurred. She searches for meaning to explain the disillusionment and she might wonder if the problem lies within her own personality. The disillusionment is usually experienced as having befallen her without any warning signal: in consequence, it is as if a bomb has dropped; from now on she believes she must be forever on guard.

Examples of this phenomenon are seen in three of the four case studies I present. I describe how Jane vividly remembers coming home from school to find her mother kneeling on the kitchen floor, overcome with grief, tears streaming down her face, totally unaware of her daughter's arrival. She remembers it as an arid time, her mother having withdrawn cathexis, locked in her own "private madness" (to use a phrase of Green's, 2005).

Similarly, Helen feels that she "lost" her mother for at least five years when, at the age of two and a half, her maternal grandmother died suddenly and her mother was overtaken with paroxysms of grief. She did not realise at this tender age what had taken her mother's attention, but she *did* notice the difference in her mother's degree of attunement to both her and her elder sibling. It was as if "she had lost all semblance of patience with us", she recalls.

An abiding sense of scarcity

For many under-mothered adults, life feels very hard. The experience means that one's vision of reality points to there being an enduring constant difficulty; that love, material possessions, relationships are all in short supply. I surmise that this is as a result of the scarcity of love in the original home; the failure-to-thrive syndrome that is often identified in orphanages in this country and is still found in Third

World countries. Frequently, this is accompanied by a tendency for the individual consequently to suffer from depressive episodes in adulthood—again something identified by André Green.

Somatisations

Naturally, it is one of the child's primary aims to engineer his mother's presence. This is the purpose of the stage identified by Bowlby as "protest": the child screams, shouts, cries, throws things, thrashes about, all carried out with the intention of motivating mother to return.

He might also become aware, consciously or unconsciously, that a way of activating mother's emotional responsiveness occurs when he suffers some illness. He then learns that illness promotes "caring", and the path opens up for him to develop somatisations: illnesses with physiological manifestations that, nevertheless, unbeknown to him, are triggered by a psychological and emotional process. These somatisations are an unconscious manipulative mechanism for eliciting caring behaviour from mother.

"Different rules apply to me"

Children who grow up feeling that they must conform if they are to be in receipt of any love from mother tend to be careful to monitor and adapt themselves, and to expect of themselves very high standards. They do not expect these perfectionist standards from others, just from themselves. This is connected to the statistical incidence that such individuals exude signs of compulsive caring and/or perfectionism. They might well develop a career where they are continually looking after the needs of others, and in their domestic lives likewise they tend to look after members of their families and their close friends, rather than eliciting caring from others.

The emotionally unavailable mother: a particular type of maternal deprivation

We have looked in this chapter at the effects on the adult child of an emotionally absent mother, due to his having, as Green so evocatively described it, a "dead mother", or because of mother's addictions, enduring poverty, or sufferance of abuse.

The effects are many and various; all are devastating. However, most fall within the context of being attachment neuroses. Most lead the adult child to suffer an attachment schema that is less than optimal, and it is likely that, at some time in his life, the individual may find his way to the door of the therapist. It is, therefore, pertinent to think about how attachment therapy can help such individuals, and whether therapy can help to heal the wounds that have been inflicted during childhood and adolescence.

It is my belief that the model of therapy that I have developed, which focuses upon the achievement of learned security, is particularly beneficial and relevant to clients who have a history such as I have described in this chapter. All of the four case studies that I present later include some elements of the individual having endured an upbringing by an emotionally unavailable mother.

CHAPTER SEVEN

Toxic parenting

Introduction

Why is it that toxic parents retain control over their children, often even into adulthood? And why do individuals who suffer toxic parenting find it so difficult to escape the emotional grasp of their parents and learn that the way forward is to eschew their help, support, and/or sense of approval in order to live their lives? The crux of the matter lies in the fact that the toxins and poisons the "child" imbibes from such a parent are usually mixed with a toxic love that masquerades as nourishment. This is often the only form of nourishment with which the emotionally starving child has come into contact. He or she latches on to it, therefore, in their state of hungry fervour. Unfortunately, this nourishment is poisonous, because of the toxic environment in which it is set.

Perhaps the most complicated of all the toxic forms of parenting is felt by the child who is sexually abused by a parent—but sexually abused "lovingly", the survivor will often emphasise to the therapist. Here, the parent's abuse, while emotionally forced upon the child, is mixed with a form of love. The child is probably treated differently from her siblings, "spoiled" by special outings and walks alone with dad, emotionally made into "his little partner", and affection is frequently entangled with the abuse. How is she to separate, in her psyche, the toxic nourishment from the abuse?

Whether these children who are in receipt of toxic parenting are sexually abused, beaten, abandoned at home for long times alone, constantly belittled and teased, treated like idiots, forced to parent their own parents via a system of role reversal, or are overprotected and suffocated, the results are surprisingly similar. Almost all of the adult children feel worthless, continuously wonder if they are lovable, and suffer from feelings of inadequacy and low self-esteem. Many are overburdened by guilt; many act out self-destructive behaviour such as cutting, or use alcohol or drugs to self-soothe, are workaholic, or have grave difficulties as parents themselves and find it impossible to maintain adult personal relationships for sustained periods of time. The underlying reason for the lack of self-esteem and feeling of being unlovable is that they rationalise that there must be something intrinsically "bad" about themselves; they believe that some of the responsibility must lie on their own shoulders. It is easier and more palatable to blame themselves than to accept that their parent, who is meant to protect and care for them as a basic human right, is lacking this capacity, and, in fact, cannot be trusted. It is very hard for any of us to accept that our parent is actually "bad"; even harder (as in the case of the sexually abusing parent) to accept that the parent is intrinsically evil. In either case, the reality is that the parent cannot be trusted. Grow up with this basic lack of trust, and one is most likely to develop an insecure–ambivalent or insecure–avoidant attachment schema.

I believe that Holmes (2010, p. 25) would not agree with me; he believes that if the individual has a reflexive function, then he or she might be able to have a sense of earned security. Personally, I feel that this is most unlikely unless and until the individual has taken part in a process of psychoanalytic therapy, or some other close healing relationship with a significant other. It is even possible, if one's parent is badly scarred and mentally ill himself (or herself), that the individual could develop an insecure–disorganised attachment schema.

Surely, an individual who comes to our consulting room will benefit hugely if he is able to learn, for the first time ever, what it is to have a sense of learned security—a belief that he really has a secure base (Bowlby, 1988) of his own, to whom he can turn in times of trouble and at times of vulnerability.

How does the adult child deal with the toxic parent before presenting in therapy?

Denial is the most common defence mechanism that individuals employ when they have been subject to toxic nourishment. While denial is the most primitive of the defence mechanisms, it is also one of the most powerful and most effective—for a time, anyway. However, as I say elsewhere in this book, and in an earlier book (2015, p. xix), all defence mechanisms fail at some point, and it is often at that point that the individual presents in the therapist's consulting room.

Nevertheless, it could well be that the individual presents in therapy relating the story of a perfect childhood, with the belief that he has had a wonderful parent. However, the individual is usually unable to substantiate this claim with any supporting evidence in the way of examples and memories of year upon year of happy family holidays or lazy Sunday lunches enjoyed together. Facts are sparse and inconclusive, and somehow the story does not add up and the jigsaw that we try to complete of the client's life will not make a full picture. We look for some triangulation (Holmes, 2010, p. 25, p. 72), some supporting evidence from a third party that the stories that we are told add up and make sense. We trawl the information provided to see if other people's stories or anecdotes substantiate the abused person's claims. In this way, it is possible for us, as therapists, to conclude that either the client's story of his life is accurate, or that he is in the grip of the defence mechanisms of denial or rationalisation.

Frequently, the client will defend the parent with what I call "faint-hope rationalisations", such as "He only spanked me to teach me right from wrong", or "He couldn't help going away to France and leaving us", or "He only had a sexual relationship with me because my mother wouldn't have sex with him, and men have to get sex from somewhere, don't they?" I have been presented with each of these rationalisations during my years as a psychotherapist.

Furthermore, the reign of terror played out by toxic parents frequently continues even after the parent's demise. There is a powerful taboo against speaking ill of the dead in Western society, and there is a tendency by others not to be prepared to hear negative feelings about the dead. In our society, society itself tends to rise up and decree that it is "not nice" to process any negative thoughts about parents once they are deceased. Additionally, there is still an overarching belief that mothers are endowed with a magical property of always being capable of attunement to their child, and that parents are always devoted to their children. The reality distinctly differs from this: some mothers positively do not wish to be mothers, or, indeed, have experienced such a deprived childhood themselves that they have no concept of how to be a good mother. In this way, toxic parenting can migrate from one generation of a family to another.

It is equally possible that the recipient of toxic abuse, speaking negatively (to her therapist, for example) about her parent just before that parent dies, becomes overtaken with guilt once the parent dies. She might suffer superstitious thoughts that she has, through some "death wish", caused the death of her parent by speaking ill of him/her. This phantasy needs to be handled compassionately by the therapist, explaining rationally and calmly that this cannot be so, while appreciating and acknowledging the very real feelings and beliefs (often unconscious) that the client is experiencing. It is vital that you give these feelings due regard and time to settle before continuing any more work, in order to avoid what Freud (1917e) named as "melancholia" (an abnormal grief reaction) developing. This is all part of the process of teaching the client to self-regulate his affect.

It is quite possible that the client may suffer from melancholia anyway, because it is very likely that the client has very mixed emotions about the death. Melancholia strikes when "the shadow of the object falls on the ego" (Freud, 1917e, p. 249). This means, in effect, that the bereaved person feels both sad (negative affect) and relieved/resentful/pleased (positive affect) that the parent has died. Perhaps she harbours resentment, remorse, memories of a slight or past hurt(s) by the deceased, and it is this that constitutes "the shadow falling upon the ego". The ego can only return to full force when the hurt is worked through and forgiven or renounced, and the bereaved person is ready to move on. Until that point is reached, the person will remain in a state of abnormal grief, that is, melancholia.

Different forms of toxic parenting

In the sections below, I shall endeavour to examine various differing forms of toxic parenting in a little more detail. All of them result, however, in the same endpoint: the adult child loses her sense of self-esteem, feels worthless, is convinced that she is unlovable, and lives constantly with the fear of being abandoned by any person to whom she dares become close in adult life. This results, of course, in insecure attachment schemas becoming the norm among such individuals. This state of affairs will continue unless some restitution in the form of an experience of learned security can be gained, and, thus, the client can experience what it means to enjoy the luxury of a secure base (Bowlby, 1988).

I examine the following forms of toxic parenting in detail:

- parentification;
- physical abuse;
- sexual abuse;
- verbal abuse
- controlling parents.

Parentification

Until the twentieth century, children were, effectively, chattels of their parents, envisaged purely as possessions that could be treated by their parents exactly as they wished. There was no legislation to protect their rights. Nowadays, the situation is very different, with legislation such as The Children Acts of 1948, 1972, 1975, 1989, 2000, 2004, 2006. The passing of this legislation is an example of gradualism—a movement to improve the rights of children sequentially alongside the gradual diminution of absolute parental rights. In harness with this legislation, the power of local authorities to take care of children who had been left without parents because of adverse circumstances has slowly been brought under sway and regularised. Children are now afforded rights as independent citizens who have an inalienable right to sustenance, shelter, and warmth, and to protection. They also have the right to be emotionally nurtured, to have their feelings respected, and to be treated in a manner that enables them to maintain their self-respect. It seems, sadly though, that children lose the right to have "fun"—to be carefree, irresponsible, and spontaneous: this is an essential quality of a happy childhood.

It is not unusual to hear rousing life narratives in which the notion of childhood fun simply does not feature. Instead, childhood consisted of housework, of shopping, of nursing a sick parent before and after school. It is not only that these children have taken on physical responsibilities; many of them have been also emotionally responsible for the family's welfare and progress. When this occurs, the child has no opportunity to enjoy carefree fun, nor is he fortunate enough to have a role model to emulate and copy.

In counselling and psychotherapy, we have a single word for this dreadful state of affairs: parentification. The child becomes an adult before her time: too fast, too soon. She is usually a parental figure to her own parent, at either a physical or an emotional level, or both. You will see in the case studies that Helen definitely suffered in this manner. She was forced to take on adult responsibilities at age thirteen when her parents each suffered nervous breakdowns. For a number of years, she felt that it was her responsibility to keep the family together, both emotionally and physically. The cost of all this? It was one of several reasons that explained why Helen lost her childhood innocence long before, ideally, she should have done.

Another client grew up with his twin brother into an existence where the two siblings became used to sharing the family's domestic chores. His mother—a single parent—had become chronically ill, suffering from myalgic encephalitis (ME). She rarely rose from her bed. From the age of ten, the two boys nursed their mother and completed the household chores before leaving for school each day, shopped for food on their way home, and then cooked the evening meal and again nursed their mother, bathing her before nightfall. This client came to see me when he was aged twenty-seven, and at that stage he was still bound to his mother emotionally, yet desperate to escape, as his twin brother had managed to do by engaging in postgraduate studies away at university. A deeply ingrained sense of guilt, however, which my client had introjected from mother, kept him tied in. He decided to come to therapy as a desperate attempt to free himself from a life of toil and torment. He had already lost his childhood and youth because, as he correctly declared, he "had never known the meaning of the word 'fun'". We tried our hardest to help him escape from his "prison of guilt" which the insecure–ambivalent attachment schema aided and abetted. This situation was all the more paradoxical because, to outsiders, he appeared to be enjoying a high-status role in the media.

When a child has habitually been inured to act as their parent's codependent during their formative years, it is very easy for them as adults to slip into becoming a co-dependent to a partner who has an alcohol, drug dependency, or eating disorder. One meets individuals in one's therapy room who "choose" very troubled partners time after time, and go on to have tumultuous relationships with a self-centred partner whom they are certain will love them in return *if only* they show him sufficient unselfish love. In reality, this is never going to happen. Narcissistic individuals who search out co-dependents are so damaged that they are not capable of real love.

A young woman in her late twenties with whom I worked for four years habitually became involved with extremely damaged partners. Despite my interventions, my interpretations, and psychodynamic links with her previous co-dependent relationship with her mother, I am sad to say that very little shifted until she finally entered into a relationship that proved to be near fatal for her. This partner was yet again physically violent and verbally abusive. After one such "fight", he fled the house believing her to be dead, having dragged her downstairs by her hair. Fortunately, she recovered consciousness and managed to call an ambulance, and, at long last, my words of the past few years echoed in her head. She began to appreciate the reality of the forewarning, and that she was effectively wasting her life. I am pleased to say that she then proceeded to choose "normal" partners. I am not sure that any of my interpretations or interventions had made much impact until this particular drama unfolded.

Once again, it is the story of someone with an insecure–avoidant attachment schema who was so anxious that she was going to be abandoned that she was prepared to go to any extremes to keep the object of her desire. She and her partners had used argument both as a means of intimate involvement and as a means of keeping some distance. Finding a man with whom she could be co-dependent had satisfied her in a perverse way because it meant that, owing to his neediness, he was less likely to abandon her. This is particularly true of the adult child who has been unfortunate enough to be reared by a narcissistic mother—she is used to "a co-dependency deal" from life, and from the mother being the centre of attention.

Physical abuse

There is an ever-continuing debate between those of us who think that corporal punishment of children should be allowed, and those of us who believe that children should never be struck physically by a person's hand or object. It is not, however, many years since we heard the dictum: "Spare the rod and spoil the child". Many of the population took this seriously and used it to defend their behaviour.

Parents who physically abuse their children often defend their actions with rationalisation. I have heard all of the following excuses: "My mother used to be just so tired, or stressed, or anxious", or "I really did deserve it!", or even, "My father was treated the same and didn't come to any harm". The reality lies in the fact that parents who beat their children lack impulse control. This might be because they suffer from uncontrollable anger for which they have never sought help, or their lack of control might be fuelled by excess alcohol or drug taking. These reasons are used to mitigate or make the abuse acceptable, but this is patently not the case.

The effect on the child and the adult child is that he or she is often never sure when or why the abuse might occur again. As one of my clients said, "I used to sit in the bedroom I shared with my sister, wondering which one of us he would pick to lash with his belt that evening." This constant state of fear is as damaging as the actual physical or sexual abuse. It leaves the victim in a constant state of anticipation and terror: "Might the bomb drop on me in a minute?" There is never any rest from being in a constant state of alert and never a moment free from fear. This, in itself, constitutes emotional abuse.

The child and the adult, once grown up, so often seeks to perpetuate the myth that he belongs to "a happy, intact family", and, in consequence, he lives in "a My Little Pony world". He is either literally sworn to secrecy by parents who beat the hell out of him, or he imbibes the message implicitly that he is not meant to tell anyone outside the family. There is often a very real fear in him that if he speaks out, the intact family will shatter, and the individual dare not take the risk of this while he is dependent upon his parents. I remember having as a client the sister of someone who has gone on to become extremely famous. She told me of an unutterable level of abuse with which she and her brother grew up, but that was never spoken about, even within the family circle. To all intents and purposes, they appeared to belong to a happy, intact family. Maintaining such secrecy is corrosive; it sets one aside from the rest of the world, setting up a barrier up between the individual and anyone else with whom he socialises, thus effectively isolating him and making intimate relationships difficult. The same arguments about the keeping of secrets and the attempt to maintain the illusion of the happy, intact family apply very closely to the next topic—that of childhood sexual abuse.

Childhood sexual abuse

Incest takes place when there is a sexual or sex-symbolising relationship between a parent and a child or adolescent, or abusive behaviour involving another family member who is in a position of trust. It is this betrayal of basic human trust that makes it so emotionally devastating for the abused person and, because of this, childhood sexual abuse is one of the cruellest and most difficult to believe acts that anyone can commit. A parent is meant to protect his child and be the person to whom the child can turn when in distress; instead the parent becomes the aggressor, the persecutor who robs the child of his innocence.

Incest used to be defined as the act of penetration by a parent, and no other act counted as such. This is not so any longer. Any act of sexual stimulation, whether involving the genitals or any other erogenous zone, or involving masturbation or exposing of the aggressor's genitalia to the child, constitutes sexual abuse.

In addition to this, you will see that above I have included in the first sentence of this section the words: "sex-symbolising relationship". By this, I mean that sexual abuse also includes any relationship where the abuser might not physically touch the child but, instead, uses language that is suggestive, repeatedly erotic in tone, or sexually harassing. It can also include the abuser attempting to create an aura of sexual excitation by his/her actions: for example, by coming into a private area of the house in order to watch a pubescent or adult daughter dress or bathe, engaging in voyeurism, or by forcing a young person to watch or make sexually graphic images.

You will read in the case studies of Helen's experience of being repeatedly subject to her father entering her bedroom and bathroom (during her adulthood) when she was naked. This is an example of a sex-symbolising relationship—there was no physical contact by this time in their relationship, but, nevertheless, the boundaries were not maintained appropriately. It is the parent's responsibility to keep the boundaries and not to give confusing messages. The result of this behaviour is that the metaphorical thorns catch one's skin, and the child or adolescent stays emotionally bound to the parent in an uncomfortable way. In summation, it means that the individual continues to suffer the disadvantages of an anxious-ambivalent or avoidant pattern of attachment.

Incest is not, in fact, a rare occurrence, and neither does it only happen in poor, uneducated, or "backward" families (as depicted in *Cider with Rosie* by Laurie Lee (2002)) with individuals who exhibit sexually deviant behaviour in a stereotypical fashion. Neither is it true that the girls who are molested are provocative and bring their fate upon themselves—they are innocent young people who deserve to be protected. The adult is unfailingly the one who should be held responsible.

Most incest stories are, unfortunately, true. As has been seen in the recent press coverage and moral panic ensuing from the Savile debacle, individuals should be believed. Their stories should not be discounted as tales of adolescents who were indulging in Freudian phantasies. It is true that Freud received a deluge of middle-class daughters of respected Viennese society who provided him with accounts of sexual relationships with parents and parental figures. When his initial treatment of them (which involved his belief in their accounts) did not yield "cure" (according to Freud), and he felt that many analyses came to abortive ends, he revised his prior belief in the veracity of these young women's stories. In a letter to his friend Fliess, he stated that he thought these young women were in the grip of phantasies (Freud, 1897b, quoted in Fear, 2015, p. 13). In my opinion, while he states that he revised his ideas because he was dissatisfied that the analyses had not concluded in a satisfactory manner, this does not adequately explain the reasons for this *volte-face* in my opinion. I think that maybe he found it worrying to countenance the backlash from high-class Viennese society if it should become common knowledge that its daughters were accusing their parents of sexual abuse. I suggest that maybe he pragmatically and cynically wanted to preserve his reputation and his income stream, so it was expedient to believe that his patients' accounts were phantasies. Unfortunately, the myth that then developed about children's "phantasy of sexual abuse" has permeated society ever since this, and, consequently, delayed the arrival of the era in which the victims of sexual abuse have started to be taken seriously.

Verbal abuse

Verbal abuse may be experienced by the child or adolescent in the form of teasing, sarcasm, repeated calling of insulting nicknames, subtle put-downs, overt aggressive remarks, or vitriolic verbal sustained attacks. It is most injurious to one's sense of self-worth to be in receipt of any of these mechanisms. All such mechanisms can have extremely negative ramifications for the person, and are a causal factor in the adoption of a dysfunctional attachment schema. The individual is likely to be so hurt that he or she vows to never again let anyone else get close, thus leading one to an insecure–avoidant attachment schema. Alternatively, the individual might cling to the faint possibility that "If just I do this . . . or that . . . then mum will love me and say something nice". If so, the child is on course to develop an insecure–ambivalent attachment schema.

Another alternative might be that parents are so perfectionist that the child or teenager can never quite match up to the parents' image of "perfection". This often happens with parents who are high achievers, or who are engaging in vicarious wish fulfilment—for example, they might be would-be actors who would like to live out their dreams through their children.

In any case, the adolescent is likely to say, "If I can't be perfect, there is no point in trying at all" and withdraw from aspirational aims completely. Another variant is for the parent to metaphorically whip the child repeatedly with the cruellest of words: "I never really wanted you", or "You were a mistake". This is often perceived as one's parent effectively saying, "I wish you had never been born!" What can be more soul-destroying than this? Is one likely to have a secure base with a parent who has uttered such words?

Controlling parents

Some parents do not allow their children to grow up and become independent. I have said for many years, as a therapist, that the most difficult job as a parent is to know how and at what time to let your adolescent grow up and go his own way. It is hard for many of us to let our children go into the adult world on their own. We might feel afraid that they will make mistakes and get hurt. We might fear that they will be damaged, literally, for example, in a road accident from which they never return to us. We might feel that once out of our sight they will forget us and never want to return, or not return frequently enough to satisfy our longing for contact with them. We might want "to put wise heads on young shoulders", but the truth is that young people have to learn some of life's lessons by experience, and need to experiment in their early years of adulthood.

We might feel that without our children at home, our life will be meaningless: we might feel that "You are my whole life", which is surely at the heart of the empty nest syndrome that so many of us experience when our children move away geographically to go to university or set up home with their first partner.

Most of us are able to self-regulate our feelings and enable our young adults to move away and have the freedom they both desire and deserve. However, some parents find this such a struggle that they seek to control their children while youngsters, and continue to do so once they are adult. There might be threats to cut off all contact with the young person unless he does as the parent says, or the parent could be even more implicitly manipulative by becoming unwell, or feigning or threatening illness or suicide. There might be overt or covert threats of suicide, or comments such as: "Your behaviour will bring on a stroke and I may die!"; "I can't live through the emotional pain that you are making me suffer!"; "My heart can't stand to be broken like this!" may be made.

In a reaction formation, the adult child might start to use illness or poor health as a way of avoiding confrontation or events that she does not want to attend. She might well not even be consciously aware that this is the mechanism that she is employing, but, in fact, psychosomatic illness is a well-known defence when an individual is in the thrall of a high degree of intrapsychic conflict. She could have learnt that illness is a way of manipulating, of getting attention, of getting one's own way, or of avoiding something unpleasant. It is likely that the adult child is not consciously aware that her illnesses have a somatic origin, but, in fact, they are a symptom of intrapsychic conflict.

Other adult children are held to ransom by the parent holding the power of the purse strings. One of my clients is kept passively loyal and obedient to her father by being in his debt. He continually drip-feeds her a few thousand at a time to help her out of financial difficulties—not enough to make her financially secure in her own right, but enough to make a significant difference to her fortunes. Another client has been forced to remain pliant and passive and "in her box" by being reliant upon her parents for help with childcare, which is especially important as she is head of a single parent household.

While a child, it is hard to do anything other than accept the controlling behaviour that is meted out to one. Perhaps the emotionally more mature survivors may be able to build up a reservoir of resilience to shake off the insults or repetitious teasing. The secret in all cases is to free oneself, once adult, by not allowing oneself to be beholden to one's parents any longer. This is hard, especially where one is probably still trying to retain the myth of the happy, intact family. This myth must be put aside in favour of reality, which, in fact, entails a steady rebirth of self-worth. Then, with steady work in long-term therapy, it will be possible to learn what it is to possess a sense of learned security—a feeling of having a secure base to return to at a day's end, when the going is tough and life seems difficult, and one wants to come in for an emotional refuel of connectedness.

Conclusion

The net effect of this toxic nourishment from parents who mix together toxic love with abuse is that the adult child undoubtedly develops an insecure–avoidant or insecure–ambivalent attachment schema. Having developed such attachment patterns, these "children" are effectively programmed to enter into repeatedly dysfunctional relationships with adult partners, with their own children, with friends, and even with work colleagues. Thus, it is likely to result in complications and emotional difficulty in all areas of their lives. Consequently, it is more likely that, at some time during their lives, they will require psychotherapy or counselling to seek some objective input in order to help them with life's unfortunate and seemingly insurmountable dilemmas. This is because they lack the resilience that a secure pattern of relating enables one to gain. It is for this reason that I have included this chapter on the subject of toxic parenting.

I am indebted to the ideas put forward by Susan Forward in her book *Toxic Parents* (1989) and to Michael Eigen in his book *Toxic Nourishment* (1999).

CHAPTER EIGHT

The physical effects of emotional nurturance on the baby's brain

Why Love Matters: How Affection Shapes a Baby's Brain *by Sue Gerhardt*

I would like to express my gratitude to Sue Gerhardt for her seminal book on the way in which the infant's experience of loving care and interaction with others is responsible for the physiological growth of his brain, and his powers to communicate with others about his feelings throughout his life. I have drawn extensively upon the information in her book in the writing of this chapter because I think that the contents are so illuminating and well expressed.

Gerhardt's book (2015) presents some seminal findings about the way that a baby's interaction with her significant attachment figures, particularly during the first eighteen months of her life, actually affects the physiological formation of her brain. Take, for instance, Romanian infants who were left in their cots all day, deprived of the opportunity for close contact with adults. Horrifyingly, they exhibited a virtual black hole instead of the growth of the orbitofrontal cortex (Chugani et al., 2001). This is believed to be as a direct result of their having no experience of nurturing social contact with adults at this crucial point in their development.

During the first few months of life, the anterior cingulate matures; it encircles the emotional core, which consists of the structures of the amygdala and the hypothalamus. The primary purpose of the anterior cingulate appears to be to help the infant to register what experiences will bring emotional pain (for example, separation, rejection, or conflict) and what experiences, at the opposite end of the spectrum, will lead to feelings of pleasure (for example, parental holding, soothing, or being spoken to tenderly). Expectations begin to be formed, and the baby begins to develop what, in economic terms, might be described as a "cost–benefit analysis": what will be the benefits of something happening, and will there be any attendant disadvantages involved in such a process?

This emerging capacity is enhanced by the developing orbitofrontal cortex. This cortex plays a key role in the individual's emotional life because, as Goleman (1996) says, it is this area of the brain that is largely responsible for what is commonly referred to as emotional intelligence. Connected as it is to the amygdala, it registers the emotions associated with facial expressions and tones of voice. Not only does the orbitofrontal cortex do this, however, it also plays a part in holding one back from impulsive action—it forms the basis of our self-control and willpower. It helps us to inhibit our rage reactions and switches off fear: in other words, the "fight or flight" mechanism that rises in us when we come into contact with a highly anxiety-provoking situation.

I was fascinated to note, however, that one is not born with this capacity to regulate self-control. As I have indicated before, the development of the size of one's orbitofrontal cortex is wholly dependent upon our social interaction with people as we mature—particularly during the first eighteen months of life. Those individuals who have large social networks have a larger orbitofrontal cortex than those of us who only engage with a small social circle. I point to the depressing findings about the Romanian orphans that I mentioned earlier. Years prior to that research, Harlow found, in the 1950s, that monkeys who were isolated for the first year of life were found to be autistic, and lacked the ability to relate socially to other monkeys.

It has been found that babies cannot develop the orbitofrontal cortex without some stimulus. It remains smaller in volume when early relationships go badly wrong, and the child is emotionally or physically abused or neglected (De Brito et al., 2013; Hanson et al.,

2010). Babies recognise smell, touch, and the sound of their parents from very early on, and respond pleasurably if the stimulus results in love being given. Sadly, if punishment follows the stimulus, the resulting neural pathways do not form.

The baby's heartbeat has been found to synchronise with the parent's heart rate. It is not sheer chance that my puppy snuggles his neck above the pulse in my neck, so that our pulses can align, when he is agitated. It soothes and calms him. He has worked this out instinctively.

"It is no accident that the image of the Madonna has become an icon in human culture" (Gerhardt, 2015, p. 58). Many of us tend to be soothed and calmed by the beatific smile of the Madonna gazing down upon the son to whom she has given birth, as if by a miracle, and whom she looks at in love and wonder. I have gone back, fascinated, time and again, over the years, to the Church of Our Lady in Bruges, to gaze upon Michelangelo's statue of the Virgin and the baby Jesus.

Allan Schore's findings

The ability to check out what to do and what not to do by reading the parents' facial expressions as a source of information is known as social referencing. This is an important skill for all of us to learn.

Schore (1994) believes, however, that looking at faces is more important even than simply to learn social referencing. He believes that looking at faces, at smiles and expressions, actually help to make the baby's brain grow. "Schore suggests that it is the positive looks which are the most vital stimulus to the growth of the social, emotionally intelligent brain" (Gerhardt, 2015, p. 59).

The baby recognises that the dilation of her mother's pupils is a physiological response to pleasure, and, in consequence, her own heart rate quickens. As a result of this, natural opioids are released, which gives the baby a "feel good" factor, and these opioids, in turn, release glucose, which promote the growth of more neurons. Dopamine is also released, and this, too, makes the baby feel good, and it also enhances the uptake of glucose, promoting growth of the brain. Thus, we see that the pleasure derived by the baby from her mother's or father's doting looks or soothing touch sets off a chain reaction that actually promotes the growth of the orbitofrontal cortex. In fact, the well-loved baby's brain doubles in weight in the first year of life.

It is vital not only that the infant possesses a certain number of neurons at birth, but that he experiences, between six and twelve months, a massive burst of synaptic connections in the prefrontal cortex. The discovery of all these theories concerning the growth of the brain provides biological, empirical evidence to support Bowlby's concept of attachment theory. Bowlby stated, from the 1950s onwards, that one's attachment experience was vital for every human being if he or she were to become a fully functioning, active, participating member of society. We now have unequivocal evidence that Bowlby's ideas have yet more scientific underpinnings than even Bowlby himself identified, and this is one of the reasons why I find Gerhardt's book so illuminating. Admittedly, Bowlby made a seminal link between attachment theory and ethology. As stated earlier, he drew on Harlow's and Lorenz's experiments.

I was remarking earlier on the importance of the baby experiencing a burst of synaptic connections: it is crucial that, at the age of six to twelve months, the baby is just becoming a social being as she realises that she is a separate entity from her parents. This separation–individuation process increases as the baby reaches toddlerhood, and goes through the exciting stage of being able to walk, and to learn other motor skills which enable her to become independent of her parents.

The toddler is using her brain all of the time as she explores her environment and her relationships with people. She begins to make connections about her experiences, by noticing what happens repeatedly and storing the information unconsciously. For example, by the age of two and a half, it seemed I had worked out intuitively that when my father did anything to upset either my sister or myself, he would incur the profound wrath of my mother.

Consequently, when he rounded the corner of the sofa with a large shovel full of coal for the fire and ran into my upper lip, cutting it open, my first thought was "I must not cry! Daddy will get into trouble for this if I make a fuss." I had already established the roots of compulsive caring at age two and a half.

This example shows how a young child stores an image and processes the visual patterns of faces, linking it with emotions. We load these images with associations. Thus, we come to the psychoanalytic concept of the association of ideas, and of unconscious process. This provides us with some theoretical underpinning of how early experiences deeply affect one's later life, one's attachment experiences, and one's reaction towards the external world.

Negative experiences and negative visual expressions also trigger biochemical responses. Unfortunately, they trigger cortisol, which, in turn, stops the endorphins and dopamine from being released. This means that neither does one feel good nor is glucose is manufactured, and, consequently, the brain does not grow because, as I have mentioned before, it needs glucose to do this. The awful feeling of shame—a feeling that is universally found difficult—leads to a sudden drop in blood pressure and shallow breathing. These are all physiological changes in the body that do not promote the growth of the brain.

It is important to realise that we need to use our brains—the more the better. This is as true for us as for infants. It has been documented recently that an excellent way of guarding against dementia as one grows older is to use one's brain: thus, the axiom "Use it or lose it!" We are being guided as retirees to engage in crossword puzzles and Sudoku, if not to read daily, and to get out and about, and to exercise, preferably in the outside world.

It is interesting to note that when Einstein's pickled brain was examined in Canada, it was found to be 15% larger than other people's brains at the same age of demise. It is surmised that this is due to the fact that Einstein avidly used his brain in developing the theory of relativity, more so than the majority of others.

The verbal self

The final stage of early emotional development of the brain is the development of the verbal self. This involves the development of the dorsolateral prefrontal cortex. This is the site of what we know as working memory, where we play around with our thoughts and feelings, thinking them through, and using language to "mull over ideas" in our heads. This linguistic ability is based in the left brain. Maybe this area of the brain develops if one is trying to mentalize and/or develop a reflexive function (RF).

If carers are able to express their feelings and are "emotionally literate", they are able to put words to the child's feeling states; that is, to express to the infant that "Now you are feeling sad, or angry, amused, bored, tearful, or tired." Thus, the toddler learns to name her feelings, and differentiates between them. She learns to express her feelings to her mother, father, and siblings and, furthermore, to negotiate the feeling of others. Otherwise, lacking such input, she might become withdrawn and unable to communicate, and could even enter adulthood unable to express to her partner what the nature of the difficulties are at work, for example, or how she feels different because she needs to cope as a new mother with the absolute dependency of a new baby. Alternatively, feelings can become expressed in some other mode: for example, they might become somatised, expressed as illness such as, for instance, by regular attacks of migraine, fibromyalgia, or irritable bowel syndrome. The person might have learnt that it is permissible to show her upset feelings by recourse to illnesses or by complaining of physical pain, rather than verbally expressing emotional pain. She will not consciously be aware that she is doing this, and she will experience the pain in reality, whether it is that of the migraine or the severe toothache-like pain of fibromyalgia. However, the pain will have a somatic origin rather than a physiological origin. It needs to be made clear, however, that the pain of psychosomatic illness is very real, and is in no way made up or imagined. The illness is frequently a result of both organic and psychosomatic factors.

The importance of the development of a sense of narrative

A part of the child's development, as she moves towards adulthood, involves the need to develop an ability to construct a narrative of her life in some sort of coherent order. She needs to be able to remember the personal events in her life in sequential order, as she also needs to have a sense of past, present, and future. Mary Main, when undertaking research into attachment security in adults, was surprised to find that what mattered was whether the adults had a sense of narrative competence: an ability to relay the sequence of events of their lives in an ordered, coherent, and consistent format, rather than oversaturated with affect. It was discovered that whether the actual happenings were traumatic or not was not of primary importance; what mattered was the sense of autobiographical competence. When an individual cannot convey a coherent narrative without getting caught up in painful, tangled memories and feelings, she is regarded as insecure, whatever her story. Similarly (as I remarked earlier when discussing the AAI), if an individual says that her relationship with her mother was "wonderful", but is incapable of reinforcing that statement with any details or memories, then her narrative is defined as inconsistent.

Thus, what is seminal in terms of attachment security and the ability to provide a secure base to a child depends upon having the capacity to have formed a coherent narrative of life to date, to have "verbal pictures" or sets of images of what constitutes one's life experiences and that these join together into a coherent whole. These images need to be connected and form a story that includes all the notable events of one's life in an ordered sequence with a beginning, middle, and end.

It seems to be that, in the process of putting feelings into words, we are helping the right and left sides of the brain to become integrated. Perhaps this is why the work of Gendlin (1978) on focusing is often found by individuals to be so fulfilling, and to leave individuals with a sense of "So that's what it's all about!" It is the very capacity of being able to express in words how one is feeling that is so satisfying, and that many of us find fulfilling in our own personal therapy when our therapist manages to encapsulate in a few sentences the very essence of how we feel at that particular time. How priceless it is to be understood so well by another human being whom we value so profoundly. It is the domain of psychoanalysis to give words to feelings and thoughts. Freud said that we simultaneously have two conversations: one involving the conscious, the other the unconscious.

Conclusion

It is hoped that this chapter, which links the development of the brain with the depth of one's emotional experiences, has helped to give a scientific basis to Bowlby's concepts in attachment theory. Neuroscience had not developed in the era in which he lived, and so he was not able to make these links. He did, of course, seek recourse to science by using findings in ethology. However, recent research into the links between biology and development of the brain has given a scientific validity to Bowlby's work.

PART III

THEORETICAL UNDERPINNINGS OF LEARNED SECURITY

CHAPTER NINE

Heinz Kohut: the psychology of the self

Introduction

If one is to research the development of Heinz Kohut's theories, one needs to understand that his studies commenced with a belief in classical Freudian analysis. Although Viennese, he taught a two-year course in the USA from 1958 to the late 1960s, during which he made a point of emphasising the evolving nature of theory building in psychoanalysis. He stressed this point partially because he believed that theory should evolve gradually and be added to by the ideas of new generations of thinkers, and partially as a defensive measure because he feared the disapproval of his colleagues and friends, whom he thought would baulk as his ideas began to diverge from classical Freudian concepts. His own notions about psychoanalysis were gradually introduced over the next couple of decades until his untimely death in 1981. At the time, many of his contemporaries in North American psychoanalysis adhered to Freudian principles with unwavering certainty, and most academic papers tended to begin with a citation to Freud in order to give the author a sense of legitimacy.

The course Kohut taught in university from the 1950s to the 1960s traced the development of Freudian principles. However, he gradually found the courage to develop his own ideas and to present them to his students, both in the classroom and in seminars where he addressed his colleagues and friends. He was, for a time, President of the American Psychoanalytical Association.

He disliked the fact that Freud had been influenced by the morals and social milieu in which he lived. It was his belief that while analysts were technically neutral in their attitude to narcissism, privtely they felt it was an obnoxious tendency in an individual. He believed that this was because we are taught, in Western civilised society, to act in a selfless manner and to love others, whereas, in contrast, to behave narcissistically means that we are thinking predominantly about ourselves, which is viewed as unseemly. Furthermore, he felt that Freud was influenced in his theory making by the biological sciences and theories such as that developed by Darwin. Thus, he argued, Freud developed his drive theory in order to be in line with the thinking of the day. I made a similar point in a previous book (Fear, 2015, pp. 11, 14) that Freud, despite the paradigmatic changes he introduced, could not escape his *Zeitgeist* and, as such, he was bound by the social mores, norms, and values of the patriarchal and paternalistic society in which he lived.

Kohut liked and gave credence to Freud's notion of the psychoeconomic point of view. He agreed with Freud that there is a tendency of the psyche to fracture under the stress of unmanageable affects. It is not, he states clearly, the content of the trauma itself that is key, but the meaning of the trauma to the individual. This is so often dependent upon the (im)maturity of the individual, in emotional terms, at the time of the actual trauma. Kohut perceived that trauma occurred when the accompanying affect overwhelms the mind's capacity to cope with the event itself. He commented that trauma can only be recognised by the report of the traumatised person or the "observer's empathic immersion" (Kohut, 1971) in the traumatic state. His use of this term heralded the way for his later well-known concept of "vicarious introspection". He deemed that the use of empathic immersion was the only method of data gathering that was legitimate in psychoanalytic enquiry.

Kohut's first paper: a signpost of things to come

The first paper that Kohut published was indicative of the nature of his interests even at that stage. Written in 1948, but not published until after the death of Thomas Mann (1957), it was entitled "Death in Venice by Thomas Mann: a story about the disintegration of artistic sublimation" (Kohut, 1957). Kohut discussed Mann's novella, which, in turn, discussed the emotional deterioration of Aschenbach, an acclaimed writer. Both Mann and Kohut recognised that Aschenbach was in the thrall of an oedipal love for an overpowering father, and, in order to try to prevent emotional disintegration, attempted to focus his affect upon an infatuation with an adolescent, a handsome boy (Tadzio), from a distance. When his love for Tadzio remained unrequited, Aschenbach sought to employ his creative powers by writing, but this did not give him freedom from feelings of angst. The purpose of my reciting this tale is to exemplify the fact that the story provides us with evidence of Kohut's fascination with Aschenbach's lack of what Kohut later came to define as a "selfobject". His writings exemplify that he had, nevertheless, identified the notion already. He points out in his writing that Aschenbach

> had no object-libidinal ties to reality. This may have served as a reassurance to Mann, who despite temporary loneliness, felt that he had sufficient emotional closeness to his family to preserve him from Aschenbach's destiny. (Kohut, 1957, p. 2)

Here, by reading Kohut's paper while employing a psychoanalytic perspective, we find a first reference to his concept of the "selfobject", which became one of his major concepts.

Another paper: on music and the concepts of the link between rupture and repair

In another of his (jointly authored) papers, "On the enjoyment of listening to music" (Kohut & Levarie, 1978), the two authors comment on the way in which musicians move from consonance to dissonance and back to consonance. In other words, musicians move from being in a state of connectedness to rupture of that connectedness, followed by a move to the joyous experiencing of repair, togetherness, and, perhaps to some extent, a feeling of "merging". We can see by analysing this paper that Kohut was playing around with the concepts of "experience-near" and "experience-distant" which are so seminal in his writings later on. One could, alternatively, put this in language different from that which Kohut uses: the concept of the connection between rupture and repair. I have stressed this concept's importance in the process of developing a state of learned security.

Forms of narcissism

Kohut puts forward the notion that the infant begins by believing in a blissful state of existence, where everything is perfect, and his needs are met instantaneously. As is not surprising in reality, mother cannot supply these perfect circumstances, so the infant develops two systems simultaneously: "the grandiose self" and "the idealised parental imago". I will explain each in turn.

"The grandiose self" comprises the system in which the infant tries to maintain that everything within the self is perfect, good, and pleasurable, and everything that is bad is outside of the self. This runs parallel to Klein's concept of the baby splitting the world into "good" and "bad". Kohut's term "grandiose" is, perhaps, unfortunate, since the word has pejorative connotations in most people's minds. He had previously called this "the narcissistic self", which perhaps has an even greater pejorative tone. Siegel (1996, p. 66), who has devoted much time to writing about Kohut, suggests that "the expansive self" might have been a more favourable term to have employed. The term "the grandiose self" brings to my mind the image of superheroes—of Superman flying across buildings, of men with Herculean strength, of mystical powers, of omnipotent control. However, my mind also jumps to the image of Black Adder and Baldrick, who were almost anti-superheroes, figures of fun, try as they might to be superheroes of their era, yet always failing. One also may remember the meanderings of Fred and Barney, the Stone Age men in *The Flintstones*, again trying so very hard to be superheroes, but failing comically. The essence of the comedy lies in their antics, which make their grandiosity look pitiful. The humour lies in the fact that real superheroes have no limits; they can leap across a building in a single bound, climb mountains in a stride, and intuit what others are thinking without needing to utter a word. One is reminded of the man clad in black in the Black Magic chocolates advertisement, delivering his gift of chocolates to an isolated mountain-top. However, the grandiose child or adult is, in actuality, more like the anti-superhero, Black Adder. It is up to the therapist, Kohut says, to admire the grandiose efforts, to have the adoring gleam in his eye, and to lovingly and gradually let the grandiose self know that there is another way of living without this illusion of greatness.

The grandiose self feels, at this stage, that he is at one with the "idealised parental imago". There is no line of demarcation between the two. This is where the concepts of merging and twinship enter the fray. Union brings to the narcissistic personality a sense of wholeness, completeness, and a feeling of being soothed.

Gradually, in good developmental circumstances, as I have said before, the parent disabuses the child of this notion of perfection, allowing the child to fractionate his awareness little by little. Kohut names this gradual process as "optimal frustration": this label encapsulates the process by which the child loses the sense of the parent's idealised state little by little. The child is frustrated, but gradually, so that he can accept this change without feeling traumatised. However, so many individuals instead are shocked into sudden awareness of the difference between reality and their idealised parental imago. In contrast, if the child gradually comes to realise that his parental figure is not perfect, and the parent—usually the mother, but not always—is able to be empathically available, and is neither too stimulating nor passive, then he will gradually learn to accept his parent's limitations and modify his idealised vision of his parent. The same process applies to the need for there not to be a sudden rupture of the child's idealised image of himself. If the child is admired and not derided, yet he is gradually brought to the realisation that he is not perfect, then the reality principle will come to the fore fractionally, and replace the grandiosity.

During this stage, exhibitionism is a part of the child's normal behaviour; it is not something to be derided by the parent. The child yearns to be admired. This stage can be likened to Winnicott's words about the need for the mother "to paint proud edges on the baby's body".

"The child needs the gleam in the mother's eye in order to maintain the narcissistic libidinal suffusion which now concerns the functions and activities of the various maturational phases" (Siegel, 1996, p. 252).

We see this same pattern that occurs between child and parent replicated in the early stages of psychoanalytic therapy between therapist and client. Indeed, the empathic immersion and the concordance of the therapist help to create this aura of mergedness in the early stages of therapy. Gradually, in both therapy and in real life, the child/client realises that he is not a part of the parental imago, and that, in fact, he is separate from the parent/therapist. The therapist moves slowly from working concordantly to complementarity: to offering the client more challenge and the possibility of doing and visualising life differently.

Under good developmental conditions, narcissism is transformed gradually through a process known to Kohut as "transmuting internalisation". This reminds me of the mourning process described by Freud in "Mourning and melancholia" (1917e). According to Freud, the libido invested in the lost object is gradually withdrawn and internalised in the form of an unconscious memory. The lost object becomes a part of the personality of the bereaved person. This also happens, in Kohut's opinion, when disappointments are gradual and of manageable proportions, and from it he perceives that the following qualities grow: creativity, humour, empathy, wisdom, transience (an understanding that the present state of affairs will not last forever).

The child's objects are experienced as part of himself, and so it is perhaps not surprising that Kohut names these objects (usually mother, and, in later life, perhaps the therapist) as the "selfobject". At first, until 1978, Kohut hyphenated the word: that is, the word was "self-object", but then he removed the hyphen to stress the idea that the object is *not* perceived—at this stage—as separate from the self. Mollon (1993, p. 17) describes the selfobject relationship as one where the client "weaves the self from the fabric of others". I think this expresses the process succinctly and poetically.

According to the timing of the trauma that occurs in the individual's life, different behaviours will result in the individual who is traumatised by sudden disillusionment. If the trauma takes place in the early pre-oedipal phase, then addictions are likely to develop. If the trauma, in contrast, occurs in the later pre-oedipal phase, then sexualised behaviour is likely to follow in adult life. Either behaviour represents an attempt to self-soothe.

The selfobject

When trauma has occurred, and the narcissistic self is clung to into adulthood, then it is quite possible that the individual will find the need to enter therapy. He needs to seek the type of therapy where the therapist can act as a selfobject: that is, for a time, to become the "idealised parental imago". Over the subsequent years in therapy, it is then hoped that three differing, but complementary, transferences develop: the twinship transference, the idealised transference, and the mirroring transference. An example of this is particularly displayed in the case study of Nick (Part IV). Let me explain each form of transference in turn.

The twinship transference

Here the client perceives the therapist "to be just like me". You will read about how my client, Nick, comments on how, in reality, I am "just a baby girl", in the identical way that he is "just a baby boy". It soothes him and provides a sense of mergedness to feel that we are at one. He is referring to the idea that we have both suffered trauma as children and still bear the scars. During this stage of the work, breaks are resented and seen as evidence of separateness.

The idealising transference

In experiencing this transference, the same client, in the earlier years of our therapy together, perceived me to be "perfect", "an ideal mother", "who knew everything" and "always knew what to do". This is a natural stage of development, but it also has its disadvantages—it tends to imbue the therapist with an unequal degree of power.

During the time of the idealising transference, the client generally finds any disruption to the therapy to be an indication of the therapist's separateness. Similarly, lack of immediate understanding is perceived as a trauma. I remember how, after one break, my client consciously expressed his dislike of my separateness by wondering whether he would continue to come to therapy twice per week, which I perceived as a sort of threat in consequence of my daring to take some time when his needs were not pre-eminent. It is important that the therapist adjusts her empathy to the level of the client's narcissistic needs at the time, and to react with understanding to the level of despondency and rage that such events bring up, rather than to respond with irritation or non-comprehension. It is necessary to look beneath the surface of the actual events for their psychological meaning, rather than to take them at face value.

The mirroring transference

While the client is experiencing this transference, he expects unquestioned control and dominance over his therapist. The therapist is experienced as an extension of oneself. In one of the composite extended case studies in my previous book (Fear, 2015, pp. 87–99), I describe how, many years ago, I woke during the night to find a client of mine in my bedroom. I now understand this client to have been in the grip of the mirroring transference, unable to distinguish where his dominance of me ended. Thus, he had temporarily lost his sense of boundary and invaded my private space. As Siegel (1996, p. 88) so rightly articulates it, "the therapist experienced as part of the self, often finds this transference oppressive and tends to rebel against its tyranny". I very nearly did rebel. Fortunately, I accepted this phase of the client's transference as something he needed to work through, and not as an act of aggression, and we continued to work together despite the shattering of the boundary.

However, looking back on the episode with the luxury of hindsight, I realise it was more luck than judgement. In fact, I have come to realise that it is not wise to emphasise to the client at this stage that his demands are unrealistic, but instead, paradoxically, to acknowledge that they are indeed appropriate at this early stage the client is working through. Through imperceptible changes, often not actually articulated by the therapist in clear language, the client gradually learns to ameliorate the mirroring transference, and to lose his grandiose vision of himself.

The central concept in Kohut's work: empathy

Kohut knew some time before his death that he was suffering from terminal leukaemia. He told no one apart from close family, but, in effect, it changed his writing, making it more "substantial": he seemed to feel more able to take a definite stance away from classical psychoanalysis and run the gauntlet of the animosity and open hostility that his theories brought forth from many of his former colleagues and friends in the American Psychoanalytical Association.

Three days before he died, he presented his final paper, "On empathy" (Kohut, 1984), in which he expressed a "serious obligation to set the record straight", having been so frequently misquoted about his views on empathy in the preceding years.

He had made the point clearly enough that only "empathic immersion" brought forth data that could be legitimately used in the gathering of psychoanalytic enquiry. He believed that the analyst immerses herself in the perception of the client's experience and then reflects upon the nature of that experience, in a reflexive way.

Kohut believed that the worst suffering that children experience comes from carers who lack any degree of empathy and have empty, vacuous personalities. You will note that the various concepts in Part II of the book explored this: for instance, Green's concept of children who experience a "dead mother", or those who are unfortunate enough to have an emotionally unavailable parent for other reasons. I have also devoted a chapter to the experience of the child who suffers maternal deprivation because of parents who are physically or emotionally unavailable as a consequence of preoccupation (due to addiction to drugs, alcohol, severe poverty, or love affair, for example).

In the therapeutic setting, it is hoped that the client experiences, from the outset, a form of "holding" by the therapist via a process of empathic attunement. Winnicott referred to this as "holding", Bion as "containing", and Stern as "attunement". In my opinion, they are all referring to a similar state.

Kohut calls this sort of empathy "experience-near": the therapist is trying her hardest to get in touch with, and articulate, how the client feels and experiences a given situation that he is anxious about at that particular time in therapy. However, from here, the therapist will move towards what Kohut terms as an "experience-distant" form of empathy. This occurs when the therapist, in order to articulate and echo her understanding of the client's feelings, provides an explanation about *why* the client thinks or feels the way he does: that is, she offers an interpretation.

Kohut's two definitions of empathy are useful in my exploration of empathy as one of the concepts that link the three theories from which

I make an integration (discussed in Chapter Eleven): Kohutian psychology of the self, Bowlbian attachment theory, and Stolorow, Atwood, and Brandchaft's intersubjective perspective. By resorting to a higher level of abstraction, I use the concept of empathy, a concept common to all three theories, to marry the three theories together. I intend to put forward a particular meaning of the concept of empathy. We shall look at this specifically in the next chapter, but I found the seeds of this idea in Stolorow and colleagues' theory of the intersubjective perspective. It is to this theory that I turn in the next chapter.

CHAPTER TEN

The intersubjective perspective

Introduction

This approach appeals to me essentially because of the relational stance it takes. It places the affective relationship between client and therapist at the heart of the therapeutic endeavour, where the purpose is seen to be the structural change in the client's self-organisation. The client, because of developmental deficit, has an incomplete self-organisation: he has not been able to develop a differentiated, individual sense of self or/and a certainty that his affective state is legitimate.

Furthermore, the appeal to me of the intersubjective perspective lies in the fact that it advocates a particular sort of therapeutic relationship; this relationship is characterised by collaboration between the therapeutic dyad. As such, it seeks to minimise the undeniable power differential that exists between client and therapist. For example, the determination to achieve the client's autobiographical competence is engaged upon in an environment of co-construction: the client leads the process as much as the therapist, if not more. In a similar intersubjective way, the therapist engages with the client within an atmosphere of sustained empathic enquiry into his affective states. This, in its turn, creates a feeling of empathic attunement; attunement is earned by the therapist continuously checking out her perceptions and level of attunement with the client himself, that is, it is co-constructed.

This approach was developed by Stolorow and colleagues (1983, 1995) in a number of books and academic papers from the 1980s and 1990s onwards. It focuses, as I have indicated above, upon the relationship between the therapist and the client, in which the authors recognise the disparity that exists during the process of the treatment as a result of the difference "between the relatively structured world of the analyst and an archaically organised personal universe of the patient" (Stolorow et al., 1995, p. 2). These three therapists came to understand that this disparity frequently leads to ruptures in the therapeutic relationship, as the therapist begins to employ her own psychological organisation of experiences (which, of course, involve her own unconscious processes) in order to "comprehend" the client's communications. In so doing, the therapist is inclined to "misunderstand" the client and, thus, respond unempathically to her client's cues. In short, the therapist neglects to use the empathic–introspective mode of enquiry (to use a phrase of Kohut's).

Psychoanalytic knowing

In traditional psychoanalysis and psychoanalytic psychotherapy, there is a strong belief, dare I say even a dominant ideology, that the analyst alone is "all-knowing". She is seen to be the only one who "knows" and holds the key to the "objective truth". It is seen that it is she alone who is capable of making the accurate interpretation because only she perceives the client's world from an objective stance. This objective stance is deemed to be crucially superior to the subjective stance of the client, whose beliefs and attitudes are viewed as being prone to distortion, and subject to various other defensive measures, such as displacement, projection, denial, resistance, and projective identification. To put it succinctly, if one is only to think in terms of objective and subjective, there is an inherent deficit comparison regarding the concept of subjective: it is generally seen to be less legitimate than an objective opinion.

This viewpoint cryptically encapsulates a dominant and insidious power discourse. If the analyst is the only one in possession of objective knowledge and truth, the only one who is aware of the "unthought known", as Bollas (1987) put it, then it follows logically that she will possess a greater degree of authority, power, and control in the relationship. If we are to follow this dictum, I question where this leaves us, as therapists, in relation to the pre-eminent belief in the world of counselling that members of the profession should at all times attempt to minimise the power differential between client and therapist. It seems to me to be inherently unhealthy to subscribe to a system where the therapist holds the power; in contrast, the intersubjective perspective seeks to remedy this by consistently employing an aura of co-construction.

On examination of the dominant ideology held by psychoanalysts and psychoanalytic psychotherapists, it seems to me that, during my training as a psychoanalytic psychotherapist, it was subtly and insidiously inculcated in me that, indeed, it was the therapist alone who was in possession of the objective truth. In other words, the dominant ideology was that "He who hath undergone such rigorous training is the only one of the dyad who is entitled to objectively know how to interpret and analyse a person's behaviour and thinking." I am very strongly of the opinion that every individual has a right to his or her own view, and to interpret events or find their own meaning for what has been overtly expressed. It is the task of the therapist not to force her interpretation on to her client, using an unequal degree of power in the relationship to hammer home and have *her* meaning taken on board. Instead, it should be the therapist's consistent task to co-construct a shared subjective reality with the client, through an atmosphere of empathic attunement and adoption of "the empathic–introspective mode of enquiry".

Thus, I support a relational, integrative approach to therapy, which includes elements of what Stolorow and colleagues (1983, 1995) entitle the intersubjective perspective. Instead of subscribing to a system of therapy that perpetuates a power differential, I have tried to work, during my years post-training, with the more contemporary concept that the therapist and client together construct a shared subjective reality of the client's experience of his life and feelings. It is of seminal importance that the therapist relies always on an attitude of what Kohut named as "vicarious introspection" (Chapter Nine), or what I prefer to call empathic attunement. Kohut, and the founders of the intersubjective perspective, also call for us, as therapists, to be "experience-near". This means that we need to strive consistently and continuously to keep as close as possible to the client's experience of his life, and the affect that accompanies his experiences. With such an outlook, if we remain attuned to the client's narrative, the therapist can try as much as possible to remain in the client's frame of reference, so that together it is possible to construct a shared narrative of the client's experience. This means, in essence, that together we construct a story that includes all of the happenings in a client's life, replete with trauma or events that he would consciously prefer to obliterate. The aim of therapist and client is to create a narrative that is coherent and complete. Additionally, it is important to duly "mark" events with their affect-laden meaning. Above all, the psychoanalytic endeavour entreats us to find meaning for the client's affective experience of his life. It is crucial, in my integrative approach to therapy, that this narrative is a co-creation because in the very making of it there is a healing process, involving a step towards learned security for the client.

This is part of the process that enables the client to build what he missed out on, developmentally, possibly because of some trauma. It is here that the client has suffered a rupture in the developmental process and, as such, the client did not reach adulthood with the "insurance policy" in which one is enveloped if one has been brought up with a secure base. Having a secure base on which to fall back reminds me of an old advertising slogan that some of you might remember from 1970s television: there was an advertisement for an insurance company where the story-board told the tale of some crisis in a family's home, and the ameliorative effect of having insurance to fall back on. The advertisement ended with the slogan, "Strong stuff, this insurance!" Well, so is having a secure base. If one has a secure base to which to return, then life can be seen as a series of excursions from that safe harbour, always aware that one can return to its calm waters. Think of the peace of mind of a fisherman, if he were always to have that safe harbour in reach. It is a priceless insurance policy that enables one to cope with almost all of life's tribulations. It is no wonder that the 66% of the population who *do* have a secure base hardly ever present in our consulting rooms.

In working towards the co-creation of the narrative, and the idea of it being a joint endeavour of client and therapist, the therapist aims, as part of the collaborative experience of narrative building, to be always experience-near. Of course, at times, it is unavoidable that the therapist (who is, after all, only human) reverts to experience-distant formulations. Such formulations, lacking in empathic attunement, are often motivated by the therapist's countertransference, sometimes arising as a consequence of the actions or affect of the client, but more often as a result of the therapist's own psychological organisation. It might well be that the therapist is whisked away into the land of her own childhood or adolescence, or possibly even to a more recent past experience, and, therefore, substitutes her empathic attunement for an identificatory feeling of how a similar event might have left her feeling or behaving. It is also possible that the therapist might be in the grip of some projective identification. When this process has occurred, a rupture ensues between the therapist and client. It is then imperative that the therapist works with the client to repair this rupture. As I have said elsewhere, it is not the rupture that is of paramount importance; what is crucial is that the therapist engages in a process of repair, and does so via collaboration with the client.

For instance, I have noticed how my therapist, on a number of occasions, has become irritated when I am recounting my younger (adult) daughter's behaviour. In the grip of projective identification, he picks up and runs with the rage that I am, in turn, defending against and find too painful and scary to acknowledge, being someone who needs to remain a trusted and consistent carer for my daughter. My therapist then tends to interpret from a position where he is imbued with rage; that is, from within his own frame of reference, though countertransferential. I think that this is countertransferential in two ways: first, my therapist has, via a process of projective identification, imbibed the projection of rage with which I cannot cope. Second, he is identifying with his own transference response to how he feels as a father, irritated and constrained from feeling free of what I refer to as "the demands of everyday parenting". Having worked together for many years, we are able to unpick the rupture, to understand the meaning of it, and repair it. Those of us with clients who are less familiar to us could lose our clients at this point, as the latter might scurry off, feeling misunderstood and hurt.

A formulation or interpretation that is experience-distant, which comes from the therapist's frame of reference rather than from that of the client, will inevitably lead to a temporary rupture in the therapeutic relationship. If we adopt an intersubjective approach, we are likely to keep these ruptures to a minimum. After such an aberration, one then redoubles one's effort to be empathically attuned, and the rupture repairs (one hopes), as the empathic attunement recommences. It is as if, metaphorically, the temperature in the room is constantly changing, moving up and down: "up" as the therapist tunes in to the client's world, and then "down" as the therapist moves out temporarily into her own frame of reference. With practice, the therapist's skills will grow in terms of empathic attunement and her ability to stay within the client's frame of reference. Her skills need also to grow in terms of her ability to communicate her understanding of this empathic attunement, to be able to articulate it clearly and unambiguously.

Working in this way helps the client and therapist together to create a new intersubjective reality. Stolorow and colleagues point this out as being a "new" reality because it has just been articulated by the dyad for the first time. However, paradoxically, it is also "old", in that, as a concept, both are somehow familiar with it already, although it has not been articulated until now (Stolorow et al., 1995, p. 8).

Through the therapist's attitude of sustained empathic enquiry, the client will come gradually to believe that his most profound internal emotional states are deeply cared about, grappled with, and understood. By introjecting this at a deep level, the client will develop the capacity for self-reflection. He will also come to experience that he, as an individual, is being held, as Winnicott expressed it. This holding environment (Winnicott, 1965) is yet another important and necessary feature of what is needed, in my view, to gain an experience of learned security.

Once more, I take you back to the work of Bowlby, and remind you of the conditions in which the infant who had the good attachment experience started out on life. He was held, literally at first by his mother, who kept him close to her in order to feed him when he was hungry and to soothe him when he was cold, tired, fractious, lonely, or had a tummy-ache or wind. The joy of human comfort is partially in the safety and security it provides, partially in the carer's ability to provide sustenance. The proximity of the care means that, as a little one, one does not have to manage life and provide one's own security or food. These needs can be answered by the carer, and this is the predominant reason that the baby or child seeks the carer's proximity. As Harlow and Zimmermann's experiment (1958) with the wire-framed and cloth-covered "monkey mothers" established, it was this need for comfort and security, rather than sustenance, that they felt was pre-eminent. The baby monkeys eschewed the wire-framed "monkey mothers", preferring cuddles to food.

The intersubjective perspective's mutations to self psychology

Stolorow and colleagues' theory has adopted much of Kohut's ideas and concepts. I will examine the overlaps in this section; some of it might seem to be a repetition of the previous chapter, but I am aiming to exemplify the way that the intersubjective perspective has mutated from Kohutian theory. Kohut put forward his theory of self psychology in two books, *The Analysis of the Self* (1971), and *The Restoration of the Self* (1977). Psychoanalysis owes an enormous debt to Kohut for the paradigmatic shift that he made in developing self psychology. Specifically, this involved the move from the mechanistic, deterministic thinking of Freudian theory, based as it was on the pre-eminence of biological constructs such as drives and instincts, to the notion that psychoanalysis is a depth psychology of human subjectivity. Kohut moved our thinking and emphasis to the study of affect in the human being, and to the study of self-experience. This emphasis of Kohut's was partially the reason that it appealed to Stolorow and colleagues.

It is pertinent to ask, at this point, "What, then, are self psychology's main contributions to psychoanalysis that Stolorow and colleagues have adopted? It seems that Stolorow and his associates answer this question when they enumerate the principal contributions under three separate headings (Stolorow et al., 1995, pp. 15–17).

1. The intersubjective perspective adopts the Kohutian idea that the empathic–introspective mode of investigation should consistently be adhered to in the consulting room by all psychoanalysts and psychoanalytic psychotherapists. Any material that is outside of this mode of enquiry is seen as outside the remit of the discipline of psychoanalysis.

   This refers to the analyst's attempt to understand a person's expressions, past and present experiences from within his frame of reference, rather than from an external perspective. Thus, the therapist must consistently attempt to be experience-near, and to avoid any tendency to become experience-distant, which could so easily happen by calling upon her own wealth of personal experience or the transference arising in her.

2. A second concept taken from self psychology is that of the emphasis on the need to focus consistently on the client's self-experience. This concept applies to the client's self-experience both historically and to his psychological state in the present, at both a conscious and an unconscious level. This concept underlines the way that Kohut moved on from Freud's motivational primacy of drives to a theory where affect and affective experience are seen as the key motivational forces (Basch, 1985, 1986; Stolorow, 1984). It is the recognition that affect and affective experience, and their derailments, are the most important factors during a client's development, which seem to me to be the single most significant theoretical contribution of self psychology. It is by investigating the client's self-experience that the therapist can enable the client to work through the developmental deficits that he has experienced in earlier years. It is also possible to repair and change the client's perceptions through his affective experiencing of the selfobject transferences.
3. The third principle that Stolorow and his collaborators adopted from self psychology was the need to attend to the selfobject and selfobject transference. The term selfobject refers to the way an object is experienced subjectively as serving certain functions; for example, caring functions, or functions that help the individual to develop what, until now, has been an aborted sense of self. It then becomes understood that the sense of self is effectively gradually engineered by the therapist, who acts as restorer, maintainer, and consolidator for the client. The therapist needs to grasp that her responsiveness is of such importance to the client because of two qualities: it is experienced subjectively, and it helps to increase the client's self-experience and self-organisation via its restorative, consolidating, and containing capacities.

If the therapist begins to appreciate this, it is unlikely that she will again listen to, and respond to, analytic material in a dispassionate, disinterested manner. I write this, having just spent an hour with a client of mine (Nick, in the case studies), who is currently engaged in doing just that—"weaving" his mature self from my experience of life, from how I experience him and mirror it back to him in the transference. I find work like this so very invigorating and, literally, life-giving; in giving within a spirit of generosity, it makes *me* feel so alive, too.

What is meant by the self?

The term "self" is open to a lot of ambiguity in self psychology, and perhaps the use of this very word is one of the reasons that self psychology is so little understood. Admittedly, another reason might well be that Kohut's own writings are extremely dense and difficult to follow. It is a pity if this makes his concepts harder to absorb, given that this man was a giant among many, whose ideas and theoretical, seismic leaps were second to none. He ranks with Freud among those who should be remembered as a great thinker whose ideas made paradigmatic shifts. He worked significantly to change the dominant world-view in psychoanalysis during his era.

Let me try to explain the somewhat ambiguous term "the self". This is not a reference to a person, an agent, or an individual who initiates an action or series of actions. It refers instead to a psychological structure. Thus, look at the idea that it is possible for one's self-experience to become fragmented. This statement refers to the way in which an individual perceives that his sense of himself as a cohesive psychological structure is beginning to break apart, and he starts to thrash about in panic. He sees his self (the psychological structure as opposed to his self as an agent in the world) as being under threat.

The selfobject transference

As stated previously, the empathically attuned therapist will always realise that the work in the transference is vital and that it is, arguably, the greatest source of mutative interpretations. Stolorow and his collaborators believe that this is as a result of the effect of the transference on the client's selfobject. I call this variance of transference, to give it its full title in line with self psychology, the selfobject transference. This means that the client perceives his therapist as his selfobject—the person to whom he assigns the role of carer, and, even more important, the role of restorer, maintainer, and consolidator of his self-experience. During the maturation of the therapeutic relationship, he has assigned to the therapist the task of making up for, and healing, the developmental deficits that he has suffered from carers in the past, particularly during childhood, but perhaps even during early adulthood as well. It is in this way that the client intuitively feels that he will be able to solve the underlying pathology from which he is suffering when he presents in therapy, and which is contributing to the issues that are consciously troubling him at that time.

The selfobject transference is the vehicle in which all the psychopathologies of the client's past will gradually come to replay themselves in the here and now of the consulting room, in the intense relationship that grows between therapist and client. The client fears that the selfobject will react in the same way as his significant other in the past. He fears, in other words, that there will be a traumatological repetition of the damaging childhood experience or catalogue of experiences, played out, this time, between himself and therapist. He waits with bated breath for the therapist to behave in a similar manner as his original carer did, and to display a similar range of affects. There are two possibilities that could occur at this point. The therapist might be coerced in the countertransference to respond in the way her client expects of her, and a "mistake" is made, and a consequential rupture follows which needs to be repaired. Such "mistakes" are commented upon by Casement in his book, *On Learning From The Patient* (1985), where he makes the worthy, and well-known, point that we all, as therapists, are wont to make such "mistakes" and that the trick is to recognise one's error, to discuss it with the client, and together to learn from the experience. The second course of action that might occur when the client is expecting a repetition of old, "worn-out tapes" to replay, is that the therapist responds quite differently. Either way, the fear of what *might* have occurred, or the trauma of re-experiencing a repetition, must be analysed fully by analyst and client together, and then an interpretation offered, linking past and present. In this way, understanding of the issues will be achieved, the toxicity defused, and healing will commence. This must be done in an experience-near manner, by an empathically attuned therapist. In this way, the selfobject tie is restored if rupture has occurred, and, indeed, consolidated at a new level of containment and durability.

It is here that the empathic–introspective mode must be adhered to in a steadfast, unswerving manner, in order to maximise therapeutic potential. The concept of the empathic–introspective mode is, to my mind, another of Kohut's major contributions to the field of psychoanalysis. It underlines the need for a process of collaboration between therapist and client.

How do we define transference in the intersubjective perspective?

Traditionally, Freud (Draft N, 31 May 1897, 1950, pp. 254–256) initially talked about transference as a hindrance to the psychoanalytic cure. He gradually came to see it as a way in which the tidal waves of the past washed over the client and the analyst in the relatively sheltered bay of the consulting room, where it can be regarded, collected, and analysed on a metaphorical beach on a lazy summer's day.

This concept of the transference "arising" is in line with the archaeological model implicit in much of Freud's writing. Even in "The claims of psycho-analysis to scientific interest" (1913j), Freud was still conceiving of psychoanalysis as a technique wherein the analyst "digs deep" (to continue the archaeological metaphor) into the unconscious to discover what lies therein.

Traditionally, psychoanalysis invariably describes transference as regression, distortion, displacement, or projection. Stolorow and colleagues posit the concept of transference as an organising activity (1995, p. 36) that helps the client to gain a new sense of self that is appropriate to his maturing sense of himself. This seems to me to fit very well into the work of the therapist who believes in working empathically in harness with the client's subjective world. The client assimilates the analytic relationship into the thematic structures of his own personal world, drawing upon his own psychological structures, and the environmental experiences that have beset him during his life. The selfobject transference develops; the client at first expects that his therapist will react to stimuli in the same way as did the original carer, with whom the traumatic event(s) and/or affect(s) led to a rupture and abrupt ending of some of the developmental pathways. The client gradually learns that another way is possible, that the therapist, as selfobject, will respond in a healthy, empathic manner. This enables the client to develop and grow psychologically.

However, it is also true to say that the therapist herself has psychological structures of her own that mean she likewise interprets events and stimuli in the present world according to what has happened in the past in her life, and this, too, should be taken into the therapeutic mix. The traditional dictum is to maintain a rule of abstinence, of neutrality and non-disclosure, so as not to "contaminate" the transference (Freud, 1915a, p. 165). I would argue that it is impossible for any therapist to remain neutral in the long term, for she will undoubtedly bring her own predilections, innate choices, preferences, and value systems to any table, whether it is in the dining room or in the consulting room. Yes, we can minimise our value systems, but we cannot simply discard them. Of course, we should never self-disclose if it is to seek discharge for our own benefit, but it is possible to share an experience, in my view, that might actually be of help to a client and from which he might learn something useful. Similarly, if we always refuse to answer questions, in order to follow the rule of abstinence, we exude the message that we are not generous-spirited and this does not assist in creating what Winnicott refers to as a "holding environment" (Winnicott, 1965).

The intersubjective perspective focuses, rightly, upon the need for the introspective–empathic approach in order to find a shared subjective experience with the client. For this to occur, the therapist must give something of herself, and this necessitates something more than her mere learnt skills as a therapist. It is essential, to my mind, that she has a generous enough spirit to give of herself, to let the client partake of her very personality, of her own sense of self. It is only by being generous enough to share some of her own sense of self that she gives the impression that she is wealthy enough, in spirit, to share some of her plenitude with another. This is true generosity of spirit, and it is the client's recognition of this that has mutative power. It encourages the client to believe that he may dare to develop his own aborted sense of self—aborted because of some developmental arrest during his formative years. It takes courage to grow one's sense of self, when it has been aborted unceremoniously at some point in the past, and it is partially due to this generosity of spirit in the therapist that the client might be able to take this leap of faith. In seeing that the therapist is confident enough to give of herself, the client gains the permission to grow and become his true self. This is opposite of the message that was imparted by his original carer, who, it is quite possible, did not wish him to become separate from herself.

The other quality that it is imperative that the therapist possesses is the capacity to act as her own secure base. She must be able intuitively to provide the message to each and every one of her clients that whatever the circumstance, whatever the trauma, she will survive and be able to withstand the pain, onslaught, temptation, etc. Above all, she needs to remain calm and dependable: able and willing to take on responsibility for the client for some extended period of time. I have talked of this quality of "mastery" in Chapter Four, and I will mention it again in Chapter Twelve.

Together with the therapist, the client thus comes to increase the sense of self-organisation that has been so traumatically and phase-inappropriately ruptured during his formative years. He can replay those times with the therapist, in the selfobject transference, and "grow" once more, this time to full maturity (in emotional terms). Once established, the selfobject transference continues to play its part throughout the therapy, sometimes in a position of figure, sometimes in a position of ground. It will oscillate from one position to the other throughout the psychotherapy.

It is my contention that the transference helps enormously to effect a "psychoanalytic cure", if such is deemed achievable. Undeniably, the mutative power of the work in the transference, it seems to me, effects the most powerful psychic change for the client. We shall see examples of how this is achieved, and to what extent "cure" is achievable, in the case studies in Part IV of the book. I would also refer you to my book on the resolution of the Oedipus complex (Fear, 2015, pp. 47–120), where I describe in detail six case studies of individuals with whom the work in the transference has been of greatest mutative effect.

As the transference is such a powerful force in the course of the client's therapy, is it true that it can be completely resolved before the end of his psychotherapy? I question whether this is a practical possibility. Personally, I think not. I speak as someone who has been in her own psychoanalytic psychotherapy for many years, and for whom the transference to my therapist has been of enormous value—sometimes of enormous pain, sometimes of enormous satisfaction. Above all, it has been the seat of enormous learning. Granted, it has mutated throughout the twenty years of therapy; my therapist has been first one thing, then another. He has accommodated and moved with me every step of the way. It has required of him great patience, forbearance, huge courage, compassion, flexibility of mind, and, above all, empathic attunement. He has "held" me in the most profound way for many years. It seems to me that it is impossible to artificially dilute and then to dissolve the transference. Admittedly, the transference will not be at the end what it was at the outset. Yet, it cannot just disappear. I guess it has gradually receded from its pre-eminent position in my life and that when therapy ends it will fade and become a faint and fond memory. But I do not think I would want to dissolve and destroy something that has meant so much to me for so long. It would seem to me to do it a disservice.

What is seen to lead to the psychoanalytic "cure"?

This question is a contentious issue, and a point at which my development of the theory of learned security, Kohutian theory, and Stolorow and colleagues' theories differ from Freudian theory.

It is possible to ponder how Freud believed that "cure" was achieved in psychoanalysis. It seems that maybe it occurs following three therapeutic benefits:

- through the provision of insight, via cognitive measures;
- through the growth of the affective relationship between therapist and client;
- through the client gradually integrating experiences in his past that he found traumatic at the time.

Freud pointed out in his writings (Freud, 1940a) that he felt that mutative change occurs via the positive transference. I am in complete agreement with Freud regarding this.

In the history of the literature and meetings of psychoanalysts, there has been a running battle between the notion that cure is achieved via the provision of insight and the alternative view that the mutative change occurs as a result of the affective relationship between client and therapist. Stolorow and colleagues (1995, p. 101) write, "We contend that the significant psychological transformations that occur in psychoanalytic treatment always involve unitary configurations of experience in which cognitive and affective components are virtually indivisible".

They point out, quite correctly to my mind, that the therapist does not offer interpretation in a disembodied way; it is an essential and indivisible part of her affective involvement with the client. I speak here as an individual who has partaken of her own analytic therapy for a long time: the mutative interpretations that my therapist has offered have been made very much as a result of his affective involvement with me. He has been affected by his countertransference, and this has led to the most outstanding interpretations and, thus, achievement of insight, largely as a function of my being fully aware that he is emotionally affected in the here and now. It is also of great import that I appreciate that my therapist understands me at a deep level, appreciating but not judging me for the "illusions" that I have tried so hard to maintain.

Each time the selfobject transference replays the archaic hurts of the past for the client, and the therapist interprets this, the client "knows" that he is understood by the therapist at a very deep level, and this leads to a healing process, which, in turn, promotes psychological regeneration and allows a new psychic structure to grow. Thus, it can be seen (and argued) that the affective involvement in psychotherapy cannot be divided from the facilitation and impact of insight. Both insight and affective experience are products of the intersubjective matrix.

Conclusion

I have attempted, in this chapter, to explain the conceptual underpinnings of the intersubjective perspective. It is apparent that it takes many of its tenets from Kohut's psychology of the self. However, this approach does explicitly stress the centrality of the concept of collaboration between therapist and client. It also makes explicit the need for a sustained empathic attitude by the therapist. Finally, this theory belongs essentially to the school of relational psychoanalysis.

We will see, in the next chapter, how these guiding principles helped to enable my integrative theory of learned security to come into being.

CHAPTER ELEVEN

The theory of learned security

Introduction

I am presenting in this chapter the integrative theory that I have developed and named "the theory of learned security". An *integrative* approach differs from an *eclectic* approach because the latter involves employing a variety of features taken from a range of theories without having any overarching concepts that link the disparate theories into a composite whole. I can best describe an eclectic therapist as reaching into her toolbox for the most appropriate tools that she believes are an optimum choice in order to help her client(s) at a particular time. In eclecticism, there is no coherent, underlying set of meta-theoretical assumptions and shared concepts that marry the disparate theories together. In contrast, any theoretical stance, whatever it may be, represents a particular ideological—if not political—position, even if it is not expressly stated (Selden et al., 2005, p. 21).

In taking an integrative approach, the therapist has engaged in a process where she has tried to develop a way of working with her clients that is derived from the combined use of two or more theories. So far, the same method applies as is used by the eclectic therapist. It is here that the paths diverge. The therapist with an integrative stance has attempted to reconcile the seeming differences of the theories she employs by recourse to a process of dialectical thinking. Much of the time, individual therapists, when in practice, adopt an established integrative theory, having discovered that their chosen theory applies to their preferred way of working. For example, cognitive analytic therapy (CAT) is an integrative therapy devised by Ryle (Ryle & Kerr, 2002), and its use has been adopted by many therapists who believe that its integrative mix of cognitive and short-term psychoanalytic therapy provides the method by which they feel that they can carry out their role most effectively. In such a case, the therapist herself does not need to engage in dialectics.

With regard to my own clinical work and the content of this book, I am promulgating here a new integrative theory (the theory of learned security) that I have, in fact, worked upon for some years. In order to devise this new theory, I have engaged in a process of dialectical thinking. Dialectics is a process (associated with Hegel) that aims to arrive at "a truth" by, first, searching for the thesis and the antithesis that underlie a particular set of theories. Second, the individual then attempts to search out a way in which the thesis and antithesis can be combined and resolved into a synthesis. In other words, it involves an analysis of the similarities and differences in two or more chosen theories by the integrative theorist, who then seeks to find a rational, theoretically grounded way that enables a reconciliation of the differences. In this way, a synthesis is created.

The three theories that are of interest to me are those that I have talked about earlier: Bowlby's attachment theory, Kohut's psychology of the self, and Stolorow and colleagues' intersubjective approach. In order to think dialectically, it is necessary for one to move to a higher level of abstraction in order to determine how best to make a synthesis from apparently disparate theories. In order to achieve this, I believe that one needs to think in depth about each of the theories, deconstructing them conceptually in one's mind. One carries out this process by first perusing each of the theories in turn at a conceptual level, in order to analyse whether they share any conceptual or philosophical underpinnings. If there are some shared concepts and, even more pertinently, some common meta-theoretical assumptions, then there exists the possibility of integration. I discovered that the three theories do have some concepts that are common to all of them, and that they also share a common world view (philosophy for life) in two ways. I was then able to set about a process of starting to construct a conceptually new theory that employs the use of the common concepts and visions of reality that the three theories share. By analysing these factors, I have been able to marry together the three theories into a single integrative theory that employs their common conceptual underpinnings. I believe that I have, in this way, created a synthesis.

In the case of the three theories that are of interest, I realise that I have been drawn philosophically to their underlying meta-theoretical assumptions. First, they all have a common *weltanschauung* (vision of reality) in the following way: they are relational theories, or theories of two-person psychology. By this, I mean that they all focus upon the therapist primarily using the relationship between herself and the client in her clinical work. In short, the therapist concentrates upon and promotes both the real relationship and the transference, and uses both as her primary method of helping the client to achieve some psychic, structural change. It is also true that, in therapy, I believe there is a need to focus upon the client's relationships with others in his external world, because these provide evidence of how he perceives his life. The two-person psychological basis of these theories is in direct contrast to Freudian theory, which has a "one-person psychology" framework: Freud did not favour the growth of an affective relationship between client and therapist.

Second, there is another common *weltanschauung* that the three theories share concerning the way in which the world works. As I stated earlier, Northrop Frye (1957, 1964) introduced a way of looking at different visions of reality. He used this typology to analyse Shakespearean literature. Messer and Winokur (1984) adapted Frye's typology in order to look at the different world views that underlie the differing theoretical orientations in psychotherapy, and Latting and Zundel (1986) similarly investigated the differing world views of therapists. I have carried out some research myself (Fear & Woolfe, 1996, 1999), as I have said before, into these world views and looked at what happens to the therapist who chooses a theoretical orientation that does not share the same meta-theoretical underpinnings as her own world view. Frye's four-part typology consists of romantic, comic, ironic, and tragic ways of seeing the world. I would like to focus here on the tragic and ironic visions of reality. All three of the theories that I have employed in my integration are underlain by a vision which is ironic, but which has elements of the tragic. It is perhaps useful to explain this. They are all, as psychoanalytic theories, to some extent tragic in their approach to life. This is as a result of the fact that they focus upon the relationship between the past and the present, and, as such, we appreciate that it is impossible for any of us to alter our past experiences in life. So, not all is redeemable; not all can be rectified. However, they all propose a way of working with the client so that he can learn to regard his past traumas in a different frame of mind; he can reinterpret them, and change his way of responding to others in consequence. In short, through his work in therapy, he can move on from the dysfunctionality that the past has created. In seeing this as possible, the three theories, while giving due credence to the effect of the past and its terrors, nevertheless believe that the past can stop affecting one negatively in the present and the future. There is hope. All is not doom-laden. Changes can be mastered. This encompasses the basic tenets of the ironic vision.

I am championing the idea that change can be accomplished by the use of the real and the transference relationship between therapist and client, and the growth of learned security. Now, learned security, as you will see in the next chapter, is partially achieved by recourse to Roger's core conditions. Rogerian, person-centred therapy adheres to the school that says that it is possible for the individual to self-actualise: to reach his optimum level of functioning. In short, this sums up the romantic vision of reality. While I counsel the use of the core conditions, I do not go so far as to say that "anything is possible; all is attainable". However, I defend the adoption of the core conditions because these go some way to enabling the individual to grasp the hope that the future can be more fruitful and satisfying. It is partly by the use of the core conditions that the therapist can help the client to achieve some change, even if we do not envisage that the changes wrought will lead to a perfect world (or a complete "cure"). This capacity and belief in the propensity for change is what makes the theory of learned security underpinned by an ironic world view, rather than a tragic view. Therefore, the fact that the three theories (attachment theory, self psychology, and the intersubjective perspective) share an ironic vision of reality is a second factor in enabling the building of an integrative synthesis.

A third factor which enables an integration to be achieved is that of a concept common to all three theories. All of them focus on the use of the transference and countertransference. I say more about this later in this chapter, where I talk about the specific manner in which I developed the use of the transference in long-term therapy in order to co-construct a state of learned security for the client. I have taken my ideas about the transference particularly from the work of Kohut.

Fourth, the overarching belief that the use of empathy is invaluable in the therapeutic relationship is a common concept found in each of the three theories. This helps to create a synthesis. Admittedly, it is not unusual for empathy to be included as an important concept in many psychotherapeutic theories. However, I am defining the concept of empathy in a particular way: I call it "intersubjective empathy". I have been guided and informed in my choice of label by the main underlying meta-theoretical assumption of Stolorow and colleagues' theory: that the therapist consistently engages with the client in an intersubjective manner.

Fifth, I firmly believe that all three theories espouse and recommend the use of a collaborative approach to the therapeutic endeavour. Collaboration and co-construction are two of the watchwords of Stolorow and colleagues' intersubjective approach. Holmes also calls upon the need for a collaborative approach in a number of his books (e.g., 1993, 2010), as does Kohut. The concept of collaboration underlies the idea that full, accurate, empathic understanding is achieved by the therapist only if she engages in empathic immersion in order to fully understand the client's internal world. She needs to work consciously and consistently, in a collaborative way, with her client, so that together they reach an understanding of the client's inscape.

Intersubjective empathy

When I first came across the work of Heinz Kohut, I was particularly intrigued by the way that he differentiated the idea of being "experience-near" from being "experience-distant". He believed that, as therapists, we need to attempt to retain an experience-near understanding of our client's frame of reference. However, he felt that when we need to *express* our understanding of our client's self-experience, that we move from being experience-near to experience-distant (otherwise known as moving from first-line empathy to second-line empathy).

In order to achieve his concept of experience-near empathy, Kohut advocated that the therapist engage in a process that he named as "vicarious introspection". To me, this means that we investigate, in depth, the experience that an(other) is undergoing, or has undergone, from outside the other's experience, by looking at it as much as possible as if one was living it oneself. However, I take this introspection a stage further: I advocate that we engage in this introspection in such a way that we repeatedly check out our understanding of what is happening or has happened to "the other". It is in this way that we engage in a process that involves an inter-subjective element.

The reason why I believe that intersubjective empathy is so crucial to our clients requires some explanation here. Normally, in trying to be experience-near, we frequently use our own experience of life, albeit from a different life situation, to bridge the gap so that we can understand the other person's inscape. This is the common manner in which we try to achieve what it is like to stand in the other's shoes. However, when we do this, a dilemma is likely to befall us upon occasions. It is possible that we will become contaminated by our own countertransference—by this, I do not mean a countertransference arising as a result of projective identification, or some projection directed at us by our client, but, instead, by countertransference that is initiated within ourselves, arising from our inner personal life. It might be our personal, syntonic transference response to the client, or, alternatively, our response in the countertransference. When this happens, it is possible that we will respond quite unempathically to our client, because his experience might be nothing like our own experience in the past. Our past experience might well have coloured our own view, and if we continue on this track it will lead to a rupture in the smooth running of our empathic attunement as we are taken over by our own affective experience of an event.

It is partly for this reason that I advocate that we take an intersubjective approach to our empathic understanding. By involving the client in the process of co-construction, we are more likely to engage in a process of accurate empathic attunement and avoid ruptures in the therapeutic relationship. When we do mistakenly cause a rupture, we can use the same co-constructive process to repair it by engaging our client in a process of healing the misunderstanding together, by talking through where we have "got it wrong" and by admitting our "mistake".

Furthermore, as I have iterated in earlier chapters, there is a distinct power differential between therapist and client. We, as therapists, need to share the position of "expert" (that is undeniably attributed to us to some extent) thus to be able to find "the client's truth" together with the client's participation. The process of co-construction and intersubjective empathy that I advocate helps to partially dissolve the inherent power differential. We actively seek to engage the client in searching for his "unthought known" (Bollas, 1987).

Let me give you a clinical example of employing this intersubjective process. This illustration shows how a rupture occurred in my own practice as a result of my not checking out my empathic understanding before venturing to make an interpretation. A little while ago, a relatively new client of mine was clearly questioning why some individuals found her to be "unacceptable" and, thus, tended to reject her in consequence. She had talked at length for some months about a number of life events (each of which featured rejection), and I had interpreted that there seemed to be a theme to the stories that she told me: she was anxious about being excluded from a group, and, even more relevantly, I felt that she was wondering (but finding it difficult to articulate) whether there was something intrinsic about her that others found unacceptable. Now we focus on this element: it is apparent that my client is of mixed race. In fact, she mentioned in an early session of our work together, almost as an aside, that her mother is Irish and her father is Egyptian.

We move now to my own life experience. Her mixed ethnicity has echoes in my own life. My sister has been married for over fifty years to a man of Nigerian ethnicity and, in consequence, my three nieces and nephews are of mixed race. My niece, in particular, has suffered a great deal in view of this with regard to her self-esteem, feeling as if she has not been accepted as being of British ethnicity or of African ethnicity. This difficulty was compounded, unfortunately, by the fact that her maternal grandparents were very rejecting of her, being verbally abusive towards her for many years. This eventually led to an extended-family-wide divisive argument in which I brought pressure to bear on her behalf.

I became caught up in the experience of my niece's trauma, that is, in my transference, originating within me and not caused by any introjection. In consequence, I unwisely offered an interpretation that perhaps my client felt that her skin colour, being different from her mother's, might have set her apart in some way. She looked thoughtful and replied, "Maybe", and then became silent. She then asked to use the cloakroom. In short, I believe that she wanted some time to recover from my ill-considered and badly timed interpretation, because the session ended shortly after this.

I ruminated upon my interpretation during the next few days until I saw her once more, and realised that I had suffered a lapse of empathic attunement by confusing my material with my client's. At the beginning of the next session, my client started by saying that she did not know where to begin. I took it upon myself to immediately explain to my client, as compassionately and gently as possible, that I felt I had spoken clumsily and been thrown off kilter due to my own life experience, rather than focusing upon hers, at the end of the previous session. This was sufficient to repair the rupture in the empathic attunement. Then something amazing happened: she felt confident enough that I deeply cared about her profound emotional self to share something with me that she had never spoken of to anyone before. She told me tearfully that I had been on the right track: she had learnt only a couple of years previously that she had been conceived as the result of a sexual encounter that her mother grew to regret deeply. So, her disquietude was affected by her parentage, but not in the way I had envisaged. She felt that this was the underlying reason that her mother had rejected her and that others found her unacceptable. Obviously, at a rational level, there was no real basis for her associated feeling of guilt. However, she had introjected a belief that she was not going to be welcomed into the world by her mother. I think she might well have picked up this message while *in utero*.

We now had the key to her difficulties, and it has enabled her to work the matter through and to move on, with a new confidence in terms of self-esteem. This was as a result of an attitude of sustained empathic enquiry, followed by its rupture (because of my ineptitude), and then the adoption of an intersubjective stance that restored the empathic environment. I employed exactly what Casement enjoins us to do in *On Learning from the Patient* (1985). Having recognised the error that I had made, through the contamination of my own countertransference, I had talked through the mistake with the patient, acknowledging the error and seeking to rectify it, so that we could learn from it *together*. We were then able to move on to a new level of collaborative enquiry and co-construction of her life narrative, both of which have led to a significant change in her psychological structure.

In fact, in the consulting room, the "emotional temperature" continually moves up and then down, as we, the therapeutic dyad, move from empathic attunement to rupture, and then, we hope, back to a state of repair of that empathic attunement. It is to be expected that we, as therapists, cannot remain in a state of empathic attunement the entire time. We are bound, in reality, to be taken over by our own countertransference, or by projective identification or projection from our client, or just to suffer the occasional "off day" when we do not feel too well, or are preoccupied with our own material.

However, the client is more interested in whether his therapist maintains an attitude of sustained empathic enquiry over a consistent period of time. If so, the client comes to recognise that his most profound internal emotional states are really cared about by his therapist and grappled with; that, in short, she seeks to understand him above all else. This entails one in a process as a therapist where one gives of oneself generously; we need to provide a loving environment at all times for our clients. This is the essence of what Winnicott expressed as "being held" (1965, 1971), and Bion called "containment" (1970). The infant is *literally* held much of the time by mother when tiny; this provides him with a feeling of safety as well as the provision of sustenance. Bowlby's comparative studies in ethology showed that animals too do not only want sustenance from mothers; they also want to feel safe, protected and emotionally nurtured. Once again, I remind you of the research of Harlow and Zimmermann (1958) with the wire-framed and cloth-covered "monkey" figures. Previous psychoanalytic theoreticians (such as Freud) had by contrast indicated that the primary instinct was survival: that is, with reference to the life and death instinct and the need for sustenance.

Thus, I would argue, to extend Bowlby's rationale, that it is extremely important for the therapist to provide empathic attunement. All three of the theories described in this part of the book have focused upon the concept of empathy. However, I have outlined a particular use of the word empathy: intersubjective empathy.

The integrative theory: a relational approach

This theory promulgates the notion that the express purpose of therapy is to promote the conditions under which the client will learn what it is to have and enjoy an experience of secure attachment for the first time in his life. This enables the client to undergo a profound healing process; in short, it heals the developmental deficits that he has suffered during his childhood and adolescent years, when, due to traumatological crisis(es), he was unable to make the necessary emotional and psychological changes necessary to reach emotional maturity at the usual stage of development.

The theory focuses upon the relationship between the therapist and the client, upon the primacy of the affect of the client and, furthermore, the derailment of affective experience that has impaired the client's development. As such, in common with its forerunners, it is a relational theory. The therapist adopts the primary role of carer in each of the three separate theories and in the integrative theory that I am putting forward here. I see my role as being that of restorer, maintainer, and consolidator of the client's self-experience. I recognise that he has passed to me the task of healing the developmental deficits that he has suffered from his carers in the past. It might be that he has given me this task only at a semi-conscious level, scarcely aware that this is one of the major reasons that he has presented in my consulting room. However, intuitively, many clients have an awareness of their reasons for coming to therapy when I start to talk candidly about these issues in words of plain English. They speak of the need to be loved and cared for with a deep longing in their voices. We need, above all, to give of ourselves in the therapeutic environment is such a way that we consistently provide loving care.

I envisage my role in the consulting room is to consistently act as a secure base, to use a Bowlbian phrase. At first, the client wants, just as the infant does, instant gratification. Just as the infant cries hoping that his hunger will be immediately assuaged, the newly attached client wants my attention between sessions as soon as he telephones or emails. Gradually, he learns that he has to wait at least until I have time to answer his email or reply to his voicemail, and maybe, he might only be able to fully process his feelings in the next session. Learning to cope with deferred gratification is the same as the Kohutian idea of optimal frustration: this is the idea that the client learns that the idealised parental imago is not perfect or ideal or exactly the same as himself, but that his selfobject does her best, and approximates well enough for him to manage. She is a real figure with her own limits. This is what I term learning to accept the less than ideal in life and in one's therapist, as I have said earlier.

If you are familiar with Ronald Britton's work (1989, 1992), or my book on the Oedipus complex (Fear, 2015), I think you might well be aware that Britton states wisely that when the individual resolves the Oedipus complex, he settles for a life that is "less than ideal" (Fear, 2015, p. 171). Although this might seem to be a disadvantage, it is actually a great gift, for the reality is that in life so much is less than ideal and, in accepting this, we come to accept reality and stop reaching for the stars.

Work in the transference

In keeping with traditional psychoanalytic psychotherapists, I believe that the client's pathologies play out in the here and now of the transference between the therapist and the client in the consulting room. The client fears that the therapist will react in the same way as his significant other did in times past, and that the traumatological crisis will re-occur. One of two things may happen: the therapist might be coerced into acting in such a way, via a process of projective identification. This then necessitates that the therapist recognises the error, reflects upon the occurrence, and talks it through with the client in order to repair the rupture to the best of her ability. However, it is more likely that the therapist will respond differently to the client in the consulting room than did his significant other in times gone by. Although finding this process unfamiliar and disorientating, he will be considerably relieved. He will gradually learn, through repeated similar experiences, that trauma is not inevitable, and healing will take place. This is all part and parcel of how the therapist becomes a secure base and the client gains an experience of learned security.

When the client is first in therapy with me, I tend to act concordantly (Racker, 1968)—that is, I fit in with his perception of the world and do not challenge him overmuch. It is like a battalion of soldiers marching together on the parade ground: they purposefully keep the same pace. Later in therapy, when the real relationship has been established, I move to complementary tactics—that is, I challenge more and enable my client to appreciate that change is possible and that my client *can* adapt his way of thinking and behaving in the world. It is harder for one to carry out the following in practice than in theory, but one must aim to offer challenge as a gift, not a punishment. As one of my clients said recently when I was pointing out a dysfunctional pattern in his life, "I know you do it with love in your heart, and my best interests in mind."

I have talked about the particular way in which I utilise the transference. Kohut delineated three types of transference (see Chapter Nine); I believe that the client searches for the mirroring transference, the twinship transference, and the idealising transference during his long-term work with me. During episodes of the twinship transference, the client sees me as the same as himself, and is reassured and emotionally warmed by a feeling that we are at one with one another. He will look for tiny signs that we are the same: this week, a client of mine commented upon the fact that we had both chosen to wear red shoes that day. She has found it comforting on other occasions, and commented that we frequently both choose to wear purple. Regarding my own therapy, I remember commenting to my therapist that we were both dressed only in grey colour co-ordinated clothes one particular day. I admit that I found it oddly comforting; I suppose it brought a sense of mergedness, which helped to assuage my past experiences of abandonment.

During the mirroring transference, my client will want to see himself reflected lovingly in my eyes. It is as if he is looking in a mirror and sees himself reflected, and, like Narcissus (gazing unknowingly at his reflection in the lake, and falling in love with himself), he wants to see an image with which he, too, can fall in love. Such clients missed out on this stage by not having a parent who thought they were the best thing since sliced bread, or that the world revolved around them, as so many parents *do* feel about their new babies. They need to experience this feeling now with their therapist in psychotherapy. Consequently, one must be admiring of their exploits, of their achievements, and encouraging of their aspirations, hopes, and plans for the future. This is not to recommend that the whole therapy becomes a *folie à deux*; it is just a stage that the client needs to pass through, where he needs to soak up this sort of attention from the therapist.

During the idealising transference, the client will see me as the perfect one. This stage approximates to Kohut's idealised parental imago and relates to the transference experienced by the client in his feelings about the therapist. During this stage of the transference, the client envisages that I am all-knowing, have an answer for everything, get everything in my own life right, have perfect children with perfect lives and a perfect marriage (if I am allowed to be married in his phantasy) to a lovely partner. Not for me (he thinks) the traumas of his life. Later, the twinship transference occurs, and the client, somewhat with relief, admits that he is glad that I, too, have my difficulties. I have spoken earlier of my client Nick, and how much closer he now feels to me owing to my possessing human frailties similar to his own.

Summary of the theory of learned security

The extent of this chapter up to now has been to elucidate the five factors which enabled me to create the integration of the theories.

1. The guiding concept of intersubjective empathy.
2. A sustained collaborative process.
3. The need to concentrate upon the client's (selfobject) transference.
4. The shared belief in an ironic view of reality.
5. The shared philosophical view of the world that it is the affective relationship (both the transference and the real relationship) that is of primary importance.

It is by focusing upon these elements in the consulting room that much of the work between therapist and client is achieved. I am constantly aware that my relationship with my client is of pre-eminent importance, and, consequently, give due gravitas to this aspect of our work together. As I have shown before, the work in the transference yields a great deal in terms of its healing power. It is possible to see this in operation in the case studies in Part IV.

I find it truly amazing to encounter the changes that clients can undergo in psychotherapy through our work. This is, undoubtedly, through the mutative power of work in the transference, but it is also a direct result, in my opinion, of the calibre of the real relationship between therapist and client. I am referring here to the way in which the therapist acts as carer and secure base for the client over a sustained period of time. This requires of her, and I will here iterate much of what I said in Chapter Four, that the therapist patiently applies herself to her task of providing a secure base in all the ways that I have described.

Attachment therapy utilising the underlying tenets of learned security is not for the therapist who does not find intriguing the high level of dependency that is likely to accompany it, for at least a proportionate period of each client's time in psychotherapy. This is not a job for those who prefer short-term work, or for those who like to go off on holiday and forget that they are therapists for four weeks at a stretch.

Last, I feel it is necessary to say that the core conditions spelled out by Carl Rogers still hold true in the twenty-first century in this integrative version of attachment theory: the theory of learned security. If the client is to learn what it is to enjoy and bask in the safe harbour of learned security, he needs to experience working with a therapist who at least tries consistently to achieve the following three qualities: intersubjective empathy, unconditional positive regard, and congruence. As I make clear in the next chapter (Chapter Twelve) with regard to all three core conditions, it is impossible for any of us to provide these conditions consistently and continuously. It is true to say of congruence and unconditional positive regard that we each achieve moments of perfection. But it is of paramount importance that we are always striving to achieve such moments. I do believe that our clients sense the level of our motivation and commitment, and our determination to succeed, and that this helps them to forgive us our mishaps. Our clients are swayed by our generosity of spirit, by how much of ourselves we are willing to give.

It is very much this quality—our generosity of spirit—that enables us to become a secure base to another. It is by the therapist acting as a secure base that a person is enabled to gain an experience of learned security. Naturally, there will come a time at the end of therapy when we cannot any longer function as that client's secure base except in the way in which he has internalised us by the end of the therapeutic relationship. It is to be hoped that he will, by then, be able to do two things. First, he will feel secure enough to have gained an internalised object as a result of his work in therapy. Second, he should then become capable of transferring his learned experience of security on to some other person in his life, or to search out a suitable individual or individuals who are capable of providing such a base. He now knows, through having learned, what sort of person to choose if he wants a satisfying, reciprocal relationship. This is at the root of why I call it a learning experience: because now he can transfer that learning and apply it to his external world.

CHAPTER TWELVE

The clinical application of the theory of learned security

Why does a client need to gain an experience of learned security?

The optimal feeling that is relevant to the client is encapsulated in the single word: *security*. His life to date will have been sprinkled with incidents or constant repeated episodes where he has suffered the antithesis—that is, insecurity. This is the word that most accurately describes one's experience when not feeling held or contained by mother or father during one's life as a child and adolescent.

When we speak of clients who need to gain an experience of learned security, we are talking about those members of society who find their way to our doorsteps because, fundamentally, they have endured a childhood of insecure attachment. This could be for one of many reasons, as described earlier. This overarching feeling of insecurity and consequent lack of self-esteem then tends to follow one as one walks down the corridors of life as an adult. Holmes (2010, pp. 25–26) states that some individuals avoid this insecure scenario because of their capacity to mentalize, which enables them to gain a feeling of "earned security" instead. I, too, would admit that of those individuals who lacked a secure base in childhood, a few seem to manage their adult lives reasonably well, but I question whether they actually feel secure, or just are resilient enough to cope with the vagaries of life via defensive measures.

Every one of our clients has his or her unique life narrative to tell. My heart breaks and my eyes could fill with tears at the thought of the trauma they have suffered. I feel the pain, viscerally, in my heart, and have done ever since clients brought to me their life stories in the early 1990s when I was still a noviate counsellor at Relate. As different therapies unravelled, the catalogue of sessions to which such clients came late directly following one of my breaks, or of sessions missed after they felt, in the transference, slighted in some way, began to teach me my trade as a psychotherapist. It was then that I decided to train as a psychoanalytic psychotherapist. I left Relate to set up a private practice and I have specialised in working long-term with clients ever since, particularly during and after my psychoanalytic psychotherapy training.

Is there a relationship between the more dysfunctional attachment schemas and the need to engage in therapy?

We do not see securely attached individuals in our consulting rooms. It is as if the securely attached members of our society are indemnified against "the slings and arrows of outrageous fortune" (Shakespeare, 1987). Individuals with a secure schema of attachment who do not find the need to come to our consulting rooms fortunately cope with, and survive, life's traumas, crises and losses. It is not that the traumas do not befall them. It is, instead, that they can endure and manage the losses and pain that the traumas bring without recourse to external help and succour. In short, they are more robust as a consequence of their secure attachment schemas.

In contrast, those individuals with insecure schemas of attachment—insecure–ambivalent and insecure–avoidant schemas—find life so much harder to manage in emotional terms. They tend to employ more robustly developed and sophisticated defensive patterns. As I have said elsewhere (Fear, 2015, p. xi), all defensive measures are employed by us as individuals to save us from unbearable pain. They work for a time—sometimes for years, sometimes even for decades. Unfortunately, these defensive structures always, without fail, break down at some time. Frequently, it is at the stage of the breakdown—sometimes involving a process of what is commonly referred to as "nervous breakdown"—that the individual presents in our consulting rooms, intuitively "knowing" that she or he cannot proceed any longer without some external form of help and succour. The actual presenting problems may be many and various, and are often relevant in some way, but principally the problem is that the individual lacks a sense of a secure base from which he can venture forth into the world, secure in the knowledge that, when fazed by the vagaries and difficult dilemmas of the external world, he has a secure base to which to return and cling while he gathers his resources to venture forth once more.

The analogy can be drawn to the toddler's behaviour at mother and toddler group, to which many parents of young children will have taken their child. Your child starts the afternoon by clinging to your skirt/trousers, and then, gaining courage, he ventures forth and starts to play with a toy car a few feet from your side. Emboldened, he gradually ventures farther away, until he starts playing with a little girl he has befriended at a nearby coffee table, her mother also sitting nearby. The two children play for a while, and every so often, your son returns to your side, for "emotional refuelling"; he pulls on your skirt (sometimes literally, sometimes metaphorically) and calls for your attention, and having checked that you are still present (both emotionally and physically) and are interested in him, he then feels free to wander off again and explore. As Bowlby wrote (and I remind you again), "All of us, from the cradle to the grave, are happiest when life is organised as a series of excursions, long and short, from the secure base provided by our attachment figures" (Bowlby, 1988, p. 62).

As a consequence of all this, we need to ask the following question: how are we as therapists to compensate for the lack of a secure base in such clients? The answer, I steadfastly believe, lies in putting into practice the theory of learned security.

Creating a secure base for the client

First of all, I do consider that, despite having undergone psychoanalytic psychotherapy training, Rogers' core conditions are essential in establishing and generating a good therapeutic relationship. The provision by the therapist of the core conditions of empathy, unconditional positive regard, and congruence are necessary if the therapist is to establish a relationship from which the client can go on to grow and develop a sense of learned security. I agree with Rogers that the core conditions are *necessary*, but I do not agree with him that they are *sufficient* for change to take place. Rogers wrote an often quoted paper in the *Journal of Consulting Psychology* (Rogers, 1957) entitled "The necessary and sufficient conditions for personality change". I believe that, as psychoanalytic therapists, it is incumbent upon us also to make interpretations. It is essential for us to make links between the client's past and his present behaviour and way of thinking and feeling. It is through our interpretations that our clients gain both cognitive and affective insight concerning their outdated modes of behaviour, and they can then change their way of thinking, feeling, and behaving if they so choose.

I am certain that one's empathic attunement to the client is one of the most important conditions that we, as psychotherapists, should aim to provide. Perhaps Stern made an important point when he said, in a paper of that name, "Empathy is interpretation (and whoever said it wasn't?)" (1994). Maybe empathic attunement in itself *is* a type of interpretation, as well as a way of showing that one appreciates the client's inscape. To extend the question posed in Stern's title, I would venture to say that maybe we need to make sure that we do not throw the baby out with the bathwater: in other words, we should be careful not to deny the essentiality of the core conditions just because we might wonder whether they qualify as interpretations. I would also add that we should not disregard the core conditions simply because they were mentioned as the *sine qua non* by Rogers.

As a consequence of the above argument, I focus now on how I think the core conditions should be utilised in order to help the client achieve a sense of learned security. I also present a transfigured form of empathy in preference to that described by Rogers, a version that I believe is more appropriate for those clients who need us to help them recover from developmental deficit.

Intersubjective empathy

Empathy, as I am sure many of you will agree, is a much overused word and concept. It is often confused by many individuals in society generally with the concept of sympathy. Sympathy involves "feeling with" another person, and is usually associated with the expression of compassion for, or commiseration with, that other person. Empathy, on the other hand, was originally defined in German as *Einfühlung* (meaning "feeling into"). It was originally used in German aesthetic philosophy to describe a process by which one could think about, and get close to understanding, the beauty and nature of inanimate objects. Study the example below of a poem by Edward Thomas, an Englishman of Welsh descent, who is known for his melancholic, whimsical, yet deep appreciation of the natural world. Thomas was trying his hardest, I think, during his life in the Victorian and Edwardian era, to get in touch with the perfection of natural beauty and our inability as humans to equal it, the quality of perfection in nature which made him both intrinsically sad and happy at the same time: perhaps bitter-sweet.

The Glory

The glory of the beauty of the morning, –
The cuckoo crying over the untouched dew;
The blackbird has found it, and the dove
That tempts me on to something sweeter than love;
White clouds ranged even and fair as new-mown hay:
The heat, the stir, the sublime vacancy
Of sky and meadow and forest and my own heart: –
The glory invites me, yet it leaves me scorning
All I can ever do, all I can be
Besides the lovely of motion, shape, and hue,
The happiness I fancy fit to dwell
In beauty's presence. Shall I now this day
Begin to seek as far as heaven, as hell,
Wisdom or strength to match this beauty, start
And tread the pale dust pitted with small dark drops,
In hope to find whatever it is I seek,
Harkening to short-lived happy-seeming things
That we know naught of, in the hazel copse?
Or must I be content with discontent
As larks and swallows are perhaps with wings?

(Thomas, 1964, p. 28)

Somehow, the poem, which is one of many of Thomas's about nature and the essential meaning of lived experience, enables me to get in touch with the way that it is impossible to hold on to, to capture, the beauty of nature; there is a melancholy, a sad tinge to the appreciation of its perfection because humans cannot equal it. So Thomas did what Theodore Lipps sought to do: to enlarge the concept of *Einfühlung* to encompass feelings/affect. Freud was, in fact, an admirer of Lipps and was also very aware of the German aesthetic movement. In *Jokes and their Relation to the Unconscious* (Freud, 1905c), he makes his first reference to the idea of *Einfühlung*. He understands that the therapist must try to put himself in the place of the patient, saying, "the analyst must adjust himself to the patient as a telephone receiver is adjusted to the transmitting microphone" (Freud, 1912e, pp. 115–116). Freud saw *Einfühlung* as being necessary in order that the therapist could establish a good rapport with the patient, so that the latter would be more receptive to his interpretations.

It is to Ferenczi, a protégé and close friend of Freud's, that we must turn to look at how he employed empathy in an atmosphere of collaboration, warmth, kindness, and acceptance. He envisaged the psychotherapeutic relationship as having a two-person psychology framework. He had a distinctive empathic demeanour that enabled him to work with all patients who were referred to him; he was known to work with the patients that other analysts deemed "unsuitable". In his use of a collaborative approach, he was a forerunner of relational psychoanalysis and therapists such as myself, who deem that collaboration between the therapeutic dyad is vital, as is the growth of an affective relationship. Only by working in a collaborative way can we hope that learned security will be gained by the client. I advocate that the therapist attempts to gain a full understanding of the client's experience by a process in which she enlists the client's co-construction in order to enter into his reality, while checking out her attempts at empathic attunement for their degree of accuracy. In this way, empathic attunement becomes an intersubjective experience. It is for this reason that I have developed the term "intersubjective empathy".

However, despite my own concept of intersubjective empathy, I accept some guidance from Rogers. I think he is absolutely correct in his belief that we should, as therapists, always try to listen and communicate empathically with our clients. We need both to listen to the overt communication that they are making and to work hard to identify meanings that are below the surface of actual speech and awareness—looking for nuances, for slips of the tongue (parapraxes), for non-verbal cues, for what gets missed out or abbreviated, for tone of voice—in other words, for what lies below what I call "the actual words of one syllable". This is the surefootedness of the emotionally attuned therapist who appreciates the nuances of advanced empathy.

However, one needs to be aware, that "others have minds similar, but never identical, to one's own" (Holmes, 2010, p. 15). As Gerhardt (in Odgers, 2014, pp. 11–26) puts it, our empathy is, first, a subjective view, and, second, we are attempting to estimate how another person might be feeling. Again, this highlights the need for an intersubjective approach to empathic understanding; we need to take note from the person we are attending to.

Rogers spoke of an empathic stance as

> . . . becoming thoroughly at home in [the client's perceptual world]. It involves being sensitive, moment by moment, to the changing felt meanings which flow in this other person, to the fear or rage or tenderness or confusion or whatever he or she is experiencing. It means temporarily living in the other person's life, moving about in it, delicately without making judgements; it means sensing meanings of which he or she is scarcely aware. (Rogers, 1980, p. 142)

I stress again that we, as therapists, need to hone our skills to the extent that we can have an awareness of meanings of which the client is not consciously aware; we then need to find a tactful way of presenting them to the client in a palatable format so that he can take them in and digest them. This is difficult; we cannot hope always to be able to achieve this. As the client has not been consciously aware of the underlying meaning that he now begins to recognise through interpretation, then we sometimes need to approach the matter by stealth. As Holmes wisely points out, "Difficulties based on a paradox require paradoxical means if they are to be overcome" (Holmes, 2010, p. 54).

Perhaps because we are forever trying to place ourselves in another's shoes, the best we can reasonably expect of ourselves and others is that we achieve empathic moments, moments when we achieve true empathy with our clients, when we are in full accord with their inner felt experience. It is through such moments that we, as therapists, help to heal the client's "dis-ease": effectively, we enable the client to feel at "ease" by healing the sorrow and anger associated with losses in the past.

I believe that there is a constant flow of rupture and repair of empathy, of coming together with the client in the same inscape followed by separation as we do not quite meet our client's high expectations that we will fully understand his felt experience. It is not indictable that there are ruptures during the therapeutic work—what makes the difference is whether we try our hardest to repair the ruptures when they occur. We can transfer the dictum that Fosha (2000) teaches us about motherhood: a child only needs her mother to be perfectly attuned 30% of the time, but what she also needs is that her mother tries to repair the ruptures in their relationship when they occur. In the same vein, this rule applies to the therapist and client. It is the ability and willingness to repair the ruptures that is essential if the relationship is to be truly beneficial.

Congruence

It is also of primary importance to us as therapists, while helping our clients to develop a feeling of learned security, to try to work congruently. It is essential, to my mind, that we do not cloak ourselves beneath the stance of "the professional", for this means that we are hiding our true selves, and put on show a "false self". If we do this, then our clients do not understand that "what they see, is what they get" and, consequently, think of us as untrustworthy.

To me, the couch used by the client and the chair by the therapist carries with it a subtle implication of a structural power differential; in reality, the therapist has the advantage of being able to watch the "patient", but the "patient" cannot make any visual contact with the therapist. This places the client at a disadvantage and, in turn, this implies a covert power differential. For similar reasons, as I have stated in the Preface, it is my choice to use the word "client" rather than "patient". I realise that the word "patient" means "one who suffers" and, as such, this is an accurate reflection of the situation. However, the word "patient" has inherent associations with the medical model. That model is imbued with a power differential, that of the surgeon being the "all-powerful giver of life and death". I do not like the power discourse in which the word "patient" is enveloped.

I am not so naïve that I believe that we can eradicate the power differential in the therapist–client relationship. Admittedly, the client has the ultimate power to walk away should he not like the treatment being offered, but that is to ignore the emotional hold that the therapist might, knowingly or unwittingly, have over the client. It is impossible, to my mind, to completely diminish the illusion that the therapist holds the role of "expert" and "specialist". It is not true, in my opinion, as I have stated before, that it is only the therapist who is aware of the "unthought known" (Bollas, 1987), by which I refer to the way the client sums up the meaning of life, his personal injunctions, myths, and phantasies. Otherwise the therapist, seen alone to know the essence of the client's mind, holds too great a power. Surely the unthought known needs to be discovered by client and therapist collaboratively?

When I trained in the late 1980s and early 1990s, it was not uncommon for analysts (and tutors) to perceive the client as "a baby" or "victim". Such language contaminates the consulting room by denigration of the client's capacity to control his own destiny. There was, in my training, a dominant ideology that the negative transference was to be focused upon above all else, which process, if followed, leads to a punitive regime. I am not the only person to criticise this ideology or provide examples of it in the 1990s. Sue Gerhardt (who trained in the same decade) tells of similar experiences with distaste, recounting how she took a client to supervision only to be told quite clearly "to destroy her masochism" (Gerhardt, in Odgers, 2014, p. 15). The covert ideology underlying this command smacks of superiority and would have been punishing of the client had it been adopted. Such language helps to perpetuate the power differential between client and therapist.

It is of paramount importance that the therapist tries her hardest to be congruent—that is, to be her real, genuine self in the room—in order to minimise the power discourse that undeniably exists. It might be useful at this point to say a few words about the use of self-disclosure. For me, this means that I *do* answer some questions asked about myself, not always parrying them with a cross-question such as, "I wonder why that is important for you to know the answer?" Or "I am wondering what you think about that?" It is sometimes disrespectful of the client's intellect and sensitivity (in that he often "knows" the answer intrinsically) to refuse to answer a question. I see a distinct difference in whether the disclosure concerns my value systems or feelings, in contrast to "facts" about my life. I need to make it clear, however, that I will only disclose any personal information *if, and only if,* it is not for my benefit or a wish to discharge emotions, but that instead I feel that the information will help the client to gain a better understanding of the issue in question.

Clients may *not* know a lot about us, in terms of the nature of our partners or our families, or how we spend our time at weekends, but they grow to know an awful lot about "the essence" of the person with whom they spend many intimate hours. They get to know what makes us tick, just as we learn what makes them tick. An example of true congruence can be seen below—a remark made by my therapist a while ago. My therapist was offering an interpretation about two seemingly conflictual aspects of my personality that I have in concert, and I replied, saying, "But you have those two characteristics, in tandem, as well as me?" He was scrupulously honest and real enough to reply, "Yes, I don't mind admitting to that. You have correctly divined that in me over our years together." That is an example of true congruence. Thankfully, he did not resort to hiding behind a professional front by remaining "blank screen".

Being congruent means that whether you see me today when I am in a good mood, or tomorrow when I am feeling angry, or seven years ago, just after my father had died, I will be the same. I use the tin of Heinz Baked Beans as a metaphor for congruence. If you were to lay the tin on its side and were to cut it through in cross-section at different points, you would get exactly the same image each time: an outer circle of metal surrounded by a paper covering, with baked beans filling the circular space. That is how I hope to appear to my clients: "a baked bean tin in cross-section!" My aim is for my clients to get the same picture of me whenever they interact with me.

The practical purpose of congruence is that it engenders a sense of deep trust in one as a person—it engenders belief in one's reliability, dependability, consistency, mastery, surefootedness. These are five of the qualities that I believe are so important if one's client is to develop a sense of learned security. I shall move on to these qualities shortly, after first talking about the last of Rogers' core conditions: unconditional positive regard.

Unconditional positive regard

Carl Rogers described this as the "non-possessive prizing" (Rogers, 1957) of the client. It entails the therapist communicating to the client that there are no conditions to her acceptance of him—she accepts the whole caboodle, good and bad together, the whole parcel. It was Rogers' belief that the root of so many pathologies lay in the individual being subjected to conditional acceptance—what I call the "If just I do this . . . then she will love me" syndrome.

Thus, Rogers felt—and I feel—that healing occurs when an individual feels fully accepted, for his "good" parts and his "bad" parts. Many individuals, especially in the early days of therapy, are enveloped in what in Melanie Klein's language is known as the paranoid–schizoid position (PS), where the individual sees life and individuals as being split between "good" and "bad". Therefore, he needs to feel that his "bad" side is acceptable as well as his "good" side, for we are all only human and possess both good and bad parts. Thus, unconditional positive regard is essential if the client is to gain a sense of learned security, a sense of having a secure base as an adult: acceptance of all of one's parts, unconditionally. It means that we need to practise a way of relating that is non-judgemental by showing tolerance of others' difference and diversity.

In reality, just like empathy, unconditional positive regard is also very hard to achieve, and it is possibly more accurate to say that we, as therapists, actually achieve it some of the time, interspersed with conditional moments. Again, it is vital that we persevere in trying to achieve unconditional positive regard.

The importance of boundary issues

The following personal qualities should be aimed for at all times:

- consistency;
- regularity;
- reliability;
- dependability;
- always being emotionally present in the room;
- always being interested in the client's material;

- prioritising the client's matters (whatever one's personal state of mind);
- containing and holding the client: keeping the frame;
- holding the client in mind during breaks and mini-breaks (between sessions).

It is taken on board all too flippantly by many noviate therapists that it is not really important to be consistently available, week-in, week-out, month-in, month-out, and to give ample notification of breaks. Of course, as therapists, we are only human beings and we, too, need to have rest and respite from the daily grind in order to recharge our batteries, but we cannot allow ourselves the luxury of taking up the economic advantage of "late deals" and jet off to the sun at a week's notice. I have known too many therapists do exactly that; in reality, their clients are left wondering whether their therapist is just saying she is "away" as an act of retribution for some "injury" the client felt that he had inflicted in the transference the previous week. These flights of fancy (for that, read phantasy) are the very reasons that it is vital that we give adequate notice of breaks and any other reason for changes to routine. It also allows our clients the time to process their feelings about such breaks should they wish to express them, and that might avoid any proclivity towards acting out. It is wise to remember that, as Kahn referred to it, there exists "co-transference" (Kahn, 1996) as part of the total relationship between therapist and client. This means that we, as therapists, must be mindful that any action taken by us may be interpreted in a very different way as a result of the client's transference neurosis.

It is just as important to be reliably and dependably available on a weekly basis—for example, to offer a session at 2.00 p.m. on a Thursday and to keep that session free for that individual for as long as that person wishes to come, apart from scheduled breaks by either party. Sessions, too, need to be kept with closely guarded time boundaries: starting promptly on time, and finishing at a set time, so that the individual feels sure of "his time" and knows the time parameters.

Such reliability and dependability also applies to the provision of the actual physicality of the consulting room: it needs to appear the same every session, unencumbered with the therapist's personal possessions. The latter can be very distracting, and I have worked with a number of supervisees who have spoken of their therapists' consulting rooms as containing an assortment of personal books and DVDs. Leaving such items on show can elicit all sorts of phantasies and anxieties about the therapist. Notwithstanding, it is important to create a room with a pleasing ambience; one needs to have some carefully selected ornaments that provide a relief from the sterile, all-white walls of the Kleinian therapist.

The term "consistency" applies not only to sessions, but also to the mood of the therapist. She needs to be engaged, ready, and willing and able to take on, listen to, and absorb the client's material, regardless of what is happening in her own personal life. She needs, even during times of difficult stress and trauma, either to take a break from work if she feels that she really cannot give her clients her full emotional self, or else she needs to be able to suspend her concerns and private anxieties for the duration of the session, and give herself over to the client's material.

Similarly, one cannot let one's mind wander, even if it seems on one particular day that the client's material seems tedious. One needs, again, to be consistent: always to maintain an interested stance, with an air, as Freud said, of "evenly suspended attention" (Freud, 1912e). Instead, if one feels bored or pressured, investigate the countertransference that is leading one to feel this way. What is it in the dynamic between the therapeutic dyad that is beneath these feelings? What projective identification is going on? What is being projected that is not happily residing there, and is engendering this feeling? In order to learn how to process one's countertransference, I direct you to read the paper by Greenson, "Loving, hating and indifference towards the patient" (1974, pp. 263–265). He suggests that when we are overcome by a feeling in the countertransference, we spend some valuable time mulling it over before we react in any way. This way, we are likely eventually to respond in an accurate and sensitive manner. For an example of how this method sometimes bears rich fruit, look at my example in the case study of Milo (Fear, 2015, pp. 54–56) concerning my client's use of the toilet facilities.

All of the points I have already mentioned help to create conditions in which we have the strength and resilience to hold and contain the client. Winnicott evocatively likens this process which we try to achieve in the therapeutic milieu to the way in which mother needs to be strong enough, both mentally and physically, to take on the baby's projections, when he feels that he cannot cope with them, and then to return them in a manageable form. One hopes that she has learnt earlier in life to self-regulate her emotions. The baby can then use mother's prefrontal cortex until his own develops. It is the development of this part of the brain that enables us to be reflexive. This is a capacity that many of our clients lack during the early days of therapy. It evidences in the way that they are enslaved by their emotions, frequently feeling overwhelmed by them and that they might fracture or disintegrate under the power of the feelings that they are experiencing. This is one of the primary reasons that the therapist must have learnt the art of containment. We, as therapists (just like Winnicott's 'mother'), must take on the client's emotional disturbance, help him to process it, and then return the feeling in what will now be a manageable, digestible form.

I have referred to the requirement for the therapist to project the feeling of certainty that she, indeed, has mastery (Slade, 2005) of her world. This is all part of the ability and determination to hold and contain the client. We need to evoke a belief in the client that, whatever life throws at us at a personal level, we can cope and remain resilient and able to function. Sometimes, I think that it is partially for this reason that the client is not informed about what happens in our private world. It might shatter his illusion if he were to feel that there are life events with which we do not cope well. It is one of the reasons that clients find it very difficult when their therapist becomes seriously ill, and can no longer work.

Power talks about such difficulties in her book, which examines therapists' retirement plans and the effects of forced endings for both client and therapist (Power, 2015). My guess is that it is extremely distressing for clients when therapists are unable to give adequate notice of their intention to retire from practice, although I recognise that this is unavoidable sometimes. The clients might know instinctively or in reality that their therapist is ill; conversely, they might phantasise about the reasons for retirement. They might imagine her prioritising other people's needs rather than their own in the future. When illness befalls us, or family matters become so pressing that we feel unable to give our full attention to our clients, we need to talk this through sensitively with our clients if at all possible, so that phantasies and reality can both be processed before the break or the end of therapy. This is all part of the process of holding and containment.

I come now to the matter of holding the client in mind between sessions, and to making oneself available between sessions, whether that is via email, telephone and voicemail, or text message. Clients in long-term therapy can become very dependent upon us as their therapists. This is because we effectively become the secure base that they never experienced when they were children or adolescents. We are providing a priceless experience for them, and it is a privilege for us as therapists to participate in this metamorphosis. We need, above all, to be dependable; dependable in terms of consistency of care and level of absorption in the client's material, but also dependable regarding our availability. I would offer a word of warning. If you do not like the level of dependency that will ensue at times, then you might find it more comfortable to engage in another type of therapy with your clients. As is one of my own therapist's favourite sayings, "If you can't stand the heat, get out of the kitchen!"

Thus, in this type of therapy, there is a great pay-off: to see someone find out what it is to have learned security for the first time in his life and to venture forth into the external world feeling really secure—there is little that is more satisfying in this world, in my opinion. However, the satisfaction and bounty of this comes at a price: the price is that you need to be reliably available, even at weekends and while on breaks. Your client, while in the dependent phase of learning what it is to have a secure base, will want to test you out, maybe again and again, and he will not distinguish between you on a working day and you on your holiday. In fact, his separation anxiety might well be heightened simply because you are away. Thus, you need to make provision for your clients to be able to contact you while you are on a break. I make provision to be available on email wherever I travel around the world and I also inform my clients when I will be available to reply by telephone to any message. I do not promise immediate gratification: my clients have to understand and learn deferred gratification, as any three-year-old should have done. The child cannot have mummy the second he clicks his fingers. He must wait until she picks him up from nursery, for instance. But she must come. He cannot wait for two weeks while she goes on her annual holiday.

Perhaps I need to say a little about the rationale for this dictum. As therapists, we are aware of attachment theory; we are aware of transference neurosis; it follows logically, therefore, that we can appreciate how dependent a client can become in long-term therapy. In contrast, most clients have no idea at all about how profound may be the process upon which they have embarked, and no conscious knowledge of attachment theory. As individual therapists, we need, therefore, to decide if we have a moral obligation to be metaphorically at a client's side, whether it is convenient or it is not, whether one is in the middle of a family dinner party or at a friend's funeral, or enjoying the best holiday ever on a trip to Machu Picchu.

Summary

In summary, I believe that those therapists who wish to help clients gain a sense of learned security need to have a sense of vocation. This is because it requires one to give an unprecedented amount of oneself in the collaborative endeavour with the client. As my therapist says, this is perhaps one of the most loving jobs in the modern world. We give our loving care; we receive unprecedented satisfaction in seeing clients grow and change as a result of a feeling of security.

It is true that we are, in fact, *quasi* secure bases, in that we cannot continue our relationship with our clients for all of their lives. First, as Holmes puts it, the intimacy between therapist and client is both real and unreal. It is, as he rightly says, "encapsulated in the ethical and physical confines of the consulting room" (Holmes, 2010, p. 57). There will come a point at which we part company. However, the therapist who involves herself and follows the rigours of the theory of learned security will have provided a seminal learning experience for her client. He is then able, at the end of therapy, to apply this learning to other relationships in which he will have the courage to involve himself. However, what is of paramount importance is that *he will have internalised his therapist*—this means that he will have the therapist, metaphorically, by his side for the rest of his life. He will be able to call upon her, in an internalised form, whenever he needs to have a quiet moment with her. He will have known her so well that he will be able to envisage the answers as if she were there beside him. This gift of internalisation is perhaps one of the most precious gifts that it is possible to give.

PART IV
CASE STUDIES

CHAPTER THIRTEEN

Nick (Part 1): moving towards a grounded belief in his own power

Introduction

This case study concerns a male whom I met some seventeen years ago. He attended therapy once weekly initially, but within months our sessions became very "full" and the transference intensified, and so we negotiated to move to twice-weekly sessions. We met twice weekly for most of the time we worked together, reverting to once-weekly sessions some time prior to a six-month-agreed ending after eight years of psychotherapy together.

During the following seven years, he contacted me a number of times by telephone, usually to tell me about significant changes in his life. For example, he telephoned me to tell me of the final termination of his relationship with his business partner (a strategy we had worked on together), when he decided to marry, then when his father died, and again to tell me of his joy when he and his wife had a daughter. During these years, he also rang me a number of times to check if I was still practising, telling me that he would like to refer someone to me. I interpret this somewhat obliquely: not only did it represent a way of offering me some recompense for the help he felt I had provided during a difficult time of his life, but it also acted as proof that he had taken a legitimate personal decision in investing such a lot of time and energy in long-term therapy, if his friends and colleagues were to have a similar experience.

Two years ago, Nick contacted me again, this time with the express wish to return to therapy. When an ex-client expresses a wish to return to therapy, I take the dynamics and previous work into account. In the case of Nick, I was aware, when we ended therapy in 2007, that it was quite possible that he would return at some point in his life; I just hoped that this point would fall before my retirement. The fact that I felt he might have this need lies in my understanding that the major underlying reason for his therapy had been to provide him with what I have now come to call an experience of learned security. I felt that when we had ended working together in 2007, the process of knowing how it feels to be sure of a secure base was not indelibly ingrained on his consciousness. I will say more of this later.

Early in Nick's therapy, my supervisor had questioned whether it was "historical truth" or Nick's "narrative truth" that he had been so damaged by his relationship with his mother. Years ago, in 1999, Nick had described a dysfunctional relationship with his mother as having occurred in the early years of his life and that it was still in evidence in adulthood. In the late 1990s, I was in training as a psychoanalytic psychotherapist, which involved intensive supervision, and my training supervisor had spent some time promulgating the possibility that maybe I was being "seduced" by his transference echoing my own syntonic countertransference. I feel that, at this time, while still a trainee psychotherapist (though an established counsellor with ten years of experience), it was a possibility that I might be "swallowing" his version of events in an undigested form, rather than appreciating it to be *his perception* of what had occurred. However, I do believe that, nowadays, I always "listen with the third ear" as a far more experienced analytic therapist. I have learnt to practise listening to all of my clients, all of the time, with what I call "the third ear": constantly to sieve through what the client tells me while calculating whether it amounts to the same sum and total as another story that they have told on a different occasion (that is, are the stories consistent in their detail?). Do the two, three, or multiple number of stories tell the same tale and reinforce one another or are they cognitively dissonant? These "sums of rationality" are the sums we learn to calculate every day of our lives if we are to become well-versed therapists and avoid credulity. Holmes (2010, p. 72) articulates this conundrum in slightly different language, referring to as "triangulation" (again using language as if a third person is present): I presume he refers to the idea of one checking things out with a metaphoric third party.

In order to tackle the dilemma from a different angle as to whether this intrapsychic damage to Nick was real or perceptual, I would like to speak of my countertransference. I am aware that my countertransference to him involves a resonance to his woundedness, and that this woundedness also evokes a syntonic transference response in me. To expand this, I need to explain: our countertransference is often in two parts: first, there is the response to the client's transference. In this case, Nick unconsciously wishes to evoke in me a particular response to his expressed woundedness, a response of tenderness and yearning for connection in order to provide a balm to heal the developmental deficits he has suffered. Second, quite unconnected with Nick, I have a transference response to him that originates within me because of my relationship with an object of my own: in short, I am speaking of my relationship with my father. The latter used his woundedness to engage me in empathic attunement, in order to create and then maintain a very close bond with me. From the time when I was a little girl, my father used to bring his "wounded child" self to me so as to receive succour (via a process which we know as parentification). In consequence of my own life experience, I recognise that I am pre-programmed to react to the "wounded" Nick in a transferential manner, although I am aware that Nick has no conscious knowledge of this. However, I am also aware that he might have sensed this vulnerability in me at an unconscious level, years ago. As you are no doubt aware, much of our communication is from unconscious to unconscious: this is reckoned to account for over 80% of our communications.

I need to beware of the fact that my pathology somehow fits with his experience and makes me feel his pain all the more acutely. After hours of intensive reflection, I eventually came to believe that his repeated recitals of his mother's purposeful neglect of him, and her wilful misinterpretation of his childish behaviour to his father as disobedience *is*, in actuality, a truthful and accurate representation of his childhood years. As McAdams states (1993), one's "narrative tone", which, in turn, displays one's myth, is generated from one's original attachment experience. Whereas an experience of optimal security provides one with a belief that one will ultimately succeed, the person with an insecure attachment history will have no such belief in happy endings, because life experience has proved that individuals do not succeed in their wishes. Nick and I are bound together by a similar life experience; partially as a consequence of this, we are very fond of each other. I think Nick will have a place in my heart for the rest of my life.

As a consequence of Nick's experience of an attachment figure that was frequently emotionally unavailable, and consistently neglectful, Nick's attachment schema fell into the realms of an insecure–ambivalent category. As I commented earlier, despite having tried my hardest to provide a reparative experience of secure attachment, I had not felt that the journey had been fully integrated into his psychic structure when we finished therapy in 2007. The dynamic between us was convoluted by the fact that Nick had sought on several occasions to take our relationship beyond the consulting room. There have been invitations to dinner, an invitation to a party, and a suggestion that we undertake some creative work together. It seems that the germ of the idea that Nick planted has finally taken root all these years later, for Nick has kindly consented to write an account of what therapy has meant to him. This account appears after the end of my case study.

At the time, Nick made these suggestions to meet outside the consulting room as innocent gestures of affection, admiration, and as a result of an idealising parental transference. I can see now, with hindsight, that, at that stage of my career, I found it difficult to explain to him the way that there was a negative aspect to these requests, because it could have led to the ending of our therapeutic relationship and professional loss of reputation for me. One gradually learns to select appropriate words so that one can offer challenge as a gift, not as a punishment: to put across the negatives to one's clients, yet to say it in a way that is not heard as a rejection but, instead, is understood as part of the therapist's determination to have the best interests of the client at heart. Nick meant his invitations with a conscious belief in their sincerity and affection, quite oblivious of any malintent. I am aware that some therapists would be inclined to focus on and interpret the negative transference, but I can now say quite confidently that I disagree, on the grounds of the effect of taking a disparaging and negative attitude towards my clients. It is not a way that I wish to work, it does not agree with my development of the theory of learned security, and I do not find it profitable in terms of the psychic growth of the client. I believe, from many years in practice and the many positive outcomes of those who have enjoined in the therapy process with me, that it is love which wins the day, not cutting interpretations that consistently focus upon the negative transference.

In consequence of a number of areas of unfinished business, some due to my own ineptitude, some due to the life stage that Nick had reached at that time, I believed that Nick would return at some point to complete the reparative experience, in order to gain what I have since named as an experience of learned security. I was excited when my opportunity to achieve this presented itself again in 2014. However, I was curious about the nature of the catalyst that led to Nick seeking my help for a second time.

This is not to say that I was not in agreement with his decision to end in 2007. Sometimes, as an experienced therapist, one recognises that it is appropriate for a client to go into the external world without the protection and guidance of their psychotherapist. This is particularly so when the client has been in therapy for a protracted period of time. Nick had entered into therapy with excellent motivation and intuitive psychological mindedness. However, in 2007, I sensed that he needed a period of time to consolidate all the psychic change he had undergone and to put into practice in the external world the work to date. In addition, Nick needed to have time to concentrate his emotional efforts upon his growing attachment to his new partner, whom he had met during his seventh year in therapy. Partially, I sensed that his attachment to me was forestalling (unconsciously) his willingness to commit to her. It was quite evident from various comments that he made, offered apparently as non-sequiturs, that she was jealous of his relationship with me, partially because it had endured for a long period of time, and that he expressed that I "had literally saved [his] life". I have found it to be true that our clients' partners are often jealous of their partner's intimate relationship with their therapist, and I think this factor needs to be taken into account.

While, as a psychoanalytic psychotherapist, I firmly believe that therapy can be vital to clients at some times in their lives, I also believe that there are times when the demands of the external world need to be given precedence. I realise that some of you who share this career with me will not be in accord. I learned, during my training, that some therapists persist in an attitude that psychotherapy should always be given precedence, but I do not accept that viewpoint, or invoke those "rules" with my clients. The external world, to my mind, does exist, and does need to be taken into account.

Nick's early history before coming to therapy

Nick is the younger of two siblings, born to an unhappily married couple who had been together since some time before his birth. He has an elder sister, to whom he was and is very attached, and whom he became reliant upon for protection against a mother who, perhaps, would have preferred her second child to have been female. Her daughter remained, and remains, her favoured child. It is painful for any of us to be the subject of a deficit comparison—forever to be compared and contrasted with someone (whom you love, too) who is purported to be so much more acceptable than yourself. However, Nick is, and was, not jealous of his sister, whose help he had found invaluable in protecting in him from his mother's wrath. She had secretly dried her enuretic brother's sheets by the fan heater at night in order to save her little brother the shame and punishment he would otherwise have unfairly endured. One wonders, of course, what level of psychic pain this bedwetting evidenced in the young Nick. Maybe it was the physiological manifestation of the fact that he sat crouched on the stairs, evening after evening, awaiting his father's return from work, in order to hear his mother recount the biased stories of her son's misdemeanours that she purported he had committed that day. As he sat there, hidden from the view of his parents, he was not able to defend himself. He realises now as a consequence that what he finds most painful is to be unjustly accused. I have interpreted to Nick that maybe this is also the underlying, unconscious reason that he dwells on any slight he might suffer in life. Admittedly, it might occur to you that a proneness to dwell on personal slights is one of the hallmarks of a narcissistic personality disorder and I have considered this. It is true that Nick does have some such characteristic of narcissism, but it is my opinion that he does not suffer from a narcissistic personality disorder. However, by now you will be cognisant of Kohut's ideas about "narcissism": he sees it as a natural stage in those who have suffered developmental deficit and that there is no negative connotation associated with it. It is for us, as therapists, to work so that the individual can move on from this natural stage of development.

I recognise that Nick possesses one other narcissistic feature. During this second period of therapy, Nick has become aware of a tendency in himself to "become puffed up in importance" quite easily, only to lose what amounts to a sense of grandiosity just as quickly. This is a result, I believe, of a man who appears outwardly confident, with a considerable public profile, who, nevertheless, at another level feels internally very unsure of himself. Much of the central meaning of our work relates to our determination to enable Nick to gain a sustainable sense of self-worth, which remains with him whatever the circumstance. The fact that his "puffed-up" sense of himself never lasts is a function of a lack of self-esteem and confidence in an individual who, since his twenties, has developed a "false self" (Winnicott, 1965) as an extremely confident man who is willing to take on whatever challenges life presents to him. It is a fact that he is extremely successful in his career as a senior professional in his chosen industry, and owns and heads a high-turnover company. In addition to this, he is frequently called upon to present motivational seminars on leadership and other human resources events, and finds himself in constant demand as a speaker. This is beneficial for his self-esteem, and he finds it very rewarding, but, unfortunately, it does not completely assuage the damage done by his attachment objects during his childhood.

I do not feel that the "puffed-upness" is evidence of narcissism, but is, rather, evidence of an individual who is trying very hard to give the appearance to the world that he is capable, in control, and "up for anything". He *is* brave, and has achieved a great deal, but only with me can he verbalise that sinking feeling inside that he is about to fall down a very deep abyss, a bottomless pit, where he may fall and fall without end. We have developed our own private "idiolect" (Lear, 1993) by referring to this feeling where he "finds himself walking down the High Street, clad in a cashmere overcoat, only to be shocked (when he divests himself of the coat) that everyone can see that, indeed, he is naked beneath it". He has felt that he was unable to legitimately have the right to speak up for himself, especially in personal relationships.

Nick's father worked very hard to provide an income for his family when Nick was a child; his mother was a stay-at-home mum. Nick idolised his father, who died just a few years ago. He hungered for his father's love, and would bitterly comment repeatedly in the early years of therapy that his father never came to watch him play football as a child; as Kohut says, Nick wanted "to see the gleam in his father's eyes" (Siegel, 1996). Nick was, even when he came to therapy in his late thirties, painfully aware that his mother had poked fun at his "stick legs", and it would have been healing for his father to have been proud of his son's athletic prowess. Nick is, in fact, tall and good-looking, quite striking, and finds no difficulty in his mid-years in attracting women. However, he modestly declares that he was "an unattractive young man who has grown into himself". He is a paradoxical mix of overinflated confidence at times, mixed with a naïve, raw sense of a wounded animal who just might have been beaten down once too often. In the countertransference, I find this appealing to the nurturing mother part of myself, and I want to soothe and protect him.

As I have intimated before, Nick displayed an insecure–ambivalent attachment schema during the first years of therapy. He had found it so difficult to win his mother's love, and felt her care of him to be so unreliable, that he had adopted a pattern which I call "if just I do this . . . then she will love me". Of course, the list of "just this . . .", "just that . . ." is endless. One needs unequivocally to surrender the hope. He needed, as Haynes evocatively names it in a case study she presents of Harry, "a parentectomy" (Haynes, in Odgers, 2014, pp. 41–54). Fortunately, through our work together during the first eight years of therapy, Nick came to the conclusion that this hope to win his mother's acknowledgement of his capabilities would never become fact, and now has withdrawn cathexis from his mother. The parentectomy has been successfully accomplished. He maintains a relationship with his mother, dutifully visiting her regularly, but without any expectation of achieving emotional satisfaction. She is now a widow and lives alone.

With regard to his father, when Nick first came to therapy, his attachment schema was also insecure–ambivalent. He longed to be cherished and adored by him. Nick feared that, in leaving his first wife, he had done the one thing that his father would never forgive. Nick's own father had been deprived of his mother at the age of three when his parents separated, and he had lost all contact with his mother. Nick felt his father would believe that Nick was replicating his own injuries as a youngster, and, consequently, he feared that his father would reject his son. This proved *not* to be the case. In fact, he proved to his father that although he was no longer living with the mother of his children, he continued to spend a great deal of time and energy on his two children, sharing the upbringing of them with his ex-wife and, above all, he has striven not to allow them to become pawns in a game of power. His father clearly observed Nick's devotion, in terms of the time, energy, thought, and finance his son expended on his children, and was immeasurably proud of his son for this. Nick also took care to involve his father in joint ventures with the children, such as outings to watch their favourite football team play at home. Before his father's death, Nick had achieved a secure and satisfying relationship with him. In consequence, I was not surprised to hear that Nick had been able to mourn his father's death without suffering an abnormal grief reaction.

In young adulthood, Nick had met and married a woman in whose shadow he lived. She had a high status career and was also a charity fund-raiser, for which she received much public acclaim. He found this difficult to match while still a young man. He was initially attracted to her as a strong, dominant woman to whom he willingly relinquished control, perhaps because she possessed some qualities that he longed to gain for himself, and hoped that she might be able to teach him. Then, as the relationship progressed, and he became more successful in his chosen career, he wished to have a more equable relationship. He found this very difficult to achieve, but still he persevered. At this point, his wife did something that he could not tolerate: she was arrogant—and angry—enough to have an affair with a colleague at work. Nick had taken his marriage vows intending them to be for life, and surmised that adultery provided him with a rationale to remove himself from the marriage. At first, his wife suggested that he should take care of the children and that she would leave; this suited Nick well. However, eventually, the estranged couple settled upon joint custody, and Nick has been an attentive and loving father to their two children, spending a good deal of his time looking after them as they matured. It is apparent that the now adult children have a high regard for their father and willingly spend time with him, and come to him for advice and guidance, and, indeed, just to spend time in his company. Interestingly, his younger son commented recently that he was very glad that his parents had separated during his childhood. This underlines my belief that children of warring parents would rather their parents separated than stay together and consign them all to living in a war-ridden battleground.

A relationship pattern becomes apparent in therapy

However, I began to be aware as the therapy unfurled that a pattern was in evidence with regard to Nick's relationships with the women in his life. When Nick first presented in therapy, he also had a female partner in business. She, too, was a dominant, powerful, matriarchal figure. Over the next decade, he became involved in a power struggle with her, as at first he admired and liked her powerful demeanour but gradually grew to dislike her, decry her domineering ways, and eventually to hate her with a vengeance. I discerned a pattern in the above two relationships and others, that each time he chose to make a relationship with strong, dominant women but then he grew to resent this inequality of power, and tried to win control—and a battle would then rage. Each time, he would find difficulty in maintaining a composed and thoughtful demeanour, unable to find the words to defend himself. Instead of being able to articulate what he wanted to change and the reasons for his anger, he would find himself reduced to silent contemplation alternating with the occasional acting out of symbolic acts of rage. For example, he would purposely not fold up the towels on the towel rail in the bathroom, or leave dirty laundry scattered on the floor rather than in the laundry bin. Nick is well aware of the underlying symbolic meaning of these seemingly small acts of defiance. However, he is then angry and frustrated with the futile nature of his own response. He wanted to be able to voice his frustration and anger in a more composed and meaningful manner, and a way that shows him to be truly "strong". This is an example of the essence of his psychopathology: a tendency to rise up and feel momentarily powerful for a few hours, or even days, and for this to be followed shortly by a disappointing feeling of deflation, of feeling small and insignificant.

Indeed, a tiny event such as described above—the taking out of his frustration by scattering the laundry—is a paradigm for his whole problem when he presented again two years ago: it encapsulates the way he felt so small, so very tiny at times. This is in contradiction to another part of him that envisages himself as a strong person, as a person of consequence who oozes self-confidence. This is the Nick who is the orator, who gives public lectures and wins acclaim. This, too, is very much a significant part of him that I would not want to see diminished.

Let us look for a few moments at some theory that might help to elucidate what is happening, and has needed to happen, for this individual to overcome his pathology. Kohut (1971, 1977) focused upon the treatment of those clients who were suffering from narcissism. He made the point, however, that to be narcissistic is not a shameful way of being, but a natural part of development. Those who suffer developmental deficit are likely to be marooned at the narcissistic stage because they have not been allowed to move on because natural development has been denied them. Narcissism is regarded derogatorily in Western society because we highly value the attribute of selflessness. Kohut developed the notion that it is not through interpretation that "cure" from narcissistic traits is achieved, but through the selfobject transference. I have, of course, talked about this earlier in Part III of this book. However, I will encapsulate Kohut's ideas here. In his 1977 book, *The Restoration of the Self*, he renames these transferences "selfobject transferences and counter-transferences". He named them selfobject transferences because of his ". . . conception of characteristic relationships of such persons to their objects, not as separate individuals but as extended parts of themselves, existing in order to meet the requirements and expectations projected into them" (Wallerstein, 1995, p. 381).

There are three types of selfobject transference: the mirroring transference, the idealising transference, and the twinship transference. I think Nick has hungered to experience all three sorts of transference at different times during our therapy together. Kohut believed that cure is achieved not through the attainment of insight but through: "the establishment of *empathic intuneness* between the self and the selfobject on mature adult levels. The gradual acquisition of empathic contact with mature selfobjects is the essence of the psychoanalytic cure" (Kohut, 1984, p. 66).

Kohut goes on to make the point that "cure" resides in the client first experiencing the mirroring and twinship transferences with the therapist, feeling the joy and the healing power of how it is to "know" a complete sense of attunement to someone; this is a feeling that the client has never experienced earlier in life. Nick, for example, had been thwarted in his wish for this experience because of a totally unsatisfactory relationship with his mother.

Having experienced this intuneness with me as his therapist, Nick will now be able to replicate this in the external world among his social milieu—perhaps in his core relationship or, otherwise, with appropriately chosen friends who are able to provide such empathic attunement.

From 1999 to 2007, I see now that I believed at that time that Nick would recover if I persevered in offering him sufficient opportunities to accomplish two things:

1. To gain insight via a process of interpretation.
2. By the provision of a relationship in therapy where he saw me as a secure base.

Nowadays, I have a greater understanding of how to help the client appreciate an experience of a secure base. I have given much thought to how psychotherapy actually helps individuals to achieve change in their lives; some clients, such as Nick, who have been damaged badly in childhood, actually need to experience the soothing and healing force of being emotionally attuned to another human being who loves them in return. It is only through this that the deficit of the early years can be healed and a new way of approaching life be learnt. If I speak in Kohution language, the client learns this through the healing power of the twinship and mirroring transferences. The client can, as Kohut says, then apply what he has learnt in the consulting room, to his everyday life, and to find such resources (of reliable alternative secure bases) in his external world. As Stolorow and colleagues stress, it is imperative to carry out this in therapy in an atmosphere of collaboration and to build a narrative of the client's life in a co-constructive manner. I believe that an integral part of the client's recovery encompasses the building of a sense of "autobiographical competence" (Holmes, 1993, pp. 122, 182).

If we look at it from the point of view of examining the client's defensive structures, Rosenfeld (1964) talks of the disturbed client having a "guru" and a "propaganda machine". I, as his therapist, represent the "guru". I function as a wise elder who "grows" his sense of self-worth, and it is also my job to keep the "propaganda machine" in check. Conversely, "the propaganda machine" has told him to be "play the fool" like Black Adder; to be outrageous, to cause offence, to have an audience laughing in the aisles as a comedian does at a comedy store. He has done this sometimes (for example, playing the fool at a wedding reception), but afterwards—the morning afterwards—in the cool light of day, he has felt vaguely embarrassed, and fallen to earth with a bump. Temporarily, his behaviour used to puff up his sense of importance, only for it to be punctured, just like a balloon with a pin in it, the very next day. He then would come to his therapy session feeling conflicted, in remorse. His opening comments would display this conflict; he would tell me that he had a wonderful time, but this was belied by his recital of an experience of notable conflict. Soon, the underlying truth of how he was feeling emerged. To use a third image of Rosenfeld's (1964), "the gang" consisted of all the little voices inside my client that clamoured to maintain the *status quo*—they did *not* want him to achieve change at *any* price.

My "guru" self has been at war with the "propaganda machine" and "the gang". I am pleased to say that, because of my perseverance, I have almost won the war. This has been a war of attrition: it is a war of repeated twinship selfobject transferences. In short, Nick wants to feel that he is loved for himself, that there is someone like him, warts and all. He wants to know that he and I are from the same mould, that we are both successful, though we have chosen different careers to follow. I understand now that his suggestion of a joint venture years ago was a part of this mirroring, selfobject transference—he wanted our relationship to be synergistic and reciprocal. From a similar perspective, in recent years I have analysed a card that Nick sent me in 2000 in which he espoused his feelings (in a self-composed poem) about the "friendship" (as he sees it) that we share. I feel that this poem, written with our relationship in mind, dwelling on all that we have shared, and stressing that I am a permanent fixture in his life, provides concrete evidence of the twinship and mirroring self-object transferences that Nick was experiencing at the time.

I have been interested to see that a psychotherapy book has just been published entitled *A Special Type of Friendship*. Years ago, I was anxious not to allow any of my feelings for a client to "leak out"—yes, it was good to be warm, empathic, understanding, but I thought then that one needed to remain objective and uninvolved. I feel that this is subtly different from the client "knowing" and "believing" that they are really loved by you, as I feel free to communicate nowadays. I was hidebound by my psychoanalytic training and of being continually reminded to remain objective and a "blank screen" at all times. I now feel that it is an integral constituent of the therapy that I show Nick that I truly care about him, that he genuinely matters to me, that he is an integral part of my life story.

Once upon a day, I might have thought that the idea of the mirroring self-object transference would lead to a *folie à deux*. I do believe that I can see beyond that now, and can see its true value, and how, as an experienced therapist, one is able to share the mirroring and twinship, yet can also challenge and confront when necessary, with love and kindness in one's heart. It is with these emotions, and with experience, that one finds the tact, and the sincerity, to say the difficult words and yet remain loving and "on side".

Recent developments in the therapy

During the first eight years of psychotherapy, I had been aware that Nick had made a number of relationships with significant others, each of them being powerful women with significant careers. At the beginning of the relationships, he admired each of these women in turn, being attracted to their success and personal power, but gradually, as he grew intimate with them, the lure of their powerfulness dissipated and he began to decry them and enter into a competitive struggle with them to wrest the power. This "war" was never successful, and invariably left him feeling inadequate and enfeebled, or, to use his term, "small".

At this moment, in the middle of 2016 (two years into the process of this time in therapy), Nick is once again unhappy with one of his relationships in his business world. This time, however, I see a great difference in him from the Nick with whom I used to be acquainted. In earlier times, Nick had an idealising, parental imago of me. He saw me at that stage as "someone perfect, mounted on a pedestal"; someone "who knew the answer to everything". I was, in his mind, "the expert". He tells me now that he used to feel "inferior". This did his tendency to lack self-worth no good whatsoever, for, rather than bolstering his faltering self-esteem, it shot his easily deflated sense of self to pieces with a bullet, and it ricocheted to earth very fast.

This time, I have moved as a therapist to be able to see his need of me to provide both a mirroring and twinship transference. I no longer believe in the necessity of the "blank screen" approach so common among traditional psychoanalysis. I have instead ensured in a number of ways that he perceives me to be flawed, just like himself, like every one of us (it is the human condition). He likes the fact that I am, as he says, "just a baby girl", "just as [he is] a baby boy". I am, at last, "human". Consequently, he is now enjoying the healing effects of the mirroring and twinship transferences: of seeing his reflection lovingly mirrored in my eyes. Nowadays, as a seasoned therapist, I do not believe that our clients can go through a long-term therapy alongside us, sharing many therapy hours in our company, without imbibing a whole raft of understanding about what makes us "tick" as individuals. They may not know specific personal details about us, such as whether we are married, or how much money we have, but they are fully aware of who we are "in essence". Nick can identify that I am like him—I, too, have my life troubles with which I contend. I, too, am less than perfect. This has enabled him to develop a true belief in a strength in his personality by accepting that we all have frailties and he is no different. No more is he forced to hide behind a shell of being the class clown. He *is* strong, and so he is feeling differently about this latest conflict with someone in his life.

He is now able to begin dealing with this conflict in a different manner from ever before. Together, we are deciding calmly what to do to enable him to once again become content with life. He is starting to put a plan into action, calmly, not with venom and malign feeling in his heart, or a need to seek revenge. He intends to be fair but to find a new way forward. No more the outbursts of rage, followed by an associated feeling of shame. He is beginning to see himself mirrored in the therapist as able to be vulnerable, empathic, warm, welcoming, yet also strong, containing, and able to withstand any onslaught. Holmes (2010) spoke of this as the therapist modelling the characteristic of "mastery"—that she can withstand any onslaught. Nick is now beginning to see that, despite his flaws, he is able to be strong—really strong. He has found a way of forgiving himself.

There has been a repetition compulsion, born of the days when his mother related those untrue tales about her little son to his father, and he was powerless—at the top of the stairs—to stop her. It might be easy for us to say that he would have been better to have left his hiding place, and to have gone down the stairs and challenged her. However, we need to remember that he was a powerless infant who needed his mother for his very survival. In reality, he had no choices then. He does have choices now.

The repetition compulsion had to end, otherwise the pattern would repeat from relationship to relationship. The answer has been to break the cycle by increasing his self-esteem, so that Nick no longer feels that "puffed-up", insecure sense of "bigness" to which he was accustomed, but instead is suffused with a sense of wellbeing, through and through. This has been brought about through the mirroring and twinship transferences described by Kohut.

As Nick achieves his belief in his own self-worth, I intend that it will be supplemented by what Holmes refers to as a growing sense of "autobiographical competence" (Holmes, 1993, p. 158). However, we shall construct this collaboratively. Heard and Lake determined that the therapy dyad need to carry this out in an atmosphere of "companionable interaction" (Heard & Lake, 1997). We shall together finish what we began in 1998; we shall co-construct the narrative of his life that includes all the relevant happenings: its vicissitudes, the good and the bad, the nostalgic bits, and the bits he might consciously choose to forget. It will be a life narrative that coherently and realistically describes his life, without being saturated with affect that belongs to another era.

Nick (Part 2): Nick's narrative of the therapeutic process

This second part of the chapter has been written by "Nick" himself.

When I arrived at Rhona's door I was thirty-eight years old, going through a divorce; I had two young sons (three and nine years old), a business that it was crucial I keep running, and a soon-to-be ex-wife who, along with her family, were hell-bent on crucifying me financially. I was scared that they might take away my livelihood: the very thing that gave me my sense of self. However, worse than even this was that they had every intention of crucifying me mentally and spiritually.

I ached with pain and a sense that I could not win against their massive force. I ached because I was no longer living with my boys. In a moment of crisis, I wrote my boys the following poem that still makes me cry to this day:

> To my darling little children
>
> I miss you oh so much.
> I miss the forming of your lives,
> They pass with such a rush.
> Will you ever understand, just why things had to be?
> I had to do what I had to do, not for you but me.
> You may feel that you've lost me and I hope you understand
> Daddy was tired, and weak, walking through deep sand.
> I cannot bear to see you hurt and watch you suffer so,
> But without my spirit, I am little use, and that is all I know.

My marriage was not happy. I had had enough of my wife (and she of me!). But I had every intention of "staying put". I did not get married with the intention of getting divorced if times were not good. Furthermore, my father's mum walked out on my Dad and his sister in 1938. This was unheard of in those days, and wreaked havoc on my Dad. In consequence, I was brought up by a man whom I loved dearly, and who had decreed that he would stay with my Mum from a belief in what was best for his family. He felt that my sister and I must not endure "the shame", the cloud that he had lived beneath. So, I "knew" in my heart that I was just going to have to "put up and shut up". My wife knew this, too, so in consequence "she had me" and could do as she liked.

However, then she announced that she was having an affair. I was not bothered emotionally by that, by a sense of betrayal. Instead, her announcement was greeted by me with great relief. I saw this as the green light to end our marriage. I was determined not to miss this chance. Not quite the reaction that she expected or appreciated! Her intention was that she would move out from the house, leaving me with the boys and her mother in the granny flat attached to our house. I thought this was a perfect solution!

Then she talked to a solicitor. He advised her to stay in the house, and to tell me to "get out" if I didn't like it. Checkmate! I considered surrendering for one last time; this, I felt, would be the biggest betrayal of my spirit! I chose to leave—if you could call it "a choice". I then embarked on the most testing time of my life that I have ever known. A period of time where I felt I was going to hell and back. This experience tested met to the full, but along the way, and in the end, it has been totally worth it. I have learnt so much.

Metaphorically, the fuel light had been on for ages; the dashboard told me that there were zero miles' petrol left in the tank. I must have been running on the reserve tank when, on the horizon, I saw a petrol station—or rather, into my life stepped Rhona Fear, my psychotherapist. I had been given Rhona's telephone number by a mutual friend who also was a therapist. In trepidation, I made the call. Sounds dramatic! It was!

I was feeling that I must be mad. I was the first person in my family to need a "shrink"! I could not tell anyone. I thought that I would keep it to myself; lie on the couch, pop on the straitjacket, and get it over with.

Just how wrong could I have been? It has been the best thing I could ever have done. At first, I found the relief of being able to "dump" all my thoughts on to someone with no axe to grind. Chatting (or moaning!) to friends is all very well, but there are real downsides, such as,

1. They feel that they have "to side" with you.
2. They give their view of the other party, only to find that you decide to give it one more "go"! That gets very embarrassing!

3. You become "a pain". A sort of "Please change the record" look comes over their faces.

On the contrary, Rhona did not take sides, and she also confirmed that

- it was all right to feel as I did;
- it was not surprising that I felt the way I did; it was a normal reaction;
- I was *not* mad;
- when I described how I felt at different times, there was a name for each feeling. She named the feelings: this meant that I had proof that it was legitimate to feel that way! Others had felt that way, too!

Even after the very first session, I felt a little better. I now had some hope. It was as if I had got a foothold now, instead of sliding, seemingly endlessly, down the hillside.

It felt as if I now had a stake in the ground. I was not on my own any longer.

Prior to having Rhona as my psychotherapist, I had started to feel very helpless, so very isolated and really, really confused. Worst of all, I was always wrong. Not with my clients or my friends, or with my two boys. But with my wife I was always in the wrong! If I dared to stand up for myself, then it would undoubtedly end in an argument. It was as if I was trying to get past someone who was already on the stairs—someone two or three steps ahead of me, and determined that I should not get past.

I used to lie in bed next to her and feel so very tiny. The bed was enormous, in my imagination, and I felt so helpless. I felt like a tiny person with a tiny voice. A tiny person like a Lilliputian in *Gulliver's Travels*. Helpless against a mighty force that could and would steamroller me emotionally.

Once with Rhona I knew that I could discuss how I felt. I found that to be such a relief. There are certain feelings that you choose not to share with friends or family in whom you might usually confide. I was (and am) very close to my sister, for example, but I would never tell her that a particular feeling I was suffering from now was a repetition of how I felt when I was growing up. Equally, I would not tell male friends about feelings that might seem soft and not very macho.

Again, with Rhona, I could just blurt it all out—say it as it was—and she accepted whatever feelings I had. The very act of just being able to state your feelings is so liberating—feelings that I had kept to myself for so long. The feelings would just surface and come out, uncensored, along with tears, real tears that were triggered by how I had felt now, and long ago, when I had those feelings originally. There were a lot of tears early on in the sessions—well, throughout really. There is something to be said for the cleansing that follows. For the fact that it is all right to cry and it is perfectly understandable.

We spent time going back to my childhood; how I used to sit at the top of the stairs after bed-time and listen to my mum's version of events to my dad when he came home from work. This was essentially a version that was only her view and did not represent the truth. Meanwhile, I had to sit in silence and take it all because I wasn't supposed to be listening, and would have been in trouble if I had been found. *Plus*—a very big plus—it would have upset my mum, and my dad always said that we must never upset my mum!

So, in a way, I judged that I had been right not to tell my sister how I felt because she didn't feel the same. While I had been at the top of the stairs, she had been tucked up in bed, and in any case she was never in the wrong, and was never the topic of conversation.

Rhona became "my friend at the top of the stairs". She listened to my point of view. The one who said it was all right to feel hurt by what had happened when I was young, and that it was all right not to like my mum much now because of what had happened then.

Of particular note was the fact that I could discuss the effect of my mum poking fun at my thin legs. It made me so self-conscious that even at the age of twenty-five, I still played tennis or football in track-suit bottoms, even in the height of summer. No one was allowed to see my legs!

So, what did therapy do for me?

- It put a stake in the ground emotionally.
- It gave me some hope; hope that I *wasn't alone* and the belief that sometimes *I am right*.
- With that belief, came the inner confidence that *I am all right actually*, and that I was going to be all right in the long run.
- It started to feel that I was doing a PhD in "Me" and how to deal with the people in my life who had been controlling me.

- We started to pre-empt *their* actions and what *they* would say and how *they* would react.
- I took control of the "remote control". Best of all, the very, very best of this was that *they* had not got a clue what armour I now had gained.
- Every way that they had used to have power over me was suddenly rendered useless. The thrill of this was quite extraordinary!
- So my mum, my ex-wife, and my former business partner could *not* control me any longer. My life was in my control: as I understand it, if you know what is coming in advance, then the other party loses the impact of their intended ambush.

I will summarise the impact of my therapy with a metaphor.

In the game of rugby, players in the North play by different rules than players in the South. Both groups call it rugby, but it has some subtle differences.

I used to think that everyone played by the same rules, and, somehow, I could never win. Then someone (Rhona) pointed out the differences in the rules, and it clicked! I started to improve on the Game of Life, and then I started to win. The opposition wondered why they were no longer winning—they did not know my new-found knowledge of "which rules to play by". Life is so much easier now I know the rules of the game.

Writing this has made me remember just how very fond I am of Rhona.

CHAPTER FOURTEEN

Emma: a flower blossoms and shares her beauty with humanity

Introduction

Emma first presented seventeen years ago, when she was in her late twenties. Upon meeting a new client, it is my habit to take a mental "snapshot" of them before I even hear them speak, and then to hold this image. I find, so often, that this initial image is in stark contrast with the way in which the individual seeks to present herself (as the "false self" (Winnicott, 1965)) in subsequent sessions. The disparity between the two images with which I am presented enables me to make a useful and perceptive interpretation that frequently pinpoints the very heart of the person's pathology.

In this case, the snapshot showed Emma to be a little lost girl, wordless, with no idea how to operate in this big world, badly wanting someone to guide her. How true this was to prove.

The transference and countertransference must have immediately struck a syntonic chord, for she much later confided in me that for a long time she had considered me as "a Mary Poppins figure". When I ventured to ask her what this meant to her (for she can be very definite sometimes that she is not prepared to discuss a certain subject) she explained that it was so for two reasons. First, it was because she perceived me to be "so posh", because I spoke without a regional dialect, had a wide vocabulary, and described myself as "psychodynamic in orientation" (the meaning of which she evidently had no grasp at the time). The above explanation was given with a slightly negative intimation, but also with an undertone of awe. Second, in contrast, she said that she believed that my Mary Poppins self would sweep her up and take care of everything in a very commanding and capable manner: just like Mary Poppins, I suppose, as the nanny in the eponymous film.

So, one can discern, even at this early point in this case study, that my client had both negative and positive transferences towards me at this stage of our relationship. Her negative transference was in the ascendency for quite some time—in short, she did not like me, any more than she liked the life she was then living. I was berated for making the wrong interpretations, for wearing a "boring pair of trousers", even for allowing "dying flowers to stay in the consulting room". I interpreted this to be that if I could not look after the flowers sufficiently well, then I was not to be trusted to take care of her assiduously. There was a sense of equivalence in her thinking at this stage—that the flowers and Emma were one and the same, and would receive an identical form of treatment.

Her negativity peaked when I was forced to take a break, shortly before Christmas, in the fourth year of her therapy, in order to undergo surgery. I readily admit, in retrospect, that I dealt with the matter clumsily. Deeply involved as I was in my psychoanalytic training at this time, I adhered by the rules that had been drummed into me, and provided minimal detail as to the reasons for my forthcoming absence. I realise now that this was an inappropriate course of action for this client, because of her attachment neurosis at that time. It allowed Emma's anxieties to rise to a high level. In fact, she feared dreadfully that I would never return to her, and that I was not accepting the gravity of the situation. However, her fear was such, as an individual with an insecure–avoidant attachment pattern, that she could not bring herself to voice her dread to me directly. Instead, she offered me what seemed like a throw-away sarcastic comment that she expected me to have cancer and die. Deeply entrenched as I was in my own fears about undergoing anaesthesia for the first time ever on the following day, I felt shocked, and I am afraid that maybe I recoiled from her, rather than staying emotionally attuned to her and understanding her distress. We parted with a distance between us.

Unfortunately, it might have seemed that I was threatening to abandon her, just as her mother had done repeatedly (as I will soon explain). In this way, I fear that maybe I inadvertently and clumsily re-abused her by not understanding the level of her distress and the way in which she covered her fear by being curt. I realise now that it would have been more appropriate to have told her some details of the process I was to undergo, and to reassure her that the diagnosis was not in any way terminal.

Christmas arrived and passed. I took three weeks off to recover from a cholecystectomy (gall-bladder removal). I pondered on Emma's interaction with me during this three-week period, and gave the matter much thought. I remembered how she is one of five children, brought up in a chaotic family in an urban environment quite some geographical distance from the town in which she now resides. Her mother clearly had found it very difficult to cope with the demands of her five offspring, and grew particularly angry when they squabbled on their trips into the city. On a number of occasions mother would give the older children some money and declare that they could telephone Social Services to inform them that mother wanted the children to be taken into care with immediate effect. First, this was a threat of cruel abandonment—a statement of conditional love: "I will only love you *if* you are good". Second, my client felt that, as a younger sibling, she personally had no control over her destiny because the money was never presented to her, but instead was given to her older siblings. She is reminded of the feeling of powerlessness that this act engendered, and ever since (until recently) has suffered from an abiding feeling that she is not in control of her life.

In consequence of this repeated gross act of rejection and threatened abandonment, Emma presented to me in her late twenties suffering from developmental arrest as a result of this, and other, traumatological incidents. Psychically, she was just a young child (as my snapshot had revealed), cast adrift and completely lacking any sense of trust, very reluctant to make any attachment again to a living soul, in case she might be cruelly rejected yet again. It was apparent to me that she had developed an insecure–avoidant attachment schema. Little wonder that she had received the prospect of my impending absence with the devastating statement that she expected me to die from some cancer I was suffering. I understand now that she feared that I would never return to her, and that this was "typical of her luck in life" to find a therapist, a "Mary Poppins figure" on whom she could perhaps rely to sweep her up and take care of her, only for that person to die and abandon her.

In the New Year, we met again, and she was conspicuously relieved that I was still a part of her life. We made our peace. From then on, the negative transference, which had ruled the consulting room for the previous four years, began to subside quite subtly, and Emma began to show signs of positive attachment to me. She has said since that in the beginning she clung to me in sheer desperation, but I feel it was also because she sensed intuitively that I was capable of containing her in a way that her mother was never able to do.

Issues arising in the therapy during the first ten years

I have spoken of the transference relationship between Emma and me, but not the content of the therapy sessions during the first decade of our work together. Despite the fact that the first four years of therapy were dominated by the negative transference, strangely, I never once felt that the therapy was threatened. I never thought that Emma would decide to discontinue her sessions. One of the few things that she never threatened to do was to cease attending sessions, and she did not miss a single session, despite the fact that at this time she needed to contend with arranging adequate childcare cover whenever she came to therapy.

My intuition that she was just a little child herself proved to be accurate because, during the first few years of therapy, Emma actively enrolled my help in learning how to mother her two young children. I think that the reason for this was as a result of her having no role model of how to be a mother. When I say this, I am referring to the emotional aspect of mothering—she was able to cope with the practical side of parenting with perfect competence. I gradually learnt that her own mother had no notion of the emotional needs of her youngsters, and was effectively counter-intuitive—thus fuelling Emma's anxiety rather than allaying it during her childhood and adolescence.

For instance, when Emma had innocently visited a male neighbour's house during the school holidays (aged about eleven), her mother made her feel that she had committed some awful crime, for which she could expect to pay a price. Mother, presumably imagining that that her pubertal daughter might have been the victim of some act of sexual abuse, projected her guilt for not having protected Emma better on her daughter, rather than accept that the guilty feelings lay within herself. This is but one of many examples of how her mother could never contain her own anxiety, but instead projected it on Emma, in a process of projective identification. Emma, then "ran with the projection injected into her", identifying with the feeling, and believing it to be of her own making. As a consequence in this instance, when Emma first told me about this event, she was convinced that maybe she had inadvertently been involved in some episode of child sexual abuse, of which she had no conscious memory. She could remember the house, the furniture, the rug, the cushions, plus she was *almost* certain that nothing had actually occurred. Nevertheless, the fear that the memory inculcated in her was palpable in the consulting room, two decades later. It took some time, and some sessions of work, to detoxify the event.

I have not yet pointed out that I found it difficult to follow what Emma was trying to convey during the first year that she came to sessions. I wondered for several years why this was occurring, until I stumbled upon the word "anacoluthon" and its meaning. It is a figure of speech indicating that the person abruptly changes the meaning of a sentence to another sentence with a different subject. The purpose of this (I think unconscious to Emma) is to confuse, or divert, the listener. I think now that Emma, at some level, wanted to confuse me and for me not to be able to understand her because she was so fearful that she would "betray" the feared belief that she was suffering from some form of insanity. The net result was that she appeared to be inchoate, and, in consequence, as I saw Emma for the first few years first thing on a Monday morning, by 10.00 a.m. I was suffering from a headache. Of course, I persevered. I knew intuitively that here was someone who really needed my help as few people do. Despite Emma's negative protestations at one level, I believed that she really needed me to convince her that I would remain true to her whatever might befall us. I interpret, in fact, that the negative transference was one way of rigorously testing me to see whether I would reject her if she was consistently negative towards me. Nevertheless, I appreciate that this was carried out by Emma at a deeply unconscious level, and so, naturally, I bore her no ill-will.

Evidently, I passed the first test when I returned to the therapy room after my operation: Emma feared that I would abandon her through death and I did not. I passed the "real test" (so she informs me) when I vowed that I would not allow her estranged husband to gain custody of their two children when he threatened to take the children. This occurred when Emma had been in therapy with me for five years. She told me, "At last in life I had an ally on my side, who would do battle for me no matter what." From that point on, the transference mutated quite quickly to become one that was positive. It would be unnatural, and something to talk through with a client, if she did not express some negative affect towards me at times, so, of course, we have a return to moments of negative transference.

In the first five years of therapy, Emma was preoccupied with the traumas that she suffered during her childhood. It was apparent that she needed to process these traumas before she could move on and begin the long journey towards enjoying her life in the present. She spoke of school years during which she was labelled as "not very bright", and "troublesome" by schoolteachers, and it was clear to her that she was not expected to achieve much when she became adult. While this was bitterly disappointing, and very difficult to hear, I think that, paradoxically, it has served her well. It has motivated her to achieve academic excellence, and to prove "them" (both parents and teachers) wrong. In addition to poor academic performance, which, incidentally, I believe was more a function of labelling as a result of the conflicted emotional preoccupation with an insecure home life than actual inability to achieve, Emma inculcated a reputation within the family for being argumentative at school. Her mother would repeatedly, day after day, ask her the same question on her return from school: "Who have you fallen out with today?" It is true to say that, in the first four years of therapy, Emma seemed to me to be consistently ill-humoured, perceiving life to be a trial and believing that fate conspired insidiously to work against her. Plaintively, she would ask, "Why does nothing ever go right for me?" But I wonder about the truth of vicious circles and self-fulfilling prophecies. If her mother and teachers prophesied that they would suffer troublesome behaviour from her, was it not likely that Emma would give up trying to win recognition, and to feel awkward and ill at ease with the world?

I interpret this, too, as a response to a childhood that represented a dire struggle to stay alive, with no opportunity at all to feel wanted or safe. Although she has four siblings, the atmosphere at home—in a small terraced house in a working class neighbourhood of a large city—was chaotic and conflictual. The pervasive air of insecurity was exacerbated during her early childhood when her mother was hospitalised for a long period of time, and father was forced to cope alone. Not only was she unable to visit her mother frequently, but the children were never told the entire truth of their mother's illness, which served to intensify Emma's anxiety. It seems that, partially consciously, partially unconsciously, she wondered whether her mother would ever return. No wonder that my sojourn in hospital was so traumatic for her, and brought forth such a sharp-mannered response. I was not aware, incidentally, of her mother's period of hospitalisation at the time of my cholecystectomy. Emma did not speak of this for many years; I suppose it was too painful to recall and was, thus, repressed or denied.

When Emma described her childhood, it was clear that her mother was suffering for some years from severe depression, and, as such, was locked in a dark, dismal, and hopeless internal world. To use André Green's metonym, Emma had to cope with a "dead mother" (Green, 1983; Kohun, 1999). Apart from her sojourn in hospital, her mother continued to function as domestic head of the household of seven, but she patently had difficulty in managing the children. For Emma, her whole childhood was a traumatological experience. A trauma is described by Sarah Benamer in an excerpt from the monograph *Trauma and Attachment* as an experience

> Where a person is faced with overwhelming feelings of helplessness and terror at the possibility of annihilation: life and death moments, accompanied by abandonment, isolation, hopelessness, shame and invisibility. These include experiences that engender a fear of disintegration and threaten a person's psychic survival long beyond the moment of actual threat. (Benamer, 2015)

When I read these lines, it immediately occurred to me that they accurately described the way that Emma's childhood impinged upon her. I have never before seen an absolutely accurate description of the effect of Emma's childhood upon her life. It is so true that the effect of the fear of annihilation has lasted long after the events have passed: it has taken seventeen years in therapy to undo the traumatological effects of her childhood. It is not sufficient, regarding Emma, to simply describe her as suffering from an insecure–avoidant attachment schema as result of her childhood attachment experiences. Emma suffered daily phantasies that it would be good to take her own life, that it would be easier to annihilate herself than to struggle on. These quotidian hallucinogenic images of death and nihilism frequently played before her eyes for the first fourteen years of therapy. At the outset of therapy, she did not admit to being plagued by these images—for fear, I think, that I would label her as insane. Then, as the years moved on, she began to confide her worst fears to me about her phantasy of dying. She would come to me and we would discuss strategies regarding her conflict and fears in association with plans to travel to certain destinations. If the route to be travelled involved passing over a high bridge, then she was doubtful that she could manage the journey, for the shocking yet stark reason that she was fearful that, faced with the reality of such "a potential suicide venue", she would actually drive her car purposely off the said bridge. This admission of what constantly plagued her started to be spoken about because I inadvertently mentioned that she would need to pass under the Clifton Suspension Bridge on a particular journey. She returned, some sessions later, enraged with me for setting such a process in motion as I have described above. It had been an innocent comment by me—mentioning Isambard Kingdom Brunel's iconic masterpiece of engineering—but it reaped such rewards in terms of the issues that arose in consequence.

I use the term "rewards" ironically. Indeed, as both client and therapist, we have learnt a lot as a result of my inadvertently mentioning this detail, but the process that we had jointly engaged upon is a metonym for the interaction that has occurred between us many times in the course of Emma's therapy. It is true, as I have said, that the process reaped "rewards" for both of us: Emma eventually gained in terms of insight into her own inner psychic world, plus there is an accompanying comfort in knowing that I understand her, and that I am committed to trying to deepen that understanding. The sense of connectedness is palpable. However, all of this is gained via a rather tortuous process. I need, above all, to employ that quality of *Einfühlung*—the process of "feeling into". I need to feel myself into her world with as much sense of emotional attunement as I can muster, regardless of any sense of rejection that I might personally be experiencing.

I need to appreciate that any angry comment to me is a function of her acute anxiety and sense that she could disintegrate if pushed too far. Her negativity is a self-survival strategy to avoid annihilation, learnt from decades of practice, a survival strategy that is too deeply ingrained to change quickly by the application of the sticking plaster strategy of cognitive behavioural techniques. It requires, instead, the painstaking, slow, patient application of emotional immersion so that I clearly demonstrate that the secure base is reliably available. This therapy is a life's work. However, the "rewards" *do* come to fruition. For example, regarding the initial mentioning of the Clifton Suspension Bridge, which brought forth a torrent of angry rebukes, we eventually won mastery of her will to take her own life. What greater reward can one ask? For Emma, this has meant that she is no longer plagued by images of her own death, and the nagging preoccupation of whether she wishes to stay alive. As her therapist who is very fond of her, I am immensely relieved and feel a sense of pride at the outcome of our work together.

The progress of therapy: other images of rebirth

When I had been working with Emma for five years, she and her husband parted. He left her because he no longer wanted the responsibility for the daily care of their two children, and she was forced, for financial reasons, to seek full-time rather than part-time work. We spent a lot of time for a number of years working through the emotional effects of the separation and eventual divorce proceedings. During the years following the marital break-up, Emma was very dependent upon me emotionally, and she never missed a single session even though she was attending psychotherapy three times per week. The whole process of becoming "a single mum", living in a geographical area of England that she had only agreed to move to in order to please her husband, and far removed from extended family and friendship networks, was devastating. It seems to me that her already shaky sense of identity was lost entirely for a while. Until then, she had clung on to the identity of being a relatively well-off wife and mother of two. During that phase of her life, she had been self-employed, before returning to being an employed member of the workforce for a large organisation. In her early mothering years, she had been happy to devote her energies to enable her husband's career to grow in terms of status and income, and it was for this reason that she had been agreeable to devote her energies to the family. It is not uncommon for women who are out of the workplace for some years while they give priority to childcare to suffer a huge loss in terms of sense of identity and self-esteem. Emma was no exception.

Together, we vowed—though by tacit agreement rather than through prolonged negotiation—that we would build Emma's self-esteem and sense of identity so strongly that it would be impregnable. In her years as a mother of under school-age children, Emma had begun to engage in further education. She had started to seek to make up for the lack of qualifications with which she left school at sixteen. Now that she was a single mother, she decided to engage in a distance-learning degree. We were both delighted when, a few years later, she achieved an Upper Second class degree. This certainly bolstered her sense of self-esteem and began to provide her with a sense of identity, particularly as her career had begun to blossom: she was promoted to a new position within the organisation for which she worked.

We talked at length about which direction she should aim to take her career. She very much aspired to gain the legitimacy that emanates from being a member of a profession. This was something that had been lacking in her family of origin. We spoke of the possibility of her following me into my profession, but, for a number of reasons, she did not proceed with this course of action. We carefully assessed all the options. By this stage, I was well aware that my client had an unusually active and quick mind. Her lack of academic achievements when she left school was, I am sure, because she was never presented with challenging work; neither was there any expectation that she would achieve, and so a vicious circle of being labelled "below average" spiralled circuitously to prove itself to be a self-fulfilling prophecy. If you feed an adolescent "crumbs" of wisdom instead of full meals, then you will be rewarded with a malnourished adult.

Consequently, extending the above metaphor, together we decided that Emma should work to become chartered within her chosen profession: to have a full meal rather than tit-bits. This meant, in the first stage, undertaking a postgraduate course, followed by a Master's degree and then a Doctorate. When Emma enrolled and started the postgraduate course, she arrived at one of her therapy sessions, feeling very downhearted. In the first semester, she feared that she had taken on a level of study beyond her. I was certain that she could cope with it, if given a little guidance, so I took it upon myself to offer some study skills. In that first year of postgraduate study, I offered a great deal of practical assistance. I do not apologise for this to those of you who believe that our realm as psychotherapists is to remain within the analytical frame. If you wish to provide a secure base, and give your client an experience of learned security, then sometimes you need to give what that individual client requires of you. This is an example of the "generosity of spirit" that I spoke of in Chapter Twelve. Often, one needs, as the therapist, to "go the extra mile" and make individual decisions, tailored to the precise needs of one's client, if one is to enter into this work fully. At that point, Emma needed a mentor and teacher, as well as an interpretative therapist.

Emma passed her postgraduate course with distinction, writing her assignments in the second semester without any help from me. She has since undertaken and passed a Master's degree, again passing with distinction, and is now well on her way to achieving a Doctorate.

In achieving all these academic qualifications, Emma has gained something far more intrinsic: a stable and deeply satisfying sense of identity. Her greater self-esteem and self-confidence has led her to shine in her career, she has been promoted again and again, and is now very senior within her workplace. The world is her oyster—she can, in a few years' time—continue to be employed or she can become self-employed within her chosen profession.

I am absolutely delighted and astounded at the metamorphosis that we have achieved together through our work. It has been a long road, to which she has given unfailing energy and devotion. This is one individual who certainly has determination to succeed at whatever task she sets herself in life. And I am so pleased that nowadays she *chooses* to be alive.

Changing a vision of reality using integrative techniques

I have mentioned earlier in this case study that Emma was strongly of the belief that she had no control over her life. Another negative script was based around her expectations of life. She felt that the straws she was drawing in life were always short ones; not for her the good fortune that seemed to shine on others.

A cognitive behavioural counsellor would no doubt identify the negative thought patterns—injunctions and scripts—and then seek to change them using thought-stopping and cognitive restructuring techniques. Having been through a CBT programme myself as a client, I can see the positive effect of this system of treatment. It served me well, but until I unearthed the root cause of my difficulties, and worked it through in analytic therapy, the matter was not laid to rest. It is my firm opinion, based upon personal experience, plus the experience of many clients who have come to me over the past quarter of a century, that cognitive behavioural techniques form a useful adjunct to psychoanalytic therapy, but that, in essence, they are but "sticking-plaster techniques": they do not heal the damage done but only serve to cover the wound until the root cause of the pain is found and tackled. If the root cause is never tackled, the scab is likely to break open again, and the wound become raw at some time in the future. Cognitive behavioural techniques are the treatment of choice in the NHS at the moment, not because CBT is truly most effective, but because it is cheap to train individuals and it is quick to administer. It does not require the long-term use of scarce resources (that is, psychodynamic and psychoanalytically trained therapists), which would be expensive. Also, a wise, politically motivated CBT industry has taken the time to provide government with a greater wealth of empirical evidence about the efficacy of CBT than exists concerning psychoanalytic therapy. This is primarily for two reasons: first, psychoanalytic therapists have not been as quick to become aware of the political requirement to provide empirical research data to reinforce their claims, plus their manner of working cannot be investigated by simple, brief standardised questionnaires. Second, the CBT research does not tackle the question of whether client difficulties recur in anything other than the very near future. It does not seek to ask the patients if they were wholly satisfied with this method of treatment, assuming from the completion of a few standardised measurement tools that the answer is apparent. But, in fact, CBT is more expensive in reality than the more in-depth psychoanalytic treatment because of its long-term cost ramifications, as clients need more mental health input and absenteeism is compounded. Yet, as is true of any set of statistics, data can "lie": it all depends upon what questions are asked of the respondent, and in what manner the questions are asked: that is, it is a question of bias introduced in the research. How many qualitative interviews are carried out, or focus groups asked to talk about their personal experience of CBT and its long-term efficacy?

A recent cartoon in the *Guardian* depicted an analyst sitting behind a patient lying on a couch with the caption that, in fact, the psychoanalytic techniques of Freud are coming back into vogue, as CBT evidences that it does not bring change in any sustainable form. A sign of the times, I hope.

During Emma's therapy, I had been faced with the fact that Emma held a number of negative beliefs about life. These, I felt, were at the root of her very pessimistic view of life. Consequently, even when life was proceeding well, she did not appreciate her good fortune. For many years, we had tackled the experience of her childhood and adolescence, which had led her to develop such a negative vision of reality. We needed to make links between the past negative experiences and her current way of thinking. I also needed to challenge her about life in the present, and help her to start to appreciate the fortunate aspects of her current life. Admittedly, she had been unfortunate enough to separate from her husband under stressful circumstances, but, if one is to take the ironic vision of reality rather than the tragic vision (Fear & Woolfe, 1999, 2000), then it is possible "to turn the coin over" and to look at it from another perspective. In this case, one can now see that one of the net effects of the marital break-up was that it proved to be a catalyst that eventually motivated Emma to feel free enough to pursue her own path to success. The break-up had motivated her to develop her own skills and aspirations in a way that she might never have embarked upon had she remained a married woman.

Gradually, Emma has learnt to perceive life from a more optimistic perspective. She has stopped adopting the "tragic vision" and instead looks at things ironically—she seeks the positive in any situation. She relishes and celebrates the "plusses", such as having two children who are both healthy and succeeding in their life choices, and who love her dearly, and to whom she is very close. She is glad that her relationship with her mother has greatly improved, and that she can rely now—in the present—upon her parents for emotional and physical support even though they live far away. She appreciates that it is beneficial that she has four siblings to whom she can turn for help and advice, and with whom she is welcome to spend leisure time. She has an excellent career, which is well paid and satisfying. Her academic abilities are superlative. Life, in short, is good, although, naturally, at times she is faced with some vicissitudes.

Next year, after a year's notice to my clients, I am intending to retire from practice. By then, Emma will have been in therapy for over eighteen years. I do believe that she has gained an experience of learned security during her relationship with me. I have tried my hardest to be reliably available, to be the mother that she did not have emotionally, to go every step of the way with her throughout the vicissitudes of life during the past eighteen years. I have answered emails and texts from all manner of foreign countries, and on many weekends and evenings. Nowadays, she rarely needs me beyond the weekly or fortnightly sessions that we still share.

Emma is very much a part of my life, as those of you who work with long-term clients will appreciate. I have probably spent more hours with her than with many of my relatives, let alone my friends. We would have been friends for quite a number of years under other circumstances, but a part of the psychoanalytic endeavour is that we forego that opportunity to satisfy personal wishes. I am immensely fond of Emma. I am also immensely proud of the work we have accomplished together.

CHAPTER FIFTEEN

Jane: challenging her world view

Introduction

Jane first consulted me fifteen years ago. She sought my care on the advice of a human resources (HR) consultant, because she had appeared overcome by tears during a training event that had concentrated upon family and loss. Frequently, when it is suggested to an individual that he or she seeks counselling or psychotherapy, the person actually presents with some level of either conscious reluctance or unconscious resistance. However, it was apparent from the outset of our relationship that Jane felt that she had been prompted to come to therapy at just the right time in her life, and that, in consequence, she was determined to enter into the process of therapy fully. She has always been very motivated to work within a psychodynamic model, and I can testify to her psychological mindedness. In fact, she seemed to be aware soon after the first assessment session that the root of her difficulties lay in her relationships within the family, though she actually named her presenting problem as a pervasive sense of anxiety.

I noted that her father brought her by car to the first session, driving away from my house for the duration of the appointment and returning for her exactly on time. Privately, I wondered about the reason for father providing a taxi service to my house, once I heard during the first session that Jane was able to drive and possessed her own car. At this point in time, she was in her late twenties, and was living with her parents and her elder sibling in their home in a nearby town. I pondered on the manner of travel, and wondered whether it indicated that here before me was a young woman who lacked the confidence to drive herself to a strange venue. This summation reinforced a growing hypothesis that Jane was suffering from a generalised diffuse anxiety disorder, but, in the first few sessions, I was not sure of my diagnosis of the underlying reason(s) for this state.

The narrative that Jane presented to me at first was of a family life that was idyllic. She appeared to be extremely reticent and unable to bring herself to criticise her parents or sibling in any way at all. I understood this to be a defensive measure, because at first it was just too painful to face the possible and likely reality that life was far from perfect in terms of her intimate relationships. With regard to personal relationships beyond the family, she had a boyfriend whom she had met some months before. She was concerned for several years that he might not reciprocate the same degree of commitment with which she was engaging in the relationship; she surmised that this was a result of his being badly hurt in a previous relationship.

At this time, she was in full employment, but engaged in manual work that was well below her obvious level of intelligence and qualifications. She had read for a degree at a university while living away from home, and had been successful in achieving the qualification after a shaky start to her first year. However, she had returned to her home town after university and, indeed, to the parental home, and it appeared that she had never searched for employment in the field in which she had qualified. I suspected that this was as a result of lack of confidence, and I was later to be proved correct.

While Jane appeared to become very anxious when faced with anything new, or that necessitated any change to routine, I became certain that she possessed a strong and determined spirit. She was highly motivated to attend her sessions with me, and relatively quickly we established a good working relationship. We soon gravitated towards working in twice-weekly therapy. She seemed to relate to me in the transference as a mother figure, but, rather than this being in the guise of her own mother, I felt that she was looking to me to be the mother she craved: someone who would hold her, contain her, and allay her anxieties as they arose. It was, in Kohutian words, an idealising parental transference at this stage. I think that the quiet atmosphere in the house, the regular session times, the consistent furnishings and ambience of the consulting room, with no additions or subtractions of accoutrements, my calm demeanour, and a relaxed style of working all helped to settle her into the therapeutic endeavour. I was aware that, at this stage of the therapy, it was important to be gentle and empathic in my relationship with her (concordant), and that it would be inadvisable at this stage to promulgate any interpretations concerning issues which, at that time, were still buried in the unconscious. I try to remember always that the timing of an interpretation is crucial in determining whether the meaning will be taken on board by the client. I am also aware of the client's tendency towards polysemy—she might say, for instance, that family life is good, but, in describing it, could be conveying something quite different from that which is spoken on the surface.

She soon confided in me and explained her difficulties with regard to travel. She admitted to extreme nervousness in travelling any road that was not known to her, and simply used her car to travel around the town where she lived. Slowly and calmly, I encouraged her—at first, just by persuading her to visualise the possibility—to take the step of driving herself to my practice in her own car. Eagerly, she took up what to her amounted to a huge challenge at that time. On the first occasion that she drove herself she was accompanied by her father, but, following this, she grew confident enough to start finding her own way to our sessions. Taking the risk of driving herself became a private metaphor, shared just between us, for taking on new challenges.

This step, in fact, deepened the emerging trust between us. Following this, she began to talk more openly about her family. Much as she loved and still, to this day, loves her mother dearly, she began to develop an objective stance about her mother's vision of reality. She began to express feeling suffocated by her mother's constant negative comments and pessimistic *weltanschauung*. It was as if everything in life involved a struggle that would need to be surmounted if it were to be achieved, or, if too difficult, mother felt that it was a wiser course of action to avoid the issue. Her mother has not been in the field of employment, except for engaging in a few hours of casual work during the girls' adolescence, since becoming a mother. I have surmised that the concept of going out to regular employment raises too many anxieties for mother to contemplate. Mother seems to feel fully at ease only when she is within her own home. For instance, contemplating a forthcoming annual holiday to the British seaside creates a feeling of unease and anxious reflection. I wondered at one stage whether her mother suffered from agoraphobia in the full sense of the word, and checked this out by asking relevant questions. However, mother does go out, but has a narrow chosen circle where she feels comfortable. It might be that she has a susceptibility towards social phobia, though this is not in a pronounced form, in that she is fine if within her chosen social circle.

Progress in the first phase of therapy

Jane gradually revealed more and more about her mother. It appears that her mother fell into a serious depressive episode when Jane was in the later years of her childhood. I believe this depression was the result of loss, as Green points out in his "dead mother" writings (Green, 1983; Kohun, 1999). In this case, however, mother was mourning the loss of security (a secure income and her family home following her husband's redundancy) rather than the loss of an object. The net effect—if the loss is of something abstract rather than concrete—in terms of melancholia is very similar, for Jane's mother was caught up in a cycle of abnormal grief. Jane remembered all too graphically returning from school one day to find her mother crouched on the kitchen floor, silently lost in a regressive state of overwhelming tears. The fact that Jane was not able to gain her mother's attention as she arrived home from school meant that, effectively, she perceived that mother was "dead". This had the effect of leaving her feeling abandoned, although, of course, her mother was still there in physical form. When this occurs, it is not that mother seeks to be dismissive of her surroundings; instead, it is that she cannot muster any sense of joy or motivation to participate in her daily life.

Thereafter, there was a period when mother was out of reach in mental and emotional terms. Jane remembers a watershed moment when she purposely cried plaintively, standing up against the dividing wall between her bedroom and her parents' bedroom. She knew her parents to be in their room, as it was during the hours of darkness. No one answered her desperate pleas for comfort. This heightened her feeling of abandonment, meaning that she felt all alone in the world with no one to rely upon in times of need. I believe that Jane's experience of the "dead mother syndrome" was seminal in the development of an insecure–ambivalent attachment schema in Jane, plus she has a genetic predisposition to suffer an anxiety state.

When Jane first sought therapy in her late twenties, her insecure–ambivalent attachment schema was very much in evidence. With regard to her feelings towards her mother, as a young adult, Jane displayed an anxious attachment, worrying constantly about whether she would say something that would upset her mother's equilibrium, anxious that she may give her mother "too much" to cope with, and that she would precipitate the other's psychic collapse again. She felt particularly guilty that her mother might not cope with the anxiety that Jane felt responsible for as a result of her regular thirty-mile journeys to a neighbouring city in order to undergo further training. At first, Jane undertook these journeys to university with many misgivings, travelling by train. However, her determination to win the qualification that would enable her to begin a new career won through, so she persevered despite her anxious state of mind and began driving to her destination. It felt to me as if Jane was acting out the repercussions of a "double dose" of acute anxiety—she was the vehicle for her own anxieties, and she was also in receipt of her mother's anxious projections. The latter offloaded her own anxious affect by a process of projective identification. I interpreted that mother projected her anxiety into her daughter by a process during which she expressed her fears, worries, and concerns and, as a result, Jane identified with the projection and "ran with it", displaying the introjection by acting out in a very nervous fashion. I think this whole process enabled her mother to achieve some degree of relief.

This process replicated itself time and time again throughout the first four years of therapy, making it very difficult for Jane to complete her three-year qualification. At times, Jane was tempted to give up the struggle. However, I was certain that with my help and understanding and through "holding" her (Winnicott, 1971), as "good mother" in the transference, by really hearing the anxiety and consistently working to rationalise it and minimise it to realistic levels, I would be able to help Jane to achieve her ultimate aim. I think she felt some degree of "twinship" transference during this period, especially as there is some overlap of skills that are required of us both in our careers. I also lent a hand to her study skills, and again this served to heighten the twinship transference, as she grew to understand herself to be alike to me in some ways.

She was successful in meeting her career aim and, in fact, after a period of internship, she achieved professional status in the fourth year of her therapy. We were both delighted with the increased self-esteem that grew alongside her qualification, and our celebration was intensified by the fact that she had surmounted all obstacles that might have prevented it in the way of persistent anxiety. With my support and consistent soothing of her anxiety state, she had learnt to overcome the disempowering nature of anxiety and to prove that life was nowhere near as dangerous as her mother's meta-communications implied. With my help, Jane had first dared to try to surmount the obstacles, and had gradually learnt that the tasks she was to undertake did not actually merit the level of anxiety with which she had previously approached such new experiences. In this way, I was able to provide the beginnings of an experience of learned security. The transference developed along the lines of Kohut's idealising transference during this first period of our work together, and there were times when Jane also felt a sense of "mirroring": that she could see herself reflected in my eyes.

In the final year of her qualification and the year after qualification, Jane grew enormously in terms of self-confidence and willingness to undertake new challenges. The blossoming of her personal relationship with her boyfriend caused the chief challenge facing her throughout this period. Her relationship with Michael grew in intensity until it seemed natural that he suggested she share his house with him. I think maybe that both thought it would be wise to live together before considering the possibility of marriage and children. We spent the final year of her first five years in therapy working upon her doubts and fearfulness about the prospect of leaving the parental home. This change effectively meant to Jane that she would no longer be prioritising her parents in life. Jane was gravely concerned that her mother would not be able to cope with the loss of her daughter's daily presence, and might fall back into a depressive state. The idea of moving away from home required the metaphorical climbing of Ben Nevis by a novice Munro climber who had never before scaled such a high pinnacle. However, with consistent support from me and a twice-weekly "injection" of therapy to calm her misgivings and to build her courage to leave the parental home, Jane finally joined Michael shortly before she ended therapy. The mirroring transference was important at this time, as Jane could envisage that she could develop her life like me, and receive my approval by "the reflective gleam in my eyes".

Imagine the delight we shared when Jane announced in therapy one day that Michael had proposed marriage. She accepted with alacrity. As she left therapy after five years of working together twice weekly, I was delighted that Jane was planning the details of her wedding day. In fact, both of her parents were very supportive of this new phase in her life. By this time, Jane had settled into full-time work in her chosen career.

The second phase of therapy

Seven years passed until I was to see Jane again. I received annual Christmas cards from her, telling me about her wedding day and then the birth of a first child, followed two years later by the birth of a sibling. She also kept me abreast of her various career moves.

Meanwhile, I had moved house twice since I had last seen her as a client, and was now settled in a rural environment in a pretty timber-framed cottage in the country. This was very different from the urban 1970s-style house in which I had lived when I was working with her before. One day, I received a telephone call from Jane asking if she might come back into therapy with me. She briefly described some of the trauma that had taken place in the past couple of years, events to which she had alluded briefly but unemotionally in her Christmas cards.

We quickly re-established a good working alliance. In the transference, I still represent "the good mother", but the relationship is substantially different from that during our first phase of therapy together. Most importantly, Jane has matured into a grown woman with wisdom, but also a gravitas that she did not possess in earlier years. I feel intuitively that I am dealing with an equal nowadays, rather than someone who was still a child in many ways when we first worked together. This has entailed my giving much thought to the transference and countertransference, and what sort of help I could best provide at this time in her life.

Since working with Jane some years ago, I had undergone some significant changes in my own life. I had, over the years since qualification as a psychoanalytic psychotherapist, grown in confidence and experience as a therapist who had chosen to specialise in working with clients on a long-term basis. Not only this, I have, in the intervening years, devoted a great deal of time to pondering the following question: what sort of therapeutic approach and underlying theoretical orientation best serves the needs of the long-term client? As a consequence, I had gradually developed my theory of learned security as an integrative development of attachment theory. In addition, as you will have divined by now, I had grown to realise that there is a real need for the therapist to work in a collaborative way, both in the co-construction of a life narrative during our therapeutic engagement and in the employment of a process of intersubjective empathy. I had discovered that the intersubjective perspective, as developed by Stolorow and colleagues (1995), coincided with concepts underlying my own reflective practice. This theoretical underpinning has helped me to develop an integrative theory to utilise in my practice. Above all, I have come to believe that there is an overarching need for the therapist working with long-term clients to consciously and purposefully enable the client to gain an experience of a secure base—to use a well-known phrase originated by John Bowlby. I appreciate that a lot of therapists think that they generally ascribe to this way of working, but I do not think that they make it the *sine qua non* of their therapy. As I have said before, it requires one to be unfailingly devoted to the ideology that it is the therapist's main purpose to provide an experience of learned security in order to heal the developmental deficits that such clients have suffered during childhood.

Jane's childhood represents a good case history of how such a developmental deficit exemplifies itself. While her mother and father were physically present throughout her growing-up years, and she suffered no physical loss of an object, she did suffer one of the maternal deprivations that I talked about in Part II: that of "the dead mother syndrome"(Green, 1983; Kohun, 1999). Her mother's diffused anxiety state also had an enormous impact upon Jane's maturation.

In fact, as an adolescent, Jane did suffer the loss of an object as well—in this case, it was her beloved grandfather who died and left a gaping hole in her life. Her grandparents had always played a major part in Jane's and her sibling's upbringing. Living within the same geographical area, she had visited them with her mother several times a week as a child, and had then taken to visiting her grandfather daily after school by herself while a teenager. Her grandfather was particularly dear to her. I think it was the air of calm resilience with which he met life's vicissitudes that attracted her to him. She described how she used to sit between his knees, on the floor, with his legs supporting her back, and it made her feel really contented and at peace, as he puffed on his pipe. He was a man of few words, but what he did utter helped her to gain a feeling of calm. At other times, she would share his company in the garden, watching him as he busied himself with the cultivation of the earth. He seemed to her, as a child and adolescent, to be the fount of all wisdom. His calm acceptance of the vagaries of life and his tranquil response to the irritating behaviour of his wife were both qualities that Jane attentively regarded. She gained relief from anxiety by watching his composure and refusal to become ruffled in the light of difficulties. When he died, quite unexpectedly in Jane's view, because she had repressed the knowledge that his illness was terminal, Jane was devastated. She fell into a state of what Freud would have termed "melancholia" (Freud, 1917e). Her grief transposed into a state of abject depression, and she could no longer summon the resources to leave home and go to university, as she had been scheduled to do. In fact, she hardly ventured outside the home for a year. Thankfully, the grief eventually abated, and she moved on by going away to university in order to read her chosen subject.

Now, on her returning to therapy once more, she was again suffering from a devastating series of losses. The loss occurred when she and her husband had been married for five years. Her husband was summarily dismissed from work on the grounds that his employers had received a "tip-off" that he was embezzling money from the company. The case was investigated by the company, and it was discovered that an accusation had been levied against him by a member of staff who was suffering from paranoia. We gradually came to understand that Jane was affected by this in two ways. First, Jane was affected at a practical level, because Michael's lack of capacity to earn a good living in the short-term meant that it was necessary for Jane to return to work, just after she had given birth to their second child. She had always envisaged that she would be "an at-home mum" during the years that her children were in their pre-school stage. I realise that plenty of new mothers choose to return to work because they do not like to be at home with the little ones, and find the lack of adult stimulation too depressing. I need to stress that the anticipation of this time at home with her children had been an essential part of Jane's abiding vision of life, and to have it taken from her involved a huge loss, and great sadness. Also, and just as crucial, there was the fact that the accusation against her husband destroyed her vision that she could hold her head up high as "a decent, law-abiding family with a traditional, middle-class value system". This world view was most important to Jane, and she felt its loss very keenly.

In consequence, both husband and wife were suffering in their private grief, which, unfortunately, they were unable to share with the other. In consequence, the greatest impact of this deliberate attempt to spoil Michael's life fell upon their marital relationship. The couple grew apart as both of them started to suffer from depressive symptoms. Each of them began to live in their own capsule, insulated from the other's help by their own preoccupations. The important consequence lay in the fact that dynamically they had stopped communicating on matters other than subjects such as "What shall we have to eat tonight?"

I learnt many years ago when training with Relate (my first experience of counselling) that the most common cause of marital breakdown is a failure in communication. By this, I mean that the couple do not literally stop speaking. Instead, they resort to talking about the humdrum aspects of adult life rather than sharing meaningful conversations. In fact, conversations and discussions about aspects of life to which one has an emotional connection maintain a sense of connectedness for a couple. It is essentially this feeling of connectedness that provides the glue of successful coupledom, and leads to continued emotional investment in one's partner. This sense of connectedness had been lost prior to Jane returning to therapy. She was correct in her awareness that their marriage was going to fail unless she took some positive steps to prevent this from happening.

The fact that Michael was cleared of the accusation, and that in time he began a new career with another company, did not heal the rift between them. Jane had lost two beliefs in how she had envisaged her life developing—in my words, her *weltanschauung* had been shaken. Instead, she returned to the dominant *weltanschauung* of her mother: "the external world is a dangerous place which one should avoid". This exacerbated her depression, and threw her back into the anxious way of relating to others in her life.

So, this time, unlike when her grandfather died, the losses were intangible as well as tangible: they comprised the tangible loss of income accompanied by the loss of her vision of reality. I suppose it was, perhaps, very difficult for her to articulate the nature of the loss to anyone other than myself, as the therapist who had acted as that secure base some years ago. By the time Jane presented herself again at my door, both she and her husband were in employment again. The allegation against Michael had been proved untrue. Unfortunately, however, the ramifications of the accusation did not recede at the same pace.

So often, in couple dynamics, one witnesses as a Relate counsellor that the couple have been metaphorically sauntering down a path together, hand in hand, enjoying their joint life, when they hit a stone in the middle of their path (the crisis: however that might present itself), and, as a consequence, they ricochet off on to two divergent paths. Continuing the metaphor, they then each continue on their way (their lives) on two ever-divergent paths. In short, the crisis that they suffer divides them rather than the alternative, where they might have been able to share their feelings and help one another through a painful period of their lives.

In this way, the crisis had served to divide Michael and Jane. They had each become locked in their lone cell of grief over the loss of the "old life" and the hurt caused by the allegation. I felt that it was my task to help Jane to re-establish the connectedness with Michael, and also to process the underlying (and only partially conscious) meaning of what had occurred. In addition, Jane had returned to me at this time because she felt that she needed the help and succour of the secure base that she had so relied upon in earlier times. Without the weekly presence of the secure base at the time of crisis, and because of the loss of her dominant world view, Jane had regressed into a pattern of anxiety-laden thoughts and feelings in response to life. In consequence, I felt that I needed to provide a new and more intense experience of learned security for two reasons: first, to superimpose the earlier experience with me and, second, because, in the seven years since I had worked with Jane, I had developed the theoretical basis of my understanding of how long-term therapy can best heal the developmental deficits that individuals all too often suffer. From this integrative stance, I had developed a pattern of working that aimed to deliver its potential to my clients in the clinical setting of the consulting room. I believed that Jane would benefit from a further "booster injection" of the provision of an experience of learned security.

This time, I feel it has been of primary importance for Jane to experience the "mirroring transference" and "twinship transference" of which Kohut speaks. Fortunately, it happens to be true that Jane's present career has a number of constructs that it shares with my own. We both have undertaken to provide care to those with whom we come into contact in our professional lives. This has helped Jane to experience both the "mirroring" and "twinship" transferences. There is a sense that "we are on the same side and wavelength". In essence, we need, as therapists, to make it clear that we speak the same language as our clients.

Jane, when she had been in therapy with me before, experienced a therapeutic input from me as an individual who was still overawed by the strictures of psychoanalytic psychotherapy training. One of the values that is promulgated is that the therapist should maintain a "blank screen" in one's relationship with the client, and concentrate on analysing the transference and providing interpretations. Consequently, at the outset of our second period of work together, Jane still had a rather "idealising transference" with regard to me. In this second phase of therapy, and taking into account the presenting problem, I felt that it was now appropriate to enable Jane to deconstruct the idealised view of me, and to perceive me both as a "mirror" and a "twin".

In order to deconstruct the idealising transference, I have, in the past three years, purposely appeared more vulnerable to Jane. This has entailed a little self-disclosure about my belief systems. More importantly, I have made a concerted effort to minimise the power differential by using all sorts of mechanisms. I have spoken in earlier chapters about the power differential that undeniably exists within the therapeutic relationship, and I have developed a very strong belief that it is healthiest for us, as therapists, to work consistently in our consulting rooms to lessen the difference in power between the two parties.

I do believe that Jane now perceives our relationship to have an equality that she did not experience in earlier times. Thus, I am careful to engage Jane in a constant process of co-construction and collaboration. One way in which such a process has been engendered has been through the building together of a narrative of Jane's life to date. The word "narrative" derives from the Greek word *gnathos*, meaning "knowledge". It is to Jane that I purposely pass the power of deciding the underlying meaning of her life story. I may suggest, or provide ideas, but they are just that, for the narrative of an individual's life is "not a crystal-clear recital of something univocally given" (Bruner, 1987). The same event, lived through by two disparate beings, can have a very different meaning to each. It was for this reason that I purposely engaged with Jane in a collaborative process to formulate the underlying and, until now, only semi-conscious meaning she had attributed to the accusation against her husband. It seems, as I have indicated earlier, that central to the despair and depression arising from this incident was the notion that it somehow destroyed the decent, law-abiding, middle-class nuclear "two-point-four-children family". It is an essential part of Jane's world view that one should always behave in a proper manner towards fellow members of society. For instance, she is very assiduous in making sure that her children say "please" and "thank you" at all appropriate times. The loss of the illusion of normality led to a deep sense of shame, and it is this feeling that was central to the depression that struck her after the event. Thus, I felt it was my task to normalise and create an atmosphere of unconditional positive regard concerning the events that had befallen her family, and to engender a revitalised sense that she could once more survive, and not merely survive, but prosper in the wake of it.

In fact, Jane has prospered, and become once again a happy member of society, overcoming the feeling of alienation and anomie that existed in her at the time she presented to me again. It was this feeling that she no longer could "hold her head up high" which needed to be challenged and eradicated before the abnormal grief cycle could come to an end.

I believe that the melancholia in which Jane was immersed was largely eradicated by the healing power of the twinship and mirroring transference, through which Jane grew to believe that she has a legitimate right to a place in "decent", "normal" British society. To paraphrase Winnicott, "the mother's [the therapist's] face is the mirror in which the child first begins to find himself" (Winnicott, 1971, p. 51).

Jane is now once again enjoying family life, and an important part of this is that her relationship with Michael is firmly back on track. She takes enjoyment from her career, but uppermost in her life is the satisfaction she reaps from being a wife and mother. She also is very much orientated towards regular interaction with her extended family structure, particularly with her continuing relationship with her parents and sibling. Although one of her close relatives unfortunately died a very painful and protracted death from cancer a year ago, she was not affected by this loss in a dysfunctional manner.

Generally, I am also very pleased with the way in which Jane has once again reverted to a less anxious experiencing of life. Since our first phase of work together, and the important separation work we concentrated upon in that five-year period of therapy, Jane has maintained a cordial and close relationship with both of her parents. In her relationship with her mother, she no longer takes on the projection of anxiety that her mother used to lob in her direction. I think this is mostly as a result of our work together. Also, her mother has come to terms with the concept that Jane's main priority lies nowadays with her own nuclear family rather than with her family of origin.

It has been a great pleasure to witness this individual young woman mature in so many ways; now she is able to face whatever vicissitudes should befall her with a sense that she no longer has an attachment schema that would be diagnosed as insecure–ambivalent. This has been, for me, a very worthwhile piece of work, and I believe that Jane would verify this.

CHAPTER SIXTEEN

Helen: on becoming a person

Introduction

Helen first consulted me twelve years ago. In the assessment appointment, she told me quite clearly that there were two major reasons why she felt she was in need of professional help: first, because she had developed a habit of befriending men, of about the same age as herself or older, whom she felt were wounded in some way. Second, she told me that she had been suffering for the past nine months from a severe depressive episode and wanted to try psychotherapy in order to recover. She had been prescribed antidepressant tablets by her GP, but, despite the fact that she had tried a number of different medications (one selective serotonin reuptake inhibitor (SSRI), and one more old-fashioned tricyclic antidepressant), these had been unsuccessful in lessening the feeling that she might as well be dead rather than alive. However, there was no evidence of suicidal ideation.

The beginnings of therapy

During the assessment session, I asked Helen what sort of time-scale she envisaged working in therapy. She replied that she believed the problems that she was encountering would take at least three years to work through. We contracted to work once weekly, but I intuitively felt that here we were faced with a set of difficulties that were quite entrenched, and that it would probably require that we work more intensively at a frequency of two or three sessions per week. However, I did not voice this at the time because I felt that this might seem too great an undertaking, and that if I did so, her resistance to treatment may become more pronounced. It was clear from what she said that it had taken her some time to reach the point at which she sought professional help. She said that she had been considering therapy for over a year, because she sensed a repeating pattern in her way of interacting with men. During the assessment sessions, I asked her whether she had undertaken any psychological help previously, for this or any other reason. She informed me that she had been encouraged to undergo analytic psychotherapy with a psychiatrist when she was twenty-two, and had attended weekly sessions (on the NHS) for six months, but had been scared off when the psychiatrist had started to make lewd jokes, and to say that he felt the root of her difficulties "lay in conflicted feelings she was encountering with regard to a man in her life". She had thought at the time that he was implying that she had made a mistake in marrying at a young age (twenty), and was now living to regret the decision. Intuitively, although at this time she had no knowledge whatsoever about psychotherapy or psychoanalysis, she had felt that the psychiatrist's boundaries were "inappropriate", and, feeling very uncomfortable about the sexual overtones apparent in the jokes, she discontinued therapy. She had enough insight to also see that her decision to end analytic therapy had been as a result of defensiveness about her marriage. She appreciated that at the time her parents had been opposed to her marrying so young and thought that "it would all end in disaster", and she felt that psychotherapy might prove their assumption to be correct.

She said that now, some twenty-five years later, she felt regretful that she had foregone the opportunity to receive psychotherapy under the auspices of the NHS. She also appreciated now that the psychiatrist had been referring to her relationship with her father, which she now recognised as "overly close" (it was, interestingly, her father who had physically taken her to the psychotherapy appointments), but she felt maybe that the psychiatrist had offered the interpretation in a disguised form to see if she had moments of insight about the irregularity of this relationship, or whether it was buried deep in the unconscious. In fact, as she quickly came to recognise in therapy with me, her insight concerning the idea that she was suffering from an unresolved Oedipus complex was non-existent when she was in her twenties, and the interpretation had the effect of confusing her, raising her resistance, and she had acted out a "flight into health". It also seems to me that the lewd jokes indicated that the psychiatrist was ill-experienced (to put forward a charitable analysis), or abusive (at worst).

However, the fact that Helen had mentioned her relationship with her father as being of a "somewhat irregular" nature, served to heighten my nascent hypothesis that here before me was a middle-aged woman suffering from unresolved Oedipal longings. I felt that the repeated flirtatious relationships with married men (in other words, making a choice of men who are in another relationship and are, thus, not likely to commit, and which might also have provided the frisson created by a breaking of boundaries) constituted the acting out of an unresolved Oedipus complex . I direct you to read an earlier book if you are interested in a perusal of this subject (Fear, 2015). The notion that my hypothesis could well be valid was heightened when Helen stated in the second of the two assessment sessions that she could not countenance life without her father, and dreaded him dying. She went on, in subsequent sessions, to describe the relationship in terms of "a partnership, though of course there is no hint of anything sexual in the relationship." It occurred to me that therein lay what Shakespeare referred to by the sentence, "the lady doth protest too much, methinks" (Shakespeare, *Hamlet*, Act III, Scene ii).

I had suggested that we need a second assessment session because Helen's first session was replete with complicated dynamics, and I felt that a second session was required to complete my assessment. This served to heighten my feeling that Helen would need more than one session each week for two reasons: first, to process all the material, and second, to commence the journey whereby I hoped to offer her containment (Bion, 1970) and an experience of a proper secure base (Bowlby, 1988). Intuitively, I foresaw that it would take quite some time and effort to gain Helen's trust, and for her to feel safely held (Winnicott, 1971) because I hypothesised that her relationship with both her parents was such that neither of them had provided the love and constancy that one needs if one is to have a secure base.

Even in the early sessions, I was aware that Helen was suffering from some profound developmental deficit that would require all my effort and growing sense of purpose to provide my client with an experience of learned security, although I had not named the process as such all those years ago.

The psychotherapy relationship develops

In fact, I believe that Helen dared to trust me to a certain extent rather more quickly than I had anticipated. Within four months, she felt trusting enough that I was certain to act in her best interests to confide some very pertinent "secrets" to me. However, despite this evidence, I cannot deny that it took almost a decade before she declared that she had grown (through her therapy with me) to feel really secure for the first time in her entire life. In terms of our therapeutic working alliance, Helen displayed an attachment schema that, for much of the time, I would tend to diagnose as insecure–ambivalent. I bear in mind what Mikulincer and Shaver (2008) state about the manner in which most insecure individuals' schemas are to be found somewhere along a continuum between insecure–ambivalent and insecure–avoidant. My diagnosis that Helen was, for a lot of the time, suffering an insecure–ambivalent schema is dependent upon several pieces of evidence. When a break of mine became apparent, she would display extremely clingy behaviour. She begged to know if I was actually going to be away from home, and her anxiety at my absence was so acute that, for at least four years, I resorted to giving her a card when we parted for a while, so that it could act as a transitional object. In fact, this worked very well, partially by its functioning as a transitional object, partially by containing some carefully chosen words to help her to feel I was "with her". I distinctly remember that one such card expressed the following interpretation so that she could think about it and absorb it during the break. It simply said: "Separation is *not* abandonment".

However, Helen also displayed her ambivalence by frequently taking exception to what I said, which evidenced her negative transference (displayed in the form of aggressive episodes) towards me alongside an ever increasing sense of positive attachment. She would become strident over relatively small differences of opinion and, on a number of occasions, she reacted with extremely vicious outbursts.

Nevertheless, one could see the ambivalence because, despite the above negativity, her dependency upon me developed very quickly. In the transference, she quickly started to relate to me as if I was her mother, but I was aware that the transference vacillated between my being a mother figure and a father figure. I started to be aware that she craved a strong, dependable father who did not ask for anything in return for his love, quite different from her actual experience of father. However, in the transference, she frequently asked me if I was angry with her, scared as she was that I would respond to her with protracted sulking or vicious rages; this represented an anticipated repetition of her father's reactions to her when she refused to comply with his demands.

As I indicated above, while Helen evidenced insecure–ambivalent behaviour for much of the time, she also displayed an insecure–avoidant schema at other times in her manner of relating to me. She tended to use humour and intellectualisation frequently, which I felt were often employed to keep me (and her own feelings) at a distance, and, for the first five years, she projected something of a "false self", trying to persuade me to accept her as how she wanted to appear, rather than as her unadulterated "true self". In early years, in the countertransference, I felt uncomfortably in receipt of flirtatious, somewhat precocious behaviour, and this, indeed, had the paradoxical effect of making me feel both enchanted and ill at ease at what I interpreted as her attempt to control me in some way. While one might think, at an overt level, that this flirtatiousness was an attempt to lessen the distance between us and create an unexpected level of intimacy, I think that it is, in fact, paradoxical. To be flirtatious is to retain a defensive structure, for it indicates a desire for intimacy but rarely creates that in the long-term, because it puts the sexual dimension of the relationship at the top of the agenda, at the expense of true emotional intimacy. I also think that Helen was unconsciously attempting to communicate to me, in the here and now, how she managed most of her relationships in life. It was, I felt, evidence of her perceiving herself as a sexual object above all other dimensions of her personality. Eventually, after quite some time mulling over my countertransference, just as Greenson advises us to do (Greenson, 1974, pp. 259–265), I made an interpretation about this way of relating. We talked in detail about how it felt for me to be in receipt of this flirtatiousness, and we explored the history of her way of relating to men.

We also talked through the effect of this behaviour, and her motivations for it, and, after some discussion, she agreed to desist from using this approach towards me. Ironically, but perhaps not surprisingly, this actually led us to a greater depth of intimacy as that particular defensive structure was challenged and broken down.

Our sessions together were vey "full" from the outset, and, within four months, Helen asked me if we could arrange for her to have another session each week as she was experiencing high anxiety levels and was full of material that she was eager to process. It was a hallmark of our work together that Helen was always highly motivated to attend her sessions, and in twelve years she scarcely missed a single session, apart from when she was recovering from two major operations.

Working intensively in therapy: a pattern emerges

Within eight months of the outset of Helen's therapy, she asked to move to three sessions each week, and we maintained this frequency for the majority of her twelve years in therapy. Within the last year of therapy, we both felt it was wise to reduce to two sessions per week, and then again to once a week as we worked towards a planned ending. Ending was a very difficult and complex process for Helen, largely because of the level of her dependency and her fear of giving up the secure base to which she had become accustomed. I think that the secure base had to be *very* secure before she was able to apply the learning to other individuals in her external world.

The first three years of the work largely focused upon Helen's relationship with various male friends. At first, Helen was working through the loss of the relationship with an older man to whom she had been very close during the Master's degree that she had undertaken in order to convert her first degree. Her male friend had been recently widowed when Helen first met him at university, and I could detect a pattern emerging concerning the way in which she compulsively sought to heal the woundedness to which she was drawn. She was aware of her pattern of relating to wounded men, but it took some time and a number of interpretations before she was able to make the link to the way she had grown up providing succour to her father's woundedness. The relationship with this fellow student had never become sexualised, but there were unspoken erotic overtones in his manner towards her and a feeling of "ownership". However, while this created for her what she described as a feeling of security in which she basked, she intentionally refrained from any sexual relationship, apart from her flirtatious behaviour. She verbalised with clarity that one of the reasons that she had sought therapy was from fear that, one day, in another relationship, she might break the boundary and put her marriage at risk. Undoubtedly, we could see that the repeated pattern of extra-marital friendships, though not fully sexualised, was putting her marriage under strain. Her husband was amazingly understanding of this need in her for some years, and loyally encouraged her to deal with it in therapy.

The first three years of therapy

In the first three years of her therapy, Helen entered compulsively into two more relationships, each of which repeated the pattern set by the prior relationship while at university. I was interested to note that the first of these relationships had come into existence following a serious argument that she had with her father caused by her decision to stop being complicit in emotionally dividing her father and mother. She had gradually, over the past few years, become consciously aware of the three-way dynamic.

In consequence, I could see that this series of relationships with members of the opposite sex represented a repetition compulsion of someone in neurotic conflict concerning their relationship with father. Each of the two men friends spoke at length to her about having been wounded during early years of their life. She began to realise that each man recited to her on early acquaintance a catalogue of events in his life that involved a difficult and conflicted relationship with father. In the case of the initial relationship made at university, her friend had lost contact with his father after his mother found another partner while her husband was away fighting in the war. Her friend had perceived his father to be "spineless". A second male friend repeatedly described to her his disgust with a father who possessed no manliness or resilience with which to face life, and a mother who repeatedly engaged in a series of extra-marital affairs, about which father was too cowardly to challenge her. Helen later made a link about a friend with whom she had been deeply in love during adolescence whose relationship with his father was hallmarked by violence and emotional abuse. She had evidently spent many hours listening to his tales of despair during teenage years.

As Helen began to tell me about her relationship with her father while she was a youngster, I grew to understand the link, in psychodynamic terms, between her current behaviour and her past. Her father had turned to Helen while she was a small child to regale her with tales of his father, who had returned from the First World War suffering what we would now recognise as PTSD but was then known as "shell-shock". Unable to forget the horrors of the war and unaware of the ramifications upon his unconscious, the father had re-enacted the aggression he had encountered in war upon his family by being physically and emotionally abusive.

Helen's father had used his daughter "as a toilet for his shit", and Helen (absorbing my interpretations) gradually came to realise that this had involved father in breaking down the appropriate boundary between parent and child. He shared with Helen what should have been shared with his real partner—Helen's mother. In this way, "the partnership between father and daughter" (as Helen named it) came into existence while she was still under five years of age. This "partnership" had continued and been solidified by the two of them doing the shopping together, by working together at his place of employment, and attending "gigs" together. Once Helen married, father and daughter together took responsibility for many household chores, the welfare of her children, and care of her dog.

As Helen grew to make links between her relationship with these men in the present and the original, unbounded relationship with father, she began to appreciate that she was acting out a repetition compulsion. As she gained this insight, her interest in these relationships began to falter. After three years, Helen brought the relationships to an end. I was indeed relieved, because I had begun to feel exasperated as she continued to put her marriage at risk.

The full reason for Helen's insecure–ambivalent schema became apparent when I heard how Helen had consistently been expected to be emotionally available to her father, ready with an empathic ear, and, as such, she had never felt loved for herself; instead, she developed a model where she only felt loved for what she provided. Thus, she had no sense of what it feels like to enjoy a secure base.

The middle years of therapy

Five months after Helen's extra-marital emotional relationships came to an end she began to have flashbacks and dreams of being involved in a sexual relationship with her father. Here, we see an example of how the stage of "remembering" and unconsciously "repeating" (Freud, 1914g) was followed by a conscious awareness of one of the causes of neurosis. These dreams stimulated her thinking, and she started to realise that her father's behaviour towards her in fact had a sexual dimension for years, since she had been a little girl of three. Freud puts it well: "When a patient talks about these 'forgotten' things (he) seldom fails to add: 'As a matter of fact I've always known it; only I've never thought of it'" (Freud, 1914g).

This applied in precisely this way to Helen. The "memories" started to flood back; she had always known a lot of these things about her relationship with her father, but never before had she seen them to be of any significance. In short, she had not been able to appreciate until now (while being securely "held") that her father's actions constituted sexual abuse.

First, she became aware of the meaning of various incidents involving sexual contact between her and father while she was a little girl. At the time, she had not possessed the language to be able to articulate or make sense of what was happening, but she had been left all her life with a sense of shame, and also a sense that she "belonged" to her father. Perhaps even more shocking was the fact that sexual contact between the two had persisted into her adulthood and during her married life. She remembered how he had, until very recently, come into her bedroom and en-suite bathroom in a voyeuristic manner while she was naked or dressed only in her underwear. She recounted how she, as an adult married woman, had been instructed to dress her father's wounds after he had an operation on his testicles. The fact that she had complied with her *mother's* command left us to understand that her mother had got some sense of excitation from the unusual relationship between father and daughter.

Helen was horrified to understand the meaning of these encounters, and felt understandably angry and a sense of disgust about the whole subject. She now understood her ambivalence about sexual relationships—she experienced excitement, but also revulsion at the idea of touching men's genitalia. It also led to her feeling extremely angry with mother, and, for some time, she projected all her rage about the reality of being abused on to her mother. It has been very hard for her to apportion blame to her father, because he remained, at some level, "her beloved father" and, understandably, she did not want to lose the feeling of being loved. We came to appreciate that only from him did she receive any loving tenderness, and, in some ways, she had enjoyed "the partnership" and considered herself "special" in consequence. She was of the belief (when she first presented in therapy, before the memories surfaced) that she was more important to him than his own wife. Yet, as I pointed out to her gently, it was to her mother's bed that he returned every night. She also gradually came to the realisation that the reality of her life had not been what is "normal" for most people. She was never self-pitying, but she became, for a time, extremely angry at the distress that his behaviour had caused her in adult life.

I move on now to another ramification of the abuse. I had noted that Helen tended to have an arrogant demeanour at times. This arrogance was not apparent in her daily pursuits, but she tended to become engaged in disagreements with those in authority. She had a feeling that she could achieve what others could not because she was "special". As Freud states, such individuals believe that

> They have renounced enough and suffered enough, and have a claim to be spared any further demands; they will submit no longer to any disagreeable necessity, for they are *exceptions,* and moreover, intend to remain so. (Freud, 1916d, p. 312)

It explained to me the reason why Helen possessed an omnipotence on occasions, which was at odds with her way of behaving the majority of the time. We worked for a great many hours upon this omnipotent stance, which had not served her well in life, and frequently led to conflict with others.

I have talked in another text about the way that experiences of repeated sexual abuse lead the individual to feel entitled and capable of getting their own way:

> Freud (1916d, pp. 316–331) speaks of those (who have been sexually abused) as "being wrecked by success" by which he refers to those who have attained the unattainable—by which I mean that the individual has won what for most is a phantasised ideal during the phallic

> stage of development: the thought of sexually winning the opposite sex parent as a partner. (Fear, 2015, p. 67)

During this protracted period of very emotional sessions, it was an acutely anxious time for Helen as these "memories" that had started with flashbacks were processed by us together. She suffered some physical manifestations, including frequent palpitations and feelings of nausea and general "dis-ease". In fact, these symptoms were repetitions of the symptoms she had originally encountered at age twenty-two, just after she had married, and which we now understood to have been as a result of the anxiety caused by having a sexual relationship with father while simultaneously having another, legitimate, sexual partner: her husband. As Freud correctly discerned, intrapsychic conflict leads to neurotic anxiety. It was these symptoms of diffuse anxiety that had led her to the door of the psychiatrist that she mentioned to me during her assessment sessions. She had, at first, been convinced that her symptoms were of organic origin, but extensive medical tests concluded that they were actually psychosomatic symptoms of underlying neurosis. So, in a convoluted way, we could see together now that the psychiatrist who offered psychotherapy had actually been on the right track.

The "discovery" of Helen's abused past constituted a difficult time in Helen's therapy. However, I employ the proverb, "Every cloud has a silver lining". Helen developed a strong erotic transference to me, and started to exhort me to abandon the therapeutic relationship in favour of a personal relationship with her. I employ the use of this proverb somewhat ironically, because, while this was extremely painful for Helen, the erotic transference nevertheless brought Helen's central difficulty into the here and now of the consulting room. I now felt that we had an opportunity to work it through in terms of immediacy and stop the repetitive acting out that had been the hallmark of Helen's behaviour for the past few years.

Helen herself was strongly of the opinion that this transference constituted wholly positive, "real" feelings towards me. I did not interpret, as I might have done, that in fact it was also a negative transference, for it represented an aggressive impulse towards me. In short, had I complied with her demands it would have ruined my professional career. Fortunately, I harboured no wish to act syntonically in the countertransference and respond by making a personal relationship with her. Helen gradually came to appreciate that she was in the grip of a powerful transference, and that this represented a way of "remembering and repeating" (Freud, 1914g) her feelings towards father. Gradually, with no encouragement that her hopes could be realised, the transference abated. It was my role, I felt, to help her with her difficult feelings, and to emphasise that she was indeed a lovely and attractive individual, while also clearly giving her the message that she could never have me as a partner. However, I also needed to make sure that Helen appreciated that she would continue to have me as a secure base without the relationship needing to become sexualised. In the same way, the oedipal father needs to give the message to his daughter that "You are lovely; I think you are wonderful and you will make some man a beautiful partner, but that person is not me, and can never be me." It was precisely because she had won her father at a sexual level that Helen perceived herself as an exception. Helen also associated the receiving of love with the idea that she had to give of herself sexually in order to get anything back. The fact that she learnt that she could receive love without having "to serve me" in some way taught Helen a very crucial lesson. Another crucial lesson was learnt that in not "being successful" in making a relationship outside of the therapy room, Helen gradually understood that she could not have what she was not supposed to have, as Bowlby said in a paper of that name: "On knowing what you are not supposed to know and feeling what you are not supposed to feel" (Bowlby, 1979b). This lesson has helped to bring to an end her tendency towards arrogance, and helped her to realise that she is not an "exception" (Freud, 1916d, p. 312).

Steiner (1985) wrote a seminal paper on the way in which those who have been in oedipal relationships tend to "turn a blind eye" to the reality of those relationships. In other words, they are prone to lack the conscious awareness of the meaning of their relationship. In the Oedipus legend (see Fear, 2015, pp. 3–10), Oedipus and Jocasta (his wife and mother) studiously ignored the difficult and questionable circumstances in which they had become a couple, as well as the recalled prophecies of the Oracle to Oedipus when he was a young man. In precisely the same way, Helen had "turned a blind eye" to the fact that, in having sex-symbolising friendships with married men, she was wilfully ignoring the injunction that one should not come between a married couple. She had also "turned a blind eye" (Steiner, 1985) to the actuality of her relationship with father.

The erotic transference continued for almost two years, and in that time I would sometimes receive telephone calls from Helen in the evening, as she was suffering such longings to recover that lost phase of her life with father that her heart literally ached. She felt that I could make up for this loss. I believe that I managed this sector of our work together with consistent care, and loving attention, while also making sure *not* to encourage her feelings, or give her any false hope. There *is* a fine line to be trodden between the two.

In this phase of our work together, we worked in such a way as to provide her with an experience of what Kohut refers to as the "twinship" and "mirroring" transferences. It is true to say that our work together was felt to be intimate by both of us. The fact that Helen had undertaken a lot of reading of psychotherapy texts by this time meant that we really had a sense of being on the same side and helped us to articulate her feelings about the process through which she was moving. I found that, unconsciously, I was mirroring Helen at a physical level, too, by contingently marking Helen's position in her chair by adjusting my position to mirror hers. We also mirrored each other psychologically, by implicitly agreeing to "butterfly" or "leapfrog" (Holmes, 2010, p. 106) from association to association, in an intimate dance. I truly believe that Helen looked on me as a "twin" in some ways.

I took the utmost care to retain the boundaries and remain consistent in all manner of ways, not only by keeping to time, by being reliably available even outside of the therapy hours, always giving her my full and complete attention, and promising that if something in my life served to distract me, I would tell her that I was experiencing difficulties, without at the same time confiding the details of my actual situation to her. It was important to Helen that she knew that I was all right, for she would detect any slight change in me—a change of mood, a slight cold or sore throat, or, as was so on one occasion, a tooth abscess. It was crucial that I was honest with her, for she had been accustomed to "keeping an eye" on her father, carefully monitoring him for signs of distress or the possibility of a sulk because she had not capitulated to him. In consequence, she had developed a very perceptive capacity to recognise nuances. I also interpret more cynically that Helen was continually looking for chinks in my armour: some way in to my woundedness. It was important for her to learn that this was not going to be achieved because, had I done so, I felt that this would have been tantamount, metaphorically, to allowing her into the marital bedroom.

It was only in the last two years of a twelve-year therapy that I felt that Helen was not aiming to please me—that she could, at last, be true to herself rather than presenting a "false self" (Winnicott, 1965) who was compulsively determined to "make things all right for me". I believe that her gaining the freedom to be herself, "warts and all", was a very healing experience. This is a direct result, I believe, of Helen experiencing what it feels like to enjoy the luxury of a secure base: it emanates from a process by which the individual learns what it means, in a series of minute steps, to truly have a secure base upon which to rely. By experientially learning what it is to enjoy a secure base as a port into which one can sail when a storm breaks, and that the ship will not sink if it is able to find a safe harbour, brought to Helen an enduring sense of calm and contentment with life. I believe that her attachment schema changed from insecure–ambivalent to secure as a result of my working in a way that focused upon the gaining of learned security for Helen.

I accept that, at times of great stress in her life now that I am no longer available, she might regress to an insecure schema on a temporary basis. There is rarely, if ever, complete "cure" in psychoanalysis or psychotherapy. One comes to realise this as a mature therapist. This is not to say that psychotherapy is not worth engaging upon. Helen is a case in point: she has a much more satisfying life, including a much happier marital relationship and a freedom from the conflictual longings that she used to suffer when she first presented in therapy.

You might wonder what happens when the therapist is no longer available as that iconic personification of a secure base. In the last two years of therapy, Helen was able to apply her learning about "knowing" how satisfying it is to have a secure base so that she could allow her husband to become the new secure base. This was something he had always wanted to be able to offer, but she had not been able to take on board. It is also true, at another level, that when one has experienced the joy and cessation of anxiety in one's life that comes with having a secure base, one developmentally internalises the secure base and thus can call on "the therapist" at any time for silent communion forever onwards in life.

We worked towards ending for a year, and so, when the time came for us to no longer meet, Helen was ready and able to face the world without the support that I had provided for a dozen years. She described her therapy as a truly mutative experience, and said something that was also expressed by Nick in his account of his therapy: "You have saved my life." But Helen added that she strongly believed that I had saved her marriage as well. I feel privileged to have been able to work with Helen (and Nick, Emma, and Jane), and to have been a part of their return to psychic health.

PART V

CONCLUDING REMARKS

CHAPTER SEVENTEEN

Conclusion

I was motivated to write this book because I wanted to share with those who have the same love of the profession the specific way that I find it is best to interact with the client. We all want the client, by the time he leaves therapy, to have lost his dysfunctional patterns of relating, and to no longer be in the grip of his major pathology or pathologies. When we are noviate therapists, we talk about "cure" for the client; as we become mature therapists, we realise that, perhaps, in the vast majority of cases, the best that we can hope for is that our work together will lead to a diminution of his pathologies, so that his life is no longer ruled by them. However, it is very likely that some residue of his pathological way of living will remain in evidence, especially at times of stress or ill-health.

I have given hundreds of hours during my twenty-seven years in practice to the thorny question of how I should function as a therapist in the consulting room in order to achieve the best outcome for the majority of my clients. In contemplating this subject, I have studied various theories. As stated earlier, my introduction into the counselling world was eclectic: at Relate, we used a toolbox of different techniques, selecting our style of intervention depending upon how we viewed its likely efficacy given the presenting problem. However, despite the fact that the training was eclectic, with very little emphasis upon the elucidation of different theories, I intuitively recognised, even at this innocent stage of training, that the psychodynamic perspective seemed most efficacious.

Perhaps my interest has always lain in investigating the theories that underlie our work. This might well be because I read first for a degree in political theory. While we are not, as therapists, in the political arena of life, I have always found the latter world interesting and challenging. I moved away from taking an active role in democratic politics and the founding of pressure groups when I became a therapist, but my fascination with analysis of theory, and with the integration and synthesis of different theories, has endured from my academic and practical life in politics. Therefore, maybe it was inevitable that I was drawn towards learning about the similarities and differences of different theories, and towards analysing these theories. It is simply that, in the past three decades, I have concentrated my interest and fascination with psychological theory rather than political theory.

During my Master's degree, I was drawn to investigate the different meta-theoretical assumptions that underlay different theoretical orientations. The central hypothesis of my dissertation was that if the individual therapist chose to adopt a theoretical orientation of which the meta-theoretical assumptions differed from those of her own world view (or *weltanschauung*), then she would tend, after a period of time, to become burned-out or choose to leave the profession. I investigated this hypothesis using qualitative analysis (narrative enquiry), and my findings strongly supported my hypothesis. During my time at Keele University, I also became interested in the integration debate and started to publish a number of journal articles (Fear & Woolfe, 1996, 1999) and chapters in edited textbooks on integration and eclecticism (Fear, 2004; Fear & Woolfe, 2000).

After completing my Master's degree, I felt strongly drawn to working within a psychoanalytic frame, and so I decided to take on what proved to be an arduous training in psychoanalytic psychotherapy. As time has progressed since I qualified, I have been motivated to investigate how we can best work as therapists in our consulting rooms in order to achieve the most favourable outcomes for our clients. For me, this could mean the adoption of concepts from theoretical orientations other than psychodynamics.

First of all, I was strongly influenced by the fact that, during my twenties, I received some excellent cognitive behavioural therapy. I shall remain eternally grateful to the psychologist who practised cognitive behavioural therapy in order to enable me to rebuild my life so that I could start to function normally in the external world. However, I suffered vestiges of my difficulties until I started to undergo psychoanalytic psychotherapy twenty years later, and gradually discovered the roots of the problem. It is only since achieving this, along with the dedication of an excellent psychoanalytic psychotherapist, that I have completely overcome these tendencies. In consequence of my own experience, and the additional evidence provided by the narratives of many clients who have passed through my consulting room, I am firmly of the belief that it is only through a psychoanalytic approach that we can hope to eradicate our difficulties. Cognitive behavioural techniques are but "sticking plasters" which usefully help us in the short-term to get back on our feet, but they do not solve the root problem. They are the therapy of choice in the NHS because they are quick and cheap, and their proponents have been most assiduous—and wise—in collating research to prove its efficacy.

In consequence of the above, I am firmly of the belief that only by psychoanalytic interventions can we best help our clients. However, since qualifying as a psychoanalytic psychotherapist, I became fascinated by the conundrum of what interventions are most successful in enabling the client to change his way of living that existed prior to his presentation in therapy.

I gradually came to the conclusion, in agreement with the received wisdom on the subject, that the answer lies in the use of the therapeutic relationship shared by client and therapist, alongside the importance of psychoanalytic interpretations. The idea that it is the therapeutic relationship that is the deciding factor is allied to "the dodo argument"—that all psychotherapies, regardless of their specific components, have equivalent outcomes. I do not subscribe to this notion. I truly believe that only in the psychoanalytic therapies does the therapeutic relationship reign supreme. I have always been attracted to Bowlby's attachment theory, and have used it to underpin my work for many years. However, I came to believe that it requires a more sophisticated way of working than Bowlby had devised. In fact, while Bowlby was at the cutting edge of relational psychoanalysis as a theorist, he was not particularly experienced or interested in being a clinician. I am, on the other hand, primarily a clinician who is fascinated by theory. I use theory to inform my practice in order to try to increase its efficacy. Furthermore, I believe "It is more effective, if not more honest, to have a praxis which is explicitly theorized than to operate from naturalised and unexamined assumptions; that such a praxis may be tactical and strategic rather than seemingly philosophically absolute" (Selden et al., 2005).

Gradually, over the past seventeen years, I have adopted a way of working that seems to reap the most efficacious rewards for my clients. Admittedly, these clients are inclined to choose to work with me in the long-term. So, as a consequence, my sample of clients is biased, and the argument put forward in this book applies only to this type of client. During my years as a therapist, I have read widely among the texts of different theorists (from Donald Winnicott to Brian Thorne). I eventually came to the conclusion in my practice that the majority of my clients suffer some form of developmental deficit. This has occurred not only because of the possible *physical loss* of an object during childhood or adolescence, but also as a result of the individual suffering an *abstract and intrinsic loss*. Such a loss might entail a resulting lack of maternal attunement. It is commonly not so much that the individual did not have a mother, but that she lacked the consistency and reliability of care that is so essential for a child to receive. In consequence, Part II of the book has concentrated upon the major ways in which an individual might have suffered such a loss in childhood, so that he subsequently develops an insecure–ambivalent or insecure–avoidant attachment schema.

The purpose of this book, then, has been to describe to you one way of working with long-term clients in order to achieve the best outcome. While I am patently aware that many therapists pay lip service to the concept of the therapist acting as a secure base, I firmly believe that the majority do not adhere to the principle that every therapeutic hour of every day one must remember to apply oneself to the task of enabling the client to experience what it means to have a secure base.

The theory of learned security requires that the therapist enter into a contract with the client where she gives of herself to an unprecedented extent. As I have said before, it requires one to have a sense of vocation. One needs to hold the client in mind for the whole period of his time in therapy, and requires that one evidences one's commitment as a therapist by making oneself available outside of one's working hours, days, and weeks. I strongly believe that one has a moral obligation to one's clients, if the choice has been made to provide a contract as a secure base. As a therapist, one has entered into a contract at an explicit level; this is because, as a therapist, one is explicitly aware of attachment theory; one knows full well how dependent a client might be for a time if he has an attachment neurosis.

I have attempted to elucidate in Chapter Twelve (and, to a lesser extent, in Chapter Four) how one is to proceed if one wishes to adopt this type of therapy. It seems to me to be a logical progression from Bowlby's attachment theory. I have not found any other text, though I have searched, that describes clearly how to adopt this theoretical approach and practise it in the consulting room. I stress the need for intersubjective empathy—one is required to consciously aim to be empathically attuned on a consistent basis. Empathic attunement has been suggested by others, but I am promulgating that one adopts an empathic approach where one proactively interacts with the client to constantly check out whether one has "got it right". Empathic attunement is, thus, the product of co-construction and collaboration between the therapist and client. Ruptures are bound to occur during one's relationship with the client; again, I am stressing the need for collaboration and co-construction to heal those ruptures. I adopt a phrase from Kohut when I stress the need for the therapist to constantly engage in an introspective–empathic mode of enquiry. One needs, literally, to "feel into" (*Einfühlung*), the client's inner world. Alongside a use of intersubjective empathy, I also believe that one should aim at all times to be congruent and to show unconditional positive regard in one's relationship with the client. This way of being is of huge importance in order to enable the client to gain a sense of learned security.

It is crucial that the client gains a sense of "autobiographical competence" (Holmes, 2010) from his time in analytic psychotherapy. It is imperative that one helps the client to build a coherent narrative of his life to date, so that he does not miss out any important events, and neither is his story oversaturated by unprocessed affect.

All of the above refer largely to one's endeavour to achieve a good therapeutic alliance that, of itself, has a huge propensity for healing to take place. However, it is also as important that the therapist and client engage in the transference. I have adopted the typology of transference as delineated by Kohut, which is that the therapist must help the client to engage, at different times, in the "mirroring", "twinship", and "idealising" transferences. At some time, usually towards the beginning of the relationship, the client will see the therapist in an ideal guise. Later on in the therapy, he might move towards envisaging the therapist as a "twin"—someone just like himself, a soulmate. At another time, he will want to see himself "mirrored" in the therapist's eyes, just as Kohut describes the baby seeing "the gleam" lovingly mirrored in his mother's eyes. It should not be forgotten that the clients who make their way to our doors have not been fortunate enough to have experienced this process during childhood.

While the real relationship is of great importance, I do feel that it is through work in the transference that the most priceless mutative changes occur. For all of the above to occur, it requires that one engages with a true generosity of spirit. This attribute is the *sine qua non*. The therapist will then be able to contain (Bion, 1970) and hold (Winnicott, 1971) the client in a sustained manner. In this way, one is able to achieve an atmosphere in the consulting room of companionable interaction (Heard & Lake, 1997).

Bowlby pointed the way to this manner of working, and I still regard the theory of learned security as a development of attachment theory. John Bowlby was a giant among men. He invented a new paradigm in the world of therapy. It is a great pity that he was scorned for so long by the analytic community, particularly in London, but maybe one can see that it is not uncommon for those who engender great change to meet resistance for the first few decades. As I stated earlier, this resistance was still palpable when I qualified in the 1990s. There was still a punitive regime in operation within analysis, where clients were seen as "victims", or, almost, as "enemies" with whom we needed to do battle in order to force them to change and to take control of their own destinies.

Fortunately, the recent growth in neurobiology has provided us with indisputable evidence that the degree to which the infant is in receipt of loving care and stimulation hugely affects the actual growth of the brain. I pay tribute to Gerhardt's book (2015), in which she presents this evidence in an accessible form. I have drawn much from her book, both in my practice and in writing this book.

I hope my promulgation of the theoretical basis of learned security has drawn, and then kept, your interest. I hope, too, that you will find useful my description of the type of therapeutic relationship that one needs to adopt in the consulting room. It is my hope that this book may stimulate debate among the attachment community, and that you personally, as a therapist, might feel the urge to adopt some of its tenets. Above all, I hope that it may further the growth of attachment theory, and add to John Bowlby's important legacy for the world of psychoanalysis.

REFERENCES

Ainsworth, M. D., Blehar, M. C., Waters, E., & Wall, S. (1978). *Patterns of Attachment: A Psychological Study of the Strange Situation.* Hillsdale, NJ: Lawrence Erlbaum.

Albee, E. (1966). *Who's Afraid of Virginia Woolf?* (Film). Warner Bros.

Allen, J., & Fonagy, P. (Eds.) (2006). *Handbook of Mentalization-Based Treatment.* Chichester: Wiley.

Allen, J., Fonagy, P., & Bateman, A. (2008). *Mentalizing in Clinical Practice.* New York: American Psychiatric Publishing.

Basch, M. (1985). Interpretation: towards a developmental model. In: A. Goldberg (Ed.), *Progress in Self Psychology, 1:* 33–42. New York: Guilford Press.

Basch, M. (1986). Clinical theory and metapsychology: incompatible or complementary? *Psychoanalytic Review, 73*: 261–271.

Bateman, A., & Fonagy, P. (2004). *Psychotherapy for Borderline Personality Disorder: Mentalization-Based Treatment.* Oxford: Oxford University Press.

Benamer, S. (2015). Sarah Benamer on why narrative of trauma is ubiquitous in contemporary society. Available at https://karnacology.com/2015/03/05/sarah-benamer-on-why-the-narrative-of-trauma-is-ubiquitous-in-contemporary-society

Bion, W. R. (1970). *Attention and Interpretation.* London: Tavistock.

Bion, W. R. (1984). *Second Thoughts.* London: Karnac.

Bollas, C. (1987). *The Shadow of the Object: Psychoanalysis of the Unthought Known*. London: Free Association Books.
Bowlby, J. (1944). Forty-four juvenile thieves: their character and home life. *International Journal of Psychoanalysis, 25*: 1–57; 107–228.
Bowlby, J. (1951). *Maternal Care and Mental Health*. World Health Organization, Monogram Series No. 2.
Bowlby, J. (1953). *Child Care and the Growth of Maternal Love* (abridged version of *Maternal Care and Mental Health*, 1951). London: Penguin Books (new and enlarged edition, 1965).
Bowlby, J. (1969). *Attachment and Loss, Vol. 1*. London: Hogarth.
Bowlby, J. (1973). *Attachment and Loss, Vol. 2, Separation: Anxiety and Anger*. London: Hogarth.
Bowlby, J. (1979a). *The Making and Breaking of Affectional Bonds*. London: Tavistock.
Bowlby, J. (1979b). On knowing what you are not supposed to know and feeling what you are not supposed to feel. *Canadian Journal of Psychiatry, 24*(5): 403–408.
Bowlby, J. (1980). *Attachment and Loss, Vol. 3, Loss: Sadness and Depression*. London: Hogarth.
Bowlby, J. (1988). *A Secure Base: Clinical Applications of Attachment Theory*. London: Routledge.
Bowlby, J. (1990). *Charles Darwin: A New Biography*. London: Hutchinson.
Bowlby, J., & Robertson, J. (1952a). A two-year-old goes to hospital: a scientific film. *Proceedings of the Royal Society of Medicine, 46*: 425–427.
Bowlby, R., & Robertson, J. (1952b). *Responses of Young Children Separated from their Mothers*. Paris: Courier, Centre Internationale de L'Enfance, II(2), pp. 66–78; II(3), pp. 131–142.
Bretherton, I. (1991). Pouring new wine into old bottles: the social self as internal working model. In: M. Gunnar & L. Stroufe (Eds.), *Self Processes and Development* (pp. 1–41). Hillsdale, NJ: Lawrence Erlbaum.
Britton, R. (1989). The missing link: parental sexuality in the Oedipus complex. In: R. Britton, M. Feldman, & E. O'Shaughnessy (Eds.), *The Oedipus Complex Today: Clinical Implications* (pp. 83–101). London: Karnac.
Britton, R. (1992). The Oedipus situation and the depressive position. In: R. Anderson (Ed.), *Clinical Lectures on Klein and Bion* (pp. 34–45). Hove: Routledge.
Bruner, J. (1987). Life as narrative. *Social Research, 54*(1): 11–32.
Casement, P. (1985). *On Learning from the Patient*. London: Tavistock.
Chodorow, N. (1978). *The Reproduction of Motherhood*. Berkley, CA: University of California Press.

Chugani, H. T., Behen, M., Muzik, O., Juhasz, C., Nagy, F., & Chugani, D. (2001). Local brain functional activity following early deprivation: a study of post-institutionalised Romanian orphans. *Neuroimage, 14*: 1290–1301.

De Brito, S., Viding, E., Sebastian, C., Kelly, P., Mechelli, A., Maris, H., & McCrory, E. (2013). Reduced orbitofrontal and temporal grey matter in a community sample of maltreated children. *Journal of Child Psychology and Child Psychiatry, 54*(1): 105–112.

Eigen, M. (1999). *Toxic Nourishment*. London: Karnac.

Fear, R. M. (2004). One training voice: reflecting on the echoes. In: V. Harding Davis, G. Aldred, K. Hunt, & G. Davis. (Eds.), *Experiences of Counsellor Training: Challenge, Surprise and Change* (pp. 108–124). Basingstoke: Palgrave Macmillan.

Fear, R. M. (2015). *The Oedipus Complex: Solutions or Resolutions?* London: Karnac.

Fear, R., & Woolfe, R. (1996). Searching for integration in counselling practice. *British Journal of Guidance and Counselling, 24*(3): 399–411.

Fear, R., & Woolfe, R. (1999). The personal and the professional development of the counsellor: the relationship between personal philosophy and theoretical orientation. *Counselling Psychology Quarterly, 12*(3): 253–262.

Fear, R., & Woolfe, R. (2000). The personal, the professional and the basis of integrative practice. In: S. Palmer & R. Woolfe (Eds.), *Integrative and Eclectic Counselling and Psychotherapy* (pp. 329–340). London: Sage.

Fonagy, P., Steele, M., Steele, H., & Target, M. (2002). *Reflective-Functioning Manual for Application to Adult Attachment Interviews, Version 4.1*. London: Psychoanalysis Unit, Sub-Department of Clinical Health Psychology, University College London.

Forward, S. (1989). *Toxic Parents*. New York: Bantam Books.

Fosha, D. (2000). *The Transforming Power of Affect*. New York: Basic Books.

Freud, S. (1897b). Extracts from the Fliess papers (1950)[1892–1899]). Letter 69. *S. E., 1*: 259–260. London: Hogarth.

Freud, S. (1905c). *Jokes and their Relation to the Unconscious. S. E., 8*: London: Hogarth.

Freud, S. (1912e). Recommendations for physicians practising psycho-analysis. *S. E., 12*: 109–120. London: Hogarth.

Freud, S. (1913j). The claims of psycho-analysis to scientific interest. *S. E., 13*: 165–190. London: Hogarth.

Freud, S. (1914g). Remembering, repeating and working-through. *S. E., 12*: 145–156. London: Hogarth.

Freud, S. (1915a). Observations on transference-love. *S. E., 12:* 157–171. London: Hogarth.
Freud, S. (1916d). Some character types met with in psychoanalytic work. *S. E., 14*: 311–334. London: Hogarth.
Freud, S. (1917e). Mourning and melancholia. *S. E., 14*: 243–258. London: Hogarth.
Freud, S. (1940a). *An Outline of Psycho-analysis. S. E., 23*: 141–207. London: Hogarth.
Freud, S. (1950)[1892–1899]. Extracts from the Fliess papers. *S. E., 1*: 177–282. London: Hogarth.
Frye, N. (1957). *Anatomy of Criticism*. Princeton, NJ: Princeton University Press.
Frye, N. (1964). *A Natural Perspective: The Development of Shakespearean Comedy and Romance.* New York: Columbia University Press.
Gendlin, E. T. (1978). *Focusing*. London: Bantam.
George, C., Kaplan, N., & Main, M. (1985). The adult attachment interview (unpublished manuscript). Berkeley, CA: University of California.
Gerhardt, S. (2014). The effort of empathy. In: A. Odgers (Ed.), *From Broken Attachments to Earned Security* (pp. 11–26). London: Karnac.
Gerhardt, S. (2015). *Why Love Matters: How Affection Shapes a Baby's Brain.* Hove: Routledge.
Goleman, D. (1996). *Emotional Intelligence*. London: Bloomsbury.
Green, A. (1983). *Narcissisme de vie. Narcissisme de mort*. Paris: Editions de Minuet.
Green, A. (2005). *On Private Madness.* London: Karnac.
Greenson, R. R. (1974). Loving, hating and indifference towards the patient. *International Review of Psycho-Analysis, 1*: 263–265.
Hanson, J., Chung, M., & Pollak, S. (2010). Early stress is associated with alterations in the orbitofrontal cortex: a tensor-based morphometry investigation of brain structure and behavioural risk. *Journal of Neuroscience, 30*(22): 7466–7472.
Harlow, H. (1958). The nature of love. *American Psychologist, 13*: 673–685.
Harlow, H. F., & Zimmerman, R. R. (1958). Affectional responses in the infant monkey. *Science, 130*: 421–432.
Hartley, L. P. (1953). *The Go-Between*. London: Hamish Hamilton.
Haynes, J., & Whitehead, H. (2014). To shed what still attempts to cling as if attached by thorns. In: A. Odgers (Ed.), *From Broken Attachments to Earned Security: the Role of Empathy in Therapeutic Change* (pp. 41–54). London: Karnac.
Heard, D., & Lake. B. (1997). *The Challenge of Attachment for Care-giving.* London: Routledge.

Holmes, J. (1993). *John Bowlby and Attachment Theory*. London: Routledge.
Holmes, J. (2010). *Exploring in Security: Towards an Attachment-Informed Psychoanalytic Psychotherapy*. Hove: Routledge.
Kahn, K. (1996). *The Political Consequences of Being a Woman*. New York: Columbia University Press.
Karen, J. (1998). *Becoming Attached: First Relationships and How They Shape Our Capacity to Love*. New York: Oxford University Press.
Kohun, G. (Ed.). (1999). *The Dead Mother: The Work of André Green*. London: Routledge.
Kohut, H. (1957). Death in Venice by Thomas Mann: a story about the disintegration of artistic sublimation. In: P. H. Ornstein (Ed.), *The Search for the Self, Volume 1, 1950–1958* (pp. 107–130). New York: International Universities Press.
Kohut, H. (1971). *The Analysis the Self*. New York: International Universities Press.
Kohut, H. (1977). *The Restoration of the Self*. New York: International Universities Press.
Kohut, H. (1984). *How Does Analysis Cure?* Chicago, IL: University of Chicago Press.
Kohut, H., & Levarie, S. (1978). On the enjoyment of listening to music. In: P. H. Ornstein (Ed.), *The Search for the Self, Volume 4* (pp. 135–158). New York: International Universities Press.
Kuhn, T. (1962). *The Structure of Scientific Revolutions*. Chicago, IL: University of Chicago Press.
Latting, J. E., & Zundel, C. (1986). World view differences between clients and counsellors *Social Casework: The Journal of Contemporary Social Work*, *67*(9): 533–541.
Lear, J. (1993). An interpretation of transference. *International Journal of Psychoanalysis*, *74*: 739–755.
Lee, L. (2002). *Cider with Rosie*. London: Vintage Classics.
Lorenz, K. (1937). The companion in the bird's world. *The Auk*, *54*(1): 245–273.
Lorenz, K. (1959). *King Soloman's Ring*. London: Butterworth
Lucas, R. (2013). *The Psychotic Wavelength: A Psychoanalytic Perspective for Psychiatry*. London: Routledge.
Lyons-Ruth, K., & Jacobvitz, D. (2008). Attachment disorganisation: genetic factors, parenting contexts and developmental transformation from infancy to adulthood. In: J. Cassidy & P. Shaver (Eds.), *Handbook of Attachment: Theory, Research and Clinical Applications*. (2nd edn) (pp. 666–697). New York: Guildford Press.

Main, M. (1990). *A Typology of Human Attachment Organization Assessed with Discourse, Drawings and Interviews*. New York: Cambridge University Press.

Main, M., & Goldwyn, R. (1984). Predicting rejection of her infant from mother's representation of her own experience: implications for the abused–abuser intergenerational cycle. *International Journal of Child Abuse and Neglect, 8*: 203–217.

Main, M., & Solomon, J. (1990). Procedures for identifying infants as disorganised/disorientated during the Ainsworth strange situation. In: M. T. Greenberg, D. Chicchetti, & E. M. Cummings (Eds.), *Attachment in the Pre-School Years* (pp. 121–161). Chicago, IL: University of Chicago Press.

McAdams, D. P. (1993). *The Stories We Live By*. London: Sage.

Melges, F., & Swartz, M. (1989). Oscillations of attachment in borderline personality disorder. *American Journal of Psychiatry, 146*: 1115–11220.

Messer, S. B., & Winokur, M. (1984). Ways of knowing and visions of reality in psychoanalytic and behaviour therapy. In: H. Arkowitz & S. B. Messer (Eds.), *Psychoanalytic Therapy and Behaviour Therapy: Is Integration Possible?* (pp. 63–100). New York: Plenum Press.

Mikulincer, M., & Shaver, P. (2008). Adult attachment and emotion regulation. In: J. Cassidy & P. Shaver (Eds.), *Handbook of Attachment: Theory, Research, and Clinical Applications* (2nd edn) (pp. 503–531). New York: Guilford Press.

Mollon, P. (1993). *The Fragile Self*. London: Whurr.

Oakley, A. (1981). *Subject Women*. Oxford: Martin Robertson.

Odgers, A. (Ed.) (2014). *From Broken Attachments to Earned Security: the Role of Empathy in Therapeutic Change*. London: Karnac.

Patrikiou, A. (2014). Empathy and earned security: reciprocal influences, ruptures, and shifts in the psychotherapeutic process. In: A. Odgers (Ed.), *From Broken Attachments to Earned Security: the Role of Empathy in Therapeutic Change* (pp. 107–125). London: Karnac.

Phelps Brown, H. (1992). Personal communication to Jeremy Holmes. In: J. Holmes, *John Bowlby and Attachment Theory* (pp. 107–125). London: Routledge.

Power, A. (2015). *Forced Endings in Psychotherapy and Psychoanalysis: Attachment and Loss in Retirement*. London: Routledge.

Proust, M. (1995). A La Recherche du Temps Perdu. In: H. Bloom, *The True Pervasion of Sexual Jealousy* (pp. 14–15). London: Western Canon.

Racker, H. (1968). *Transference and Counter-transference*. London: Hogarth Press.

Richards, E. (2014). "What happens after this quiet bit? I may have to leave now." The risks of empathy. In: A. Odgers (Ed.), *From Broken Attachments to Earned Security: the Role of Empathy in Therapeutic Change* (pp. 91–106). London: Karnac.

Rogers, C. (1957). The necessary and sufficient conditions for personality change. *Journal of Consulting Psychology, 21*: 95–103.

Rogers, C. (1961). *On Becoming a Person: A Therapist's View of Psychotherapy*. London: Constable and Robinson.

Rogers, C. R. (1980). *A Way of Being*. New York: Houghton Mifflin.

Rosenfeld, H. A. (1964). On the psychopathology of narcissism. A clinical approach. *International Journal of Psychoanalysis, 45*: 332–337.

Rutter, M. (1981). *Maternal Deprivation Reassessed* (2nd edn). London: Penguin.

Ryle, A., & Kerr, I. B. (2002). *Introducing Cognitive Analytic Therapy: Principles and Practice*. New York: John Wiley.

Safran, J., & Muran, J. C. (2000). *Negotiating the Therapeutic Alliance: A Relational Treatment Guide*. New York: Guilford Press.

Schore, A. (1994). *Affect Regulation and the Origin of the Self*. Hillsdale, NJ: Lawrence Erlbaum.

Selden, R., Widdowson, P., & Brooker, P. (2005). *A Reader's Guide to Contemporary Literary Theory*. London: Pearson Education.

Shafer, R. (1976). *A New Language for Psychoanalysis*. New Haven, CT: Yale University Press.

Shakespeare, W. (1987). *Hamlet*. Oxford: Oxford University Press.

Shostrom, E. (1964). *Three Approaches to Psychotherapy* (Film). Corona Del Mar, CA: Psychological and Educational Films.

Siegel, A. M. (1996). *Heinz Kohut and the Psychology of the Self*. Hove: Routledge.

Slade, A. (2005). Parental reflecting functioning: an introduction. *Attachment and Human Development, 7*: 269–282.

Steiner, J. (1985). Turning a blind eye: the cover up for Oedipus. *International Review of Psycho-Analysis, 12*: 161–172.

Stern, D. (1985). *The Interpersonal World of the Infant*. New York: Basic Books.

Stern, D. (1994). Empathy is interpretation (and whoever said it wasn't?). *Psychoanalytic Dialogues, 4*(3): 441–471.

Stolorow, R. D. (1984). Varieties of selfobject experience. In: P. Stepansky & A. Goldberg (Eds.), *Kohut's Legacy* (pp. 43–50). Hillsdale, NJ: Analytic Press.

Stolorow, R. D., Brandchaft, B., & Atwood, G. E. (1983). Self psychology—a structural psychology. In: J. Lichtenberg & S. Kaplan (Eds.), *Reflections of Self Psychology* (pp. 287–296). Hillsdale, NJ: Analytic Press.

Stolorow, R. D., Brandchaft, B., & Atwood, G. E. (1995). *Psychoanalytic Treatment: An Intersubjective Approach*. London: Routledge.

Thomas, R. S. (1964). *Selected Poems of Edward Thomas*. London: Faber and Faber.

Van IJzendoorn, M. H., & Kroonenberg, P. M. (1988). Cross-cultural patterns of attachment: a meta-analysis of the strange situation. *Child Development, 2*: 147–156.

Van IJzendoorn, M., & Sagi-Schwartz, A. (2008). Cross-cultural patterns of attachment: universal and contextual dimensions. In: J. Cassidy & P. Shaver (Eds.), *Handbook of Attachment: Theory, Research, and Clinical Applications* (pp. 880–905). New York: Guilford Press.

Wachtel, P. L., & McKinney, M. K. (1992). Cyclical psychodynamics and integrative psychodynamic therapy. In: J. C. Norcross & M. R. Goldfried (Eds.), *Handbook of Psychotherapy Integration* (pp. 335–370). New York: Basic Books.

Wallerstein, J. S. (2004). *Second Chances: Men, Women and Children a Decade after Divorce* (2nd edn). London: Houghton Mifflin Harcourt.

Wallerstein, R. S. (1995). *The Talking Cures: The Psychoanalyses and Psychotherapies*. New Haven, CT: Yale University Press.

Winnicott, D. W. (1965). *The Maturational Processes and the Facilitating Environment*. London: Karnac

Winnicott, D. W. (1971). *Playing and Reality*. London: Routledge.

INDEX

For Product Safety Concerns and Information please contact our EU representative GPSR@taylorandfrancis.com
Taylor & Francis Verlag GmbH, Kaufingerstraße 24, 80331 München, Germany

www.ingramcontent.com/pod-product-compliance
Ingram Content Group UK Ltd.
Pitfield, Milton Keynes, MK11 3LW, UK
UKHW022204190926
475702UK00003B/201

* 9 7 8 0 3 6 7 3 2 3 3 7 0 *